Thanks for Your Service

BRIDGING THE GAP

Series Editors
James Goldgeier
Bruce Jentleson
Steven Weber

The Logic of American Nuclear Strategy:
Why Strategic Superiority Matters
Matthew Kroenig

Planning to Fail:
The US Wars in Vietnam, Iraq, and Afghanistan
James H. Lebovic

War and Chance:
Assessing Uncertainty in International Politics
Jeffrey A. Friedman

Delaying Doomsday:
The Politics of Nuclear Reversal
Rupal N. Mehta

Delta Democracy:
Pathways to Incremental Civic Revolution in Egypt and Beyond
Catherine E. Herrold

Adaptation under Fire:
How Militaries Change in Wartime
David Barno and Nora Bensahel

The Long Game:
China's Grand Strategy to Displace American Order
Rush Doshi

A Small State's Guide to Influence in World Politics
Tom Long

Cyber Persistence Theory:
Redefining National Security in Cyberspace
Michael P. Fischerkeller, Emily O. Goldman, and Richard J. Harknett

Beyond the Wire:
US Military Deployments and Host Country Public Opinion
Michael A. Allen, Michael E. Flynn, Carla Martinez Machain, and Andrew Stravers

Deploying Feminism:
The Role of Gender in NATO Military Operations
Stéfanie von Hlatky

Thanks for Your Service:
The Causes and Consequences of Public Confidence in the US Military
Peter D. Feaver

Thanks for Your Service

The Causes and Consequences of Public Confidence in the US Military

PETER D. FEAVER

OXFORD
UNIVERSITY PRESS

Oxford University Press is a department of the University of Oxford. It furthers the University's objective of excellence in research, scholarship, and education by publishing worldwide. Oxford is a registered trade mark of Oxford University Press in the UK and certain other countries.

Published in the United States of America by Oxford University Press
198 Madison Avenue, New York, NY 10016, United States of America.

© Peter Feaver 2023

All rights reserved. No part of this publication may be reproduced, stored in a retrieval system, or transmitted, in any form or by any means, without the prior permission in writing of Oxford University Press, or as expressly permitted by law, by license, or under terms agreed with the appropriate reproduction rights organization. Inquiries concerning reproduction outside the scope of the above should be sent to the Rights Department, Oxford University Press, at the address above.

You must not circulate this work in any other form
and you must impose this same condition on any acquirer.

Library of Congress Cataloging-in-Publication Data
Names: Feaver, Peter D., 1961– author.
Title: Thanks for your service : the causes and consequences of public confidence in the US military / Peter D. Feaver.
Description: New York, NY : Oxford University Press, [2023] |
Series: Bridging The Gap series |
Includes bibliographical references.
Identifiers: LCCN 2022060632 (print) | LCCN 2022060633 (ebook) |
ISBN 9780197681138 (paperback) | ISBN 9780197681121 (hardback) |
ISBN 9780197681145 (epub)
Subjects: LCSH: United States—Armed Forces—Public opinion.
Classification: LCC UA23.F373 2023 (print) | LCC UA23 (ebook) |
DDC 355/.033573—dc23/eng/20230206
LC record available at https://lccn.loc.gov/2022060632
LC ebook record available at https://lccn.loc.gov/2022060633

DOI: 10.1093/oso/9780197681121.001.0001

CONTENTS

List of Figures vii
List of Tables xi
Acknowledgments xv

1. Introduction 1

PART I   WHO HAS CONFIDENCE IN THE MILITARY?

2. Confidence in the Military over Time and Today 15
3. Confidence and the Gaps: Knowledge, Education, Media, and Social Contact 44

PART II   WHY DO PEOPLE HAVE CONFIDENCE IN THE MILITARY?

4. Comparing Public Confidence across the Military and Other Institutions 69
5. Performance, Professional Ethics, and Public Confidence in the Military 91
6. Politics, Politicization, and Public Confidence 119
7. Social Desirability Bias: A Silent Prop Undergirding Public Confidence in the Military 161

PART III WHY CONFIDENCE IN THE MILITARY MATTERS

8. Whether and How Confidence Shapes Concrete Support for Raising and Maintaining the Military   175

9. Whether and How Confidence Shapes Views on the Military as an Instrument of Foreign Policy   202

10. Whether and How Confidence Shapes Intangible Benefits Enjoyed by the Military   223

11. Conclusion   261

References   283
Index   299

FIGURES

2.1. Total Public Confidence in the Military since 1972   16
2.2. Public Confidence in the Military over Time by Gender of Respondent   18
2.3. Public Confidence in the Military over Time by Race of Respondent   19
2.4. Public Confidence in the Military over Time by Generation of Respondent   20
2.5. Public Confidence in the Military over Time by Region of Respondent   21
2.6. Changes in Mean Self-Reporting by Party ID of Respondent   22
2.7. Public Confidence in the Military and Public Assessments of Whether Wars are "Going Badly"   26
2.8. Public Confidence in the Military Tracked against War Events by Party   27
2.9. Predicting Confidence in the Military by Demographic Features of Respondents   34
2.10. Predicting Confidence in the Military by Combined Demographic Profile   36
2.11. Percentage of Public Who Correctly Identified the Serving Status of Senior Military Leaders   41
3.1. Whether Most Military Look Like Me by Race and Confidence Levels   47
3.2. The Link between Knowledge about Military Affairs and Public Confidence   51
3.3. Predicted Confidence in the Military by Education and Party ID   52
3.4. Perceptions of the Military's Partisan Makeup by Education Level and Party ID   53
3.5. Most Common Media Source for Political News   55

3.6. Confidence in the Military by Most Common Political News Source   56
3.7. Primary Source of What Respondents Learned about Military   57
3.8. High Confidence in Military by Source of Learning about Military   58
3.9. Confidence in the Military by How Closely One Follows Military News   59
3.10. Family Connections to the Military by Age Cohort and Dates of Service   62
3.11. Change in Public Confidence in the Military in the Abstract versus Known by Personal Connection   63
4.1. Public Confidence in Various Institutions over Time   70
4.2. Public Confidence in the Military versus Average of Other Institutions over Time   71
4.3. Predicted Confidence in the Military against Confidence in Other Institutions   73
4.4. Public Confidence in Various Institutions over Time by Party   74
4.5. Percentage Agreeing an Institution Exhibits Various Attributes   80
4.6. Percentage Agreeing an Institution Exhibits Various Attributes   81
4.7. Percentage Agreeing Others Have Confidence in an Institution   83
4.8. Principal Component Analysis of Institutional Attributes   84
4.9. Predictors of Overall Confidence in Institutions, Agencies, and Professions   87
5.1. Treatment Effects for Public Confidence in the Military   98
5.2. Treatment Effects for Public Confidence in the Military Conditioned on Partisan Status of Respondents   100
5.3. Treatment Effects for Ethics Prompt in the Aggregate   106
5.4. Treatment Effects for Ethics Prompt Broken Down by Partisan ID   107
6.1. Effects of Political Treatment on Public Confidence in the Military   136
6.2. Effects of Political Treatment by Respondent Partisanship   138
6.3. Treatment Effect of the Military Cue on Vote Choice   147
6.4. Treatment Effect of the Military Cue on Vote Choice by Respondent Partisan ID   148
6.5. Treatment Effects for Border Deployment by Respondent Partisanship   151
6.6. Treatment Effects for Trust in the Military by Border Deployment by Respondent Partisanship   151
6.7. Treatment Effects for Insurrection Act by Respondent Partisanship   153
6.8. Support for Criticizing President by Partisan ID of Respondent   156
6.9. Support for Criticizing President by Respondent Party ID and Confidence Level   157

LIST OF FIGURES

7.1. Public Confidence in the Military Varied by Pressure to Support the Troops   165
7.2. Multivariate Estimates of Aggregate and Subgroup Social Desirability Bias from List Experiment   170
8.1. Percentage of Americans Who Report They Have Learned Most of What They Know about the Military from Movies and Television Shows   180
8.2. Percentage of Americans By Age Who Report They Have Learned Most of What They Know about the Military from Movies and Television Shows (2020)   181
8.3. Change in Propensity to Serve in the Military and Change in Perception of Whether the Military Is Doing a Good Job for the Nation   182
8.4. High School Seniors Saying They Will Join the Military by Satisfaction with the Job the Military Is Doing on Behalf of the Country   183
8.5. Percentage of Respondent Who Would Advise a Close Friend or Relative to Join the Military by Confidence and Military Service Connections   189
8.6. Public Confidence in the Military and Support for Increased Military Spending over Time   191
8.7. Support for Increased Military Spending by Feelings toward the Military and Party before and after September 11, 2001   194
8.8. Effect of Confidence on Defense Spending Attitudes Conditioned on Party   198
8.9. Responses to Questions about the Size of the Budgets for the Departments of Defense and State   198
8.10. Percentage of Responses to a Factual Question about the Size of the Department of Defense Budget by Confidence Level   199
9.1. Overall Importance and Usefulness of Military Missions by Confidence Level   209
9.2. Importance of Different Military Missions by Confidence Level   210
9.3. Importance of Domestic Military Missions by Confidence Level   211
9.4. Importance of Military Missions Categories by Confidence Level and Party   213
9.5. Importance of Humanitarian and Civil War Interventions by Confidence and Party   214
9.6. Usefulness of Humanitarian and Domestic Disaster Response Missions by Confidence Level and Party   214
9.7. Support for Iran Strikes and Domestic Missions by Confidence Level and Party   218
10.1. Treatment Effects for Iran Strike and Transgender Ban Questions   244

10.2. Treatment Effects for Handguns in Schools   245
10.3. Effect of Military Cues as a Function of High versus Low Levels of Confidence in the Military   246
10.4. Support for Transgender Ban in Response to Military Cue by Party ID and by Level of Confidence in the Military   248
10.5. Views of War Performance of Civilian and Military Leaders by Partisanship of Respondent   257

TABLES

2.1. Changes in the Ideological Composition of the Parties from 1974 to 2021   23
2.2. Public Confidence in the Military by Party Identification   31
2.3. Public Confidence in the Military by Ideology   32
2.4. Percentage of American Public with "A Great Deal" or "Quite a Lot" of Confidence in the Military by Demographics   33
2.5. Comparing Predicted Public Confidence across Branches of the Military   38
2.6. Comparing Public Confidence across Types of Military   39
2.7. Perceived Closeness of Views of Retired Generals and Admirals to Active-Duty Counterparts   42
3.1. Whether Most Members of the Military "Look Like Me" by Race   46
3.2. Accuracy of Responses to Knowledge Questions   50
3.3. High Confidence in the Military by Trust/Distrust in News Media Sources   57
4.1. Percentage Expressing Confidence in Institutions   77
4.2. Percentage Expressing Confidence in Departments and Agencies   77
4.3. Percentage Expressing Confidence in Professions   78
5.1. Public Attitudes on Military Competence Attributes by Party Identification   94
5.2. Public Attitudes on Military Ethics Attributes by Party Identification   103
5.3. Public Agreement with Other Military Attributes by Experimental and Party Conditions   110
5.4. Average Causal Mediation Effects   113
5.5. Views on Candor of Senior Military Leaders by Level of Confidence   116
6.1. Public Beliefs about Whether the Military Has a Political Affiliation by Party Identification of Respondent   124

LIST OF TABLES

6.2. Public Beliefs about Which Political Affiliation the Military Has by Party Identification of Respondent   125
6.3. Public Beliefs about Military Political Ideology by Party Identification of Respondent   126
6.4. Whether the Military "Looks Like Me" by Party Identification   127
6.5. Public Attitudes on Military Political Attributes by Party Identification   127
6.6. Perceptions of Partisanship in Civilian Society and in the Military by Partisanship of Respondent   129
6.7. High Confidence in the Military by Party Identification of Respondent and Perceived Political Affiliation of the Military   130
6.8. Public Agreement with Other Military Attributes by Experimental and Party Conditions   142
6.9. Average Causal Mediation Effects   144
7.1. Public Confidence in the Military as Revealed by the Social Desirability List Experiment   166
7.2. Multivariate Analysis of the List Experiment and the Direct Question   168
8.1. Overall Responses to a Question about Whether a Respondent Would Advise a Close Friend or Relative to Join the Military by Confidence   186
8.2. Overall Responses to Feelings about Family Member Joining the Military Questions by Confidence   186
8.3. Responses to Question about Whether a Respondent Would Advise a Close Friend or Relative to Join the Military by Military Service Connections   188
8.4. Predictors of Support for Increased Military Spending over Time   192
8.5. Support for Military Pay by Level of Confidence   195
8.6. Support for Trading Funding for the Department of State to Increase Funding for the Department of Defense by Level of Confidence   196
9.1. Range of Potential Mission Priorities for the Military   205
9.2. Mapping Questions onto the Potential Mission Priorities of the Military   207
9.3. Views on Whether Diplomacy or Military Force Causes More Problems   215
9.4. Support for Drone or Special Operations Forces Attacks against Overseas Threats   216
9.5. Retrospective Attitudes about the Afghanistan and Iraq Wars in 2019 by Confidence Level   219
9.6. Support for Withdrawing Troops from Afghanistan and Iraq in 2019 by Confidence Level   220

LIST OF TABLES

10.1. Responses to Privilege Questions by Level of Confidence in the Military 229
10.2. Thanks for Your Service by Veteran Status 230
10.3. Public Pedestalizing of the Military by Confidence Level 233
10.4. Attitudes about Guilt for Not Serving by Veteran Status and Confidence 234
10.5. Attitudes about the Military Role in Policymaking by Level of Confidence 238
10.6. Public Views on Success of the Wars in Iraq and Afghanistan 251
10.7. Public Views on Whether the United States Has Accomplished Its Goals in Afghanistan 252
10.8. Public Views on Criticism of the Military by Level of Confidence 253
10.9. Public Views on Who Deserves Blame/Credit 254
10.10. Perceptions of Civilian Leaders' Performance in Afghanistan 255
10.11. Perceptions of Military Leaders' Performance in Afghanistan by Confidence in the Military 256
11.1. The Six Determinants of Public Confidence in the Military 263

ACKNOWLEDGMENTS

This book builds on work developed in close collaboration with Dr. James Golby. He and I came up with the idea for the book based on our earlier published work and we jointly developed the research design and the survey instrument. He had the lead in conducting the analyses, and we shared in coming up with our interpretations and then solidifying them in written form. Prior versions of the chapters have been circulated and presented as coauthored pieces reflecting his extensive contributions to every aspect of the project. Dr. Golby requested that he be removed as listed coauthor so he could better attend to a personal matter unrelated to this research project. However, this book would not have been possible without his substantial contributions, and I owe him a significant intellectual debt.

I also owe a significant debt to Robert and Marion Oster, who provided the financial resources necessary to collect the high-quality data. I am grateful for their investment—and for their patience with the slow pace of academic research. I thank Kori Schake for making this fruitful connection.

The National Opinion Research Center team, especially Dan Constanzo and Suzanne Howard, were fabulous partners in this project. Their professionalism reassured us that the surveys would meet the exacting standards we aimed for, though of course they bear no blame for any inferential errors made with that data.

It has been a privilege to work with Oxford University Press and the Bridging the Gap series editorial team. I thank Emily Benitez, Jim Goldgeier, Bruce Jentleson, David McBride, Kathryn Urban, Vinothini Thiruvannamalai, Steve Weber, and Madison Zickgraf.

This project would not have been possible without an excellent squad of research assistants. Each one of them—Dr. Robert Allred, Rebecca Dudley, Spencer Kaplan, Dr. So Jin Lee, Zoe Spicer, and Ritika Saligram—provided invaluable experience that improved literally every page of this project. Each one of them seems destined for a high-impact career touching on international relations, and I hope they will be as proud of their work on this project as I am proud to have had the chance to work with them.

Portions of this work were presented in draft form at professional conferences. Chapter 2 was presented at the American Political Science Association annual meeting in 2019 and the Inter-University Seminar in 2019. Chapter 4 was presented at APSA 2020. The manuscript also benefited from feedback from the expert participants at the following workshops and academic speaker series: Security, Peace and Conflict Lab at Duke University; International Institute for Strategic Studies in London; All Souls College, Oxford University; Nuffield College Political Science Seminar, Oxford University; the International Relations Colloquium, Oxford University; the MIT Security Studies Program; and the Civil-Military Relations Workshop.

At the risk of forgetting someone important, I want to thank the anonymous reviewers at OUP as well as some who were especially generous with their feedback, including Holger Albrecht, Victor Asal, David Burbach, Lindsay Cohn, Pepper Culpepper, Erica DeBruin, Martin Dempsey, Brett Gall, Jane Green, Sunshine Hillygus, Christopher Johnston, Michael Kenwick, Ron Krebs, Danielle Lupton, Max Margulies, Jim Mattis, Sam Neill, Andrew Payne, Michael Robinson, Laura Samotin, Kori Schake, and Heidi Urben. The long-suffering students in Political Science 667, American Civil-Military Relations, the course I co-taught with General Martin Dempsey, were heroic in reading and discussing the entire manuscript in draft. I especially thank Anne Crabil, Paul Framel, Jonathan Griffin, and Alice Shih for going above and beyond to offer feedback.

I greatly benefited from my pandemic-sabbatical as a Visiting Fellow at All Soul's College and an Associate Fellow at Nuffield College in Oxford University. Most of the book was written under lockdown conditions, but I hope it will mostly be read with the pandemic well behind us.

Of course, I owe a great debt to my family—Karen, Samuel, Kelsey, Ellie, and PJ—a debt they rightly remind me of from time to time. If they read this book, I hope they will see why I find American civil-military relations so interesting and so worth the considerable investment of time I have given it.

Finally, I thank the thousands of men and women in and out of uniform with whom I have had the privilege to converse on civil-military topics over the years—especially the hundreds of general and flag officers at CAPSTONE and PINNACLE, and the other senior commanders and civilian leaders in the Department of Defense, the Department of State, the White House, and the Congress who have reached out to discuss these topics. As a citizen, I owe a great debt of gratitude to them and to their families for their service to this country. As a scholar, I am also grateful for how seriously they take their collective professional responsibility as custodians of the health of civil-military relations.

I dedicate this book to all who serve, both in and out of uniform.

1

Introduction

> This reverent but disengaged attitude toward the military—we love the troops, but we'd rather not think about them—has become so familiar that we assume it is the American norm.
> —James Fallows (2015)

This book is about high levels of confidence in the armed forces of the United States, as expressed by the American public over the last several decades. What explains this confidence? Does having a high level of confidence in the military matter for anything else of importance? And, more speculatively, what do answers to those questions suggest about the future trajectory of public attitudes toward the military?

The answers offered in this book draw on proprietary survey data collected expressly to probe these questions and can be summarized briefly. Public confidence in the military is heavily shaped by what may be called the "Smith Barney" factor, recalling the old television advertisement for Smith Barney Wealth Management: "They make money the old-fashioned way—they earn it." That is, part of public confidence in the military is this "old-fashioned way," in which the military earns it with high competence, adherence to high professional ethics, and a determination to stand apart from the bitter divisions of partisan politics. As the analyses in this book show, that is undoubtedly part of the story, and it suggests that if the military stops "earning it"—if the military performance slips, if the public sees the military falling short of ethical standards, and if the military joins the partisan food fight—then public confidence will drop accordingly.

However, a central finding in this book is that public confidence has been propped up by other factors as well, ones that do not fit neatly within this comfortable story of complete deservedness. Importantly, public confidence in the military already is shaped by partisan considerations—in particular a blame game in which the military is at least a passive participant—and by social desirability bias, the idea that some individuals express confidence in the military because they believe that is the socially approved attitude to hold. This suggests that the still-high confidence the military enjoys today could well be more tenuous than a superficial glance at poll numbers might suggest.

It is worth preserving the public's high confidence in the military, if deserved, because high confidence reinforces other attitudes of interest, including support for raising and maintaining the defense forces the country needs and support for using the military to defend important national interests. High confidence is not an unalloyed benefit, however, since it can lead to a desire to use the military in the service of policies for which the military tool may not be well suited. Even more problematically, high confidence does not bring with it an understanding of, nor support for, the best practices in democratic civil-military relations and can even lead to situations where the military is put on a pedestal from which it might look down on civilian society. This perch might also offer some unwelcome insulation from accountability for its performance when such accountability devolves into a partisan blame game.

To break this down a bit more concretely, the American public has confidence in its military because of six primary drivers: *Patriotism, Performance, Professional Ethics, Party, Personal Contact,* and *Public Pressure.* There is no guarantee this public confidence will remain elevated, however, and trends in these underlying drivers are uncertain and impermanent. Even in retrospect, these trends can be difficult to identify precisely; in part, the lack of detailed, precise data about the drivers of public confidence in the military—beyond the topline confidence ratings that Gallup, the National Opinion Research Center (NORC), and the General Social Survey have collected in recent decades—is a major reason why these new surveys provide real value. Whenever possible, though, I do trace broad trends across a number of different longitudinal data sources to reinforce that the proprietary surveys offer not only a glimpse, but also a deeper understanding, of why confidence increased in recent decades. Of particular importance, surveys conducted after the ones that are the focus of this book largely reinforce the main arguments presented here.

Regarding the specific drivers I identify, high levels of public confidence seem to be partly an artifact of the indefinite quasi-war footing the country has been on since late in the Cold War and the patriotic ceremony that has come with it (*Patriotism*). Periodic high-profile uses of the military—Desert Storm, the Kosovo War, and especially the myriad interventions after the 9/11 terrorist attacks—have all made the military salient in the public's mind. And while those interventions have yielded uncertain strategic results in geopolitical terms, the public has judged the military's performance in those operations quite favorably (*Performance*). When the public has identified shortcomings, it has not attributed them to failures in the military but rather to defects in the civilian political leadership of the wars. Yet it seems clear that the public has confidence in the military in part because it believes the military holds itself to a high ethical standard (*Professional Ethics*). These attitudes have been heavily conditioned on partisanship, with Republicans showing much higher levels of confidence, higher estimations of performance and ethics, and greater willingness to shield the military from blame than Democrats (*Party*). These attitudes also reflect a marked degree of what social psychologists call social desirability bias—what is colloquially understood as something like "political correctness." A significant portion of the public appears to express high levels of confidence primarily because that seems to be the socially approved opinion (*Public Pressure*). To a certain extent, social connection and familiarity with the military boosts confidence, though not uniformly so; having a direct connection to the military props up confidence, but having no connection leaves attitudes somewhat unmoored (*Personal Contact*). The surveys show that confidence does move up or down in mostly intuitive ways when they present respondents with information intended to nudge their opinions up or down. Information that frames the military as incompetent or unethical leads respondents on average to have somewhat lower levels of confidence (*Performance* and *Professional Ethics*). Likewise, being told that the military is a political supporter of the opposing party leads partisans to lower their level of confidence in the military, whereas being told that the military supports one's own party does not (*Party*). The public does not want a partisan military but seems to define "partisan" down to mean only "aligns with the party opposite my own."

Regarding the effects, high levels of confidence obviously provide the military with the intrinsic utility that any institution might derive from being viewed favorably. When confidence declines in response to adverse information about the military, it has the potential to affect public attitudes to the military across the board. Thus, hearing about questionable ethical behavior by the military lowers estimations that the military is truthful and thereby lowers overall confidence in the military—but awareness of unethical behavior also lowers estimations of the competence of the military and its ability to win the wars it fights. In other words, the public seems not to worry about partisan, unethical, or dishonest behavior just because people see those things as bad in and of themselves; rather, they worry that such behavior shows that the military will not be able to do its job well and that it does not share their values.

But beyond that, these results suggest that military leaders are wise to care about maintaining the public's confidence because along with it come other tangible and intangible benefits. High confidence is correlated with support for higher defense expenditures and a willingness to recommend to others that they join the military. In an era when the Department of Defense faces tough fiscal choices and must scramble to attract the highly qualified recruits on which military strength depends, it is surely a significant boon that the public views the military so favorably. Likewise, high public confidence helps contribute to a permissive environment for the use of the military in support of foreign policy objectives; whether this is a boon or a bane depends on one's own opinions regarding the utility of military force, but it surely gives policymakers more latitude than they would have if they faced implacable skepticism from the public regarding what the military can or should accomplish. High levels of public confidence also appear to contribute to an environment in which the military enjoys perquisites and prerogatives unlike any other institution in American public life. Here, as explained in much greater detail in Chapter 10, the ultimate consequences are more ambivalent, since it is not at all clear that being put on a pedestal in this fashion is conducive to healthy civil-military relations in a democratic republic. But it seems clear that this confidence has insulated the military from criticism that it might otherwise have received. More troublingly, it seems clear that the high confidence has become associated with some of the more pernicious developments in American political life, particularly intense partisan polarization.

Although the analysis here should provide greater insight into what factors to watch going forward, I am less confident in predicting the future course of public attitudes. After all, one of the motivations for the present study was the fact that public confidence had remained persistently high despite signs of its fragility that were noticeable some two decades ago (Gronke and Feaver 2001; Gourley 2014). Betting against the public's admiration for the military has been something of a fool's game for a long time. And yet it is impossible not to notice the warning signs in the details presented throughout this book. To the extent that high public confidence in the military is an artifact of salient combat operations, if the gradual decline in high-intensity combat interventions over the past half decade extends into the future, then some decrement in public attitudes should follow regardless.

Moreover, just as partisan polarization has poisoned public attitudes across a wide spectrum of government activities, it seems unlikely that the military can avoid experiencing a similar corrosion if present trends continue. It is striking just how prominent the military was in the public's imagination during the extraordinarily divisive 2020 presidential campaign and its aftermath. Although military leaders worked hard and with some success to keep the institution out of playing a pivotal role in the drama, they could not keep the military out of the limelight altogether. By the time President Biden's administration was securely launched, the military could not completely escape the tarnish that stained virtually every political actor in the tragedy. It is also not clear how long attitudes that are based on a social connection to the military can remain robust as demographic trends lead inexorably to a smaller and smaller percentage of Americans having direct ties to the military. At the same time, senior military leaders rightly care about what the public thinks about the organizations they lead and have it within their power to make reforms that might help shore up public confidence. As discussed in the concluding chapter, a military that is assiduous about being competent, ethical, and uninvolved in partisan politics is more likely to be seen in that way, and that should help shore up public confidence in the face of other downward pressures.

Plan of the Book

The chapters that follow analyze a raft of data to reach these conclusions. In this chapter, I lay out a bit more of the background to the questions I seek to answer and sketch out what answers prevailed before this study was launched.

The main body of the book is broken into three sections. Part I, comprising Chapters 2 and 3, considers public attitudes about the military in general and shows how those attitudes vary across key demographic groups. Chapter 2 examines the changes in public confidence over time, drawing on the General Social Survey—and, to a lesser degree, the Gallup survey—which together have tracked this issue since the early 1970s. Chapter 2 also conducts a detailed analysis of a snapshot of American opinion in 2019 and 2020, exploring how this basic confidence question varies by the political affiliation and ideology of the respondent, as well as by other standard demographic factors that are important in public opinion research, and assessing the extent to which the public draws much of a distinction between the active duty force as a whole versus prominent military leaders, the individual military services, retired generals and admirals, and veterans. Chapter 3 examines how attitudes about the military covary with how well a respondent "knows" the military—the respondent's base of information on military matters, the media channels by which the respondent gets information about the military, the respondent's education level, and the degree to which respondents have some social or personal connection to the military.

The next major section of the book, Part II, comprised of Chapters 4, 5, 6, and 7, goes beyond simple demographics to consider other reasons *why* the public holds the level of confidence in the military that it professes to hold. Chapter 4 compares confidence in the military to confidence in other public institutions and begins to explore why public confidence in the military surged even as it dropped among other national institutions. Chapter 5 uses survey experiments to test various hypotheses for why the public might believe the military is worthy of high confidence, including basic arguments about the military's competence or professionalism. Chapter 6 uses similar techniques to dig into how confidence is shaped by the perceived politicization of the military. Chapter 7 uses other techniques to explore the extent to which public confidence is a function of social desirability bias.

The final section, Part III, probes why confidence in the military matters and what we can do about it. Chapter 8 examines the extent to which confidence in the military seems to matter for the tangible needs of the military—budget and manpower. Chapter 9 examines how confidence is linked to views about military force as an instrument of foreign policy. Chapter 10 digs into the intangible benefits that come with high confidence and social esteem. Chapter 11 closes the book with a discussion of how policymakers can best make use of the arguments I advance.

Throughout, the book rests heavily on proprietary data collected for this project by NORC. A technical appendix available online (https://dataverse.harvard.edu/dataverse/pfeaver) describes the data collection in much greater detail, but in brief the process consisted of two waves of surveys, one in the early summer of 2019 and one in the early fall of 2020. NORC surveyed some 4,500 American adult respondents each time, with a large oversample of some 900 veterans to allow for more precise comparisons across veteran and nonveteran groups. Each respondent received an internet-based survey instrument that took roughly 15 minutes to complete. With the publication of this book, these responses are now available for anyone to use and are also at https://dataverse.harvard.edu/dataverse/pfeaver. They comprise some of the most detailed and up-to-date survey data on American public attitudes to the military ever collected.

Background

During his State of the Union address in 2012, President Barack Obama highlighted the killing of Osama bin Laden and the then-recent (but short-lived) removal of US troops from Iraq before directing his praise to the men and women who carried out his orders. Obama stated:

> These achievements are a testament to the courage, selflessness and teamwork of America's Armed Forces. At a time when too many of our institutions have let us down, they exceed all expectations. They're not consumed with personal ambition. They don't obsess over their differences. They focus on the mission at hand. They work together. (Obama 2012b)

The president paused for a moment and then concluded, "Imagine what we could accomplish if we followed their example." In a rare moment of bipartisan unity, legislators on both sides of the aisle sprung to their feet and delivered the longest-sustained applause of the night.

That an American president would praise the bravery of American service members is not surprising. The US public's high professed confidence in the military is an oft-quoted statistic. But, in a democracy with a strong tradition of civilian control of a military, it was nonetheless striking to see a progressive Democrat calling for the American people—and their political institutions—to become more like the military.

In praising the military, Obama was trying to invoke things on which Americans might agree—love of Mom, apple pie, and the military. He was reminding Americans of what they already knew, which is that most other Americans hold the military in high esteem. Indeed, the public's generally high esteem for the military is one of the facts about American public opinion that most Americans seem to know. Put another way, public confidence in the military may be something of a mystery, but it is certainly not a secret. The result is trumpeted repeatedly after it is reconfirmed in new polls, and anecdotally I have found that it is all but impossible to have a conversation about civil-military relations with military or political leaders for very long without the interlocutor providing the statistic unprompted.[1]

Part of its salience is due to the fact that very few other public institutions in the United States enjoy such standing. In 2022, according to Gallup, the military was one of only two institutions in which a near supermajority of the public (64%) had "a great deal" (32%) or "quite a lot" (32%) of confidence—not the church, Congress, the Supreme Court, or the presidency, not organized labor or big business, not public schools or the medical system or HMOs, not newspapers or television news or news on the internet, and not the criminal justice system or the police. Only small businesses at 68% enjoyed comparable levels of confidence, split evenly between "a great deal" and "quite a lot" (Gallup 2022). Increasingly, it seems, support for the military may be one of the few things on which Americans can agree in these polarized times.

Part of its salience may also be due to the fact that it was not always so—that as recently as the post-Vietnam era, the military was held in much lower esteem (25% "a great deal" and 29% "quite a lot" of confidence). And, indeed, for much of US history, the military was viewed with some suspicion, especially during peacetime (King and Karabell 2003; Huntington 1957; Ekirch 2010; Kohn

---

[1] For just one example, see Murray (2016). The claim of public confidence in the military also was the foundation of two prominent policy conferences: "Command Climate: The State of U.S. Civil-Military Relations" at the Center for Strategic and International Studies (see CSIS 2017) and "Blurred Lines: Civil-Military Relations and Modern War" at the Modern War Institute at West Point (Modern War Institute 2018).

1999). These two factors work in tandem to make the military stand out: while Americans lost confidence in other institutions over the last several decades, public confidence in the military bucked the trend and actually increased.

And, of course, part of the salience of the statistic is that the military as an institution is itself quite salient in American public life. The military plays a central role in American foreign and national security policy, and rising prospects of a military confrontation are the fastest way that a "problem" becomes a "crisis" that commands public attention. More distinctively, the military occupies a privileged position in the public consciousness, whether in the form of popular film and television productions, or the quasi-ritualistic role the military plays at sporting and other major civic events, or even in the regular reminders for airline travelers that the military qualify for the special benefit of early boarding on planes. To be sure, some of the most salient manifestations are symbolic (sporting events) or even fantasy (Hollywood), which makes the interaction of the average citizen today with the military qualitatively different from the way it was at the height of the Vietnam War, let alone the mass mobilization of World War II and the Civil War. The military is not ubiquitous, as it was during the age of total mobilization, and fewer and fewer Americans have a personal connection to it. Yet if you compare the present day to the pre–Civil War era, or the 1870–1910 era (outside of the brief Reconstruction period), or even the post-Vietnam "malaise" era, then the US military is more prominent. America's global geopolitics makes the military relevant and salient in a real way—and not just a fantasy way—that the Framers of the Constitution would have found disconcerting. In short, the military is hard to ignore altogether in American culture.

For all these reasons, most Americans know that most other Americans have high confidence in the military. (In my survey, some 70% agreed or strongly agreed that "most members of American society have confidence in the military.") What is less well understood is why this is true.

Findings from Earlier Work

This book is by no means the first effort to understand the dynamics of public confidence in the military. The public's on-again, off-again affair with the military has long interested historians (Ekirch 2010; Kohn 1975; Bacevich 2005). King and Karabell (2003) is perhaps the most comprehensive examination of the question using the tools of social science until this work. I explored a detailed snapshot of data from early in the Cold War (Gronke and Feaver 2001). And more recently, Burbach (2017, 2018) has sought to bring that earlier work up to the contemporary era, extending the earlier analyses up to 2016. All of these efforts contributed to the baseline understanding of the dynamics of public confidence and undergirded the expectations I sought to test with the new data collected.

The key findings from other studies include the following:

- Public confidence, especially when focusing on respondents who select the strongest response option—"a great deal"—has moved up and down in response to world events, but remained remarkably and consistently high for decades (King and Karabell 2003; Burbach 2017).
- There are at least three plausible and potentially complementary explanations for this persistent high public confidence: perhaps the military is very good at what it does; perhaps the military exhibits a high level of ethical standards; and perhaps the military's advertising efforts, designed to draw in recruits, have persuaded the public to rate the military highly (King and Karabell 2003).
- Perceptions of battlefield prowess are probably part of the story, since public confidence climbs somewhat in the wake of good news from the front and dips somewhat when the wars are going poorly. But it is not all of the story: the same public that expresses confidence also believes the United States has been losing the wars the military is fighting (Burbach 2017).
- Perceptions of high military ethics and the positive effects of recruiting efforts are also probably part of the story, since the public does tend to believe good things about military ethics, but it is not clear how much this props up confidence (Golby, Cohn, and Feaver 2016; Hill, Wong, and Gerras 2013).
- The aggregate poll result masks important, if intuitive, variation among subpopulations. Men show higher confidence than women; whites more than nonwhites; older people more than younger; people with personal or social connections more than those with none (Burbach 2018).
- Perhaps of greater significance, public confidence seems highly conditioned on partisanship. Today, Republicans have much higher confidence than Democrats or independents, but in the late 1970s the reverse was true (Liebert and Golby 2017). Unlike most other issues on a traditional left-right scale, independents do not fall in between Republicans and Democrats, however—partisans of either stripe have more confidence than self-identified independents (Burbach 2018). Strongly partisan Democrats condition their confidence on whether the president is a Democrat (producing higher confidence) or a Republican (producing lower confidence) (Burbach 2018).
- There is some evidence that the public feels social pressure to express promilitary attitudes. Support for increased spending on veterans benefits might be 10 points higher than the "true" underlying level of support overall, perhaps 25 points higher among African Americans (Kleykamp, Hipes, and MacLean 2018).

Some of the earlier arguments have been harder to maintain as public confidence in the military has remained high while the underlying conditions have changed markedly. Early research (Gronke and Feaver 2001; King and Karabell 2003; Hill, Wong, and Gerras 2013) suggested that increased public confidence was partly a function of whether the public viewed an institution as above partisan politics. Institutions that the public viewed as nonpartisan, like the military and the Supreme Court, fared better in polling than did institutions that the public viewed as unavoidably partisan, like Congress or the presidency. According to this theory, the drop in public confidence in the Supreme Court—dropping from a high of 50% in 1997 saying that they have a great deal or quite a lot of confidence to a low of 30% in 2014—coincided with the changing perception of the Supreme Court as a nonpolitical legal body seemingly above partisan politics into something that looked more like four Democrats, four Republicans, and one less predictable, perhaps even confused, individual (Gallup 2020).

Confounding this explanation, however, is evidence that the military—especially the officer corps—has also become more partisan (Feaver and Kohn 2001; Dempsey 2009; Urben 2010, 2021; Liebert and Golby 2017) and that the public has become increasingly aware of these changes (Golby, Dropp, and Feaver 2012). And yet public confidence in the military has not declined proportionately. Furthermore, in lieu of an overall decline in confidence driven by dismay over rising partisanship, there is evidence of a growing confidence gap perhaps driven by rising partisanship in the general public. Liebert and Golby (2017) demonstrate that a large confidence gap has developed since the mid-1970s, with Republicans now far more likely to express confidence than either Democrats or independents. Burbach (2018) suggests that the party of the president also may impact partisans' assessments of the military.

King and Karabell (2003) also argued that increased public confidence reflected underlying changes in views about the competence of the military compared to other institutions, partly due to better performance and partly due to better public relations. After the Vietnam War, the military implemented reforms that helped it rebuild itself as an institution. But it also rebuilt its relationship with the press and—perhaps more importantly—with Hollywood. The Department of Defense partnered with television and movie studios on high-budget films, like *Top Gun*, that portrayed the military in a very positive light. As a result of changes in both competence and persuasion, the US military seemed good at what it was supposed to do—fight and win the nation's wars—whereas Congress and other institutions simply appeared dysfunctional.

After nearly two decades of prolonged wars with a disastrous outcome in Afghanistan and at best an unsatisfying outcome in Iraq, however, the suggestion that perceptions of military competence are driving high military confidence deserves greater scrutiny (Burbach 2017). Moreover, the media landscape has also undergone fundamental changes over the last two decades, with the advent of the internet and the introduction of streaming services. Even if King and Karabell (2003) were correct that increased confidence among millennials—driven largely by their exposure to positive portrayals of the US military on television and in the movies—was the driving factor behind increased military confidence, that explanation is on much flimsier ground today.

Collectively, the existing literature leaves unresolved many questions related to the causes, consequences, and future trajectory of public confidence in the military. In the following chapters, I aim to provide the most systematic and up-to-date answers available. Along the way, however, I have found new questions worth exploring, which I flag for further research in the conclusion.

PART I

WHO HAS CONFIDENCE IN THE MILITARY?

2

Confidence in the Military over Time and Today

> We're at war while America is at the mall.
> —Anonymous marine grunt (Klay 2018)

Most Americans know that the public expresses a high degree of confidence in the US military. Fewer Americans seem to know that it was not always so. Since the founding of the Republic, there has always been a strong undercurrent of suspicion about what the constitutional framers called "a standing army" (Kohn 1975; Ekirch 1956). And as the military grew in size and power beyond anything the Framers imagined, concerns about a "standing army" gave way to concerns about a "garrison state" (Lasswell 1941) and a "military industrial complex" (Eisenhower 1961). Yet, over the past 50 years, these concerns receded somewhat in the public imagination, giving way to a striking level of public optimism and embrace of the military.

Today that confidence is broad, but not universal—and, I would argue, deep but not unbreakable. This chapter explores the ebb and flow in public confidence in the military over the past five decades and then looks closely at a recent snapshot of public opinion to identify which parts of the population express the highest and the lowest levels of confidence.[1] Although the public's confidence in the military remains quite high in the aggregate, there is far more variation across demographic groups than is usually recognized. The analysis in this chapter will draw primarily on underexploited data on American institutions that has been collected as part of the General Social Survey since 1972, as well as the data collected in the new proprietary surveys.

---

[1] This chapter draws on Golby and Feaver (2018) and Golby and Feaver (2019b).

Thanks for Your Service. Peter D. Feaver, Oxford University Press. © Peter Feaver 2023.
DOI: 10.1093/oso/9780197681121.003.0002

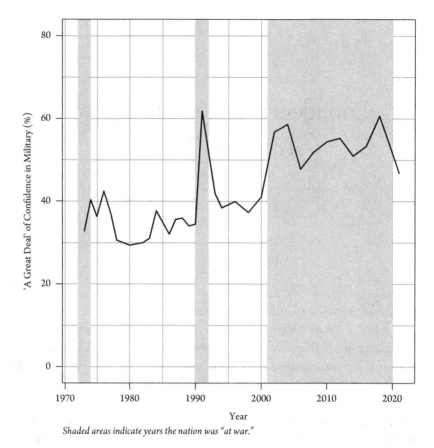

Figure 2.1 Total Public Confidence in the Military since 1972 (General Social Survey, % a great deal of confidence)

Looking at Public Confidence in the Military over Time

The public's confidence in the military did not increase gradually and steadily over time; rather, it occurred in a series of steps—from the 1980s to the 1990s, and from the 1990s to the post-9/11 era—with periods of elevated confidence highly correlated with the years the US military has been in high-intensity combat. Figure 2.1 displays the percentage of the public expressing "a great deal" of confidence in the military from 1973 to 2021, the highest level of confidence available in the Gallup version of the question.[2]

---

[2] All percentages discussed in this section should be interpreted as the percentage of a group expressing "a great deal" of confidence in the US military according to the General Social Survey (1972–2021). Analyses elsewhere in the book may group respondents who report "a great deal" with

In 1976, one year after the end of the Vietnam War, 42% of Americans expressed a great deal of confidence in the military. As fallout from that war became apparent over the next few years, public confidence began to fall. It reached its nadir at 28% in 1980, only months after the humiliating debacle Operation Eagle Claw was ordered by President Jimmy Carter in an attempt to rescue 62 embassy personnel and end the Iranian hostage crisis. Although the number of respondents expressing a great deal of confidence in the US military briefly rebounded to as high as 37% after the successful invasion of Grenada in 1984, public confidence remained mired in the mid-30s until spiking to 61% immediately after Operation Desert Storm in 1991. Public admiration again fell quickly after the war, though it remained in the upper 30s throughout the 1990s—slightly higher than the low-30s average of the 1980s. After the terrorist attacks on September 11, 2001, however, public confidence precipitously spiked to 55%, and since then has only fallen below 50% once, during the height of the Iraqi civil war in 2006.

Confidence in the military increased among all demographic groups, but topline numbers mask significant variation within these groups over time. Although the percentage of men and women expressing a great deal of confidence in the military tracked closely in the late 1970s and early 1980s, the percentage of women giving this response began to fall in 1984 and a gender gap began to emerge, as Figure 2.2 shows. By 1990, confidence among women had dropped to its lowest point on record at 28%. Since that time, men have consistently expressed solidly higher confidence than women, with the gap ranging between 4 and 12 points. Similarly, Figure 2.3 displays change by race. African Americans reported higher confidence than whites as late as 1986, but the number of blacks stating they had a great deal of confidence in the US military fell to a paltry 26% just before the Gulf War in 1990. A clear gap has persisted between whites and blacks since. Nevertheless, it is noteworthy that over the course of the Obama administration the gap between white and black professed confidence closed from 16 points in 2008 to only 3 points in 2016.

Figure 2.4 shows that the millennial generation (those born in the 1981– 1996 years) clearly no longer deserves the "generation of trust" label King and Karabell (2003) gave it, though it likely did in the early 2000s. Although

---

those reporting "quite a lot" of confidence, as is more customary in media discussions of this topic. The focus here is just on those expressing the absolute highest amount of confidence to better illustrate how attitudes move in response to world events. Since I do not have access to panel data, I cannot say for certain what is the new attitude that those who previously reported "a great deal" of confidence might have after some salient news event, but it seems likely that in response to adverse information their confidence drops down one level to "quite a lot." If that is correct, some of the movement would be obscured if I combined responses in the conventional way the media does.

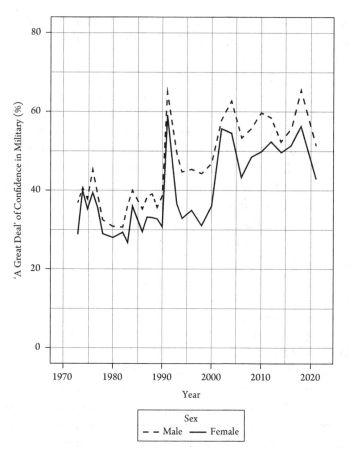

Figure 2.2 Public Confidence in the Military over Time by Gender of Respondent (General Social Survey, % a great deal of confidence)

millennials continued to express extremely high levels of trust until 2004, their confidence in the military has plummeted since. Millennials now express far less confidence than other generations. This change is unsurprising, as evidence of stagnating military campaigns in Iraq and Afghanistan finally seemed to contradict years of positive portrayals of the military in movies and television shows, but it remains in stark contrast to the older baby boomers, the Silent Generation, and Generation X, who have all seen their confidence rebound since 2010. It also is an ominous harbinger of future trends. The fact that younger people show markedly lower levels of confidence than older people suggests that the military may be losing ground with the people who will matter the most over the long term. Although not depicted in a figure, a different type of reversal also took place among those who earned incomes greater than $150,000. During the 1980s and 1990s, this group routinely expressed lower confidence than did

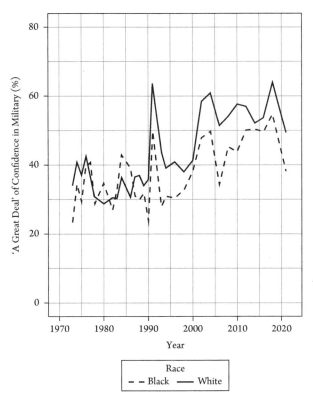

Figure 2.3 Public Confidence in the Military over Time by Race of Respondent (General Social Survey, % a great deal of confidence)

Americans at the bottom of the income ladder. After September 11, 2001, however, these high earners consistently have expressed more confidence than other Americans.

As Figure 2.5 demonstrates, differences in confidence have also persisted across different regions of the United States. Since 1972, southerners consistently have expressed more confidence in the military than have Americans from other regions. Somewhat surprisingly, however, this gap has not grown over time, and midwesterners have rivaled—and even surpassed in some years—the southerners' confidence since September 11, 2001. More surprising perhaps is the significant 11-point surge in support for the military among Americans from the Northeast between 2016 and 2018 (because of data availability, the figure just reports through 2018). Nevertheless, the most enduring regional patterns are those of high support among Americans living in the South and the support among those living in the western states.

The largest and most persistent changes emerged across partisan and ideological lines, however, beginning with the Reagan years. Republicans (25%)

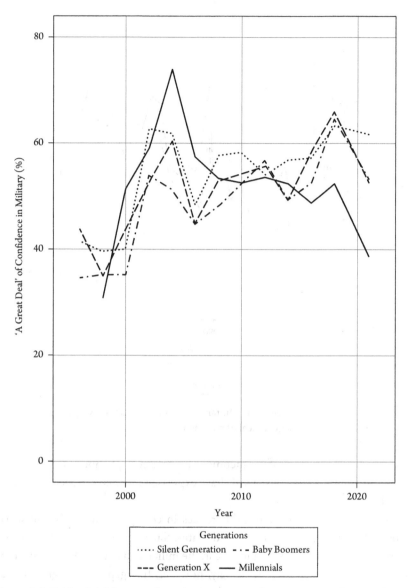

Figure 2.4 Public Confidence in the Military over Time by Generation of Respondent (General Social Survey, % "a great deal of confidence")

were 6 points less likely to express a great deal of confidence in the military than Democrats (31%) just prior to the election of Ronald Reagan in 1980. In 2018, confidence in the military among Republicans (72%) was 20 points higher than confidence among Democrats (52%). The partisan differences in 2018 were virtually indistinguishable from the differences between conservatives (71%) and liberals (51%). It is notable, however, that the ideology gap has grown much

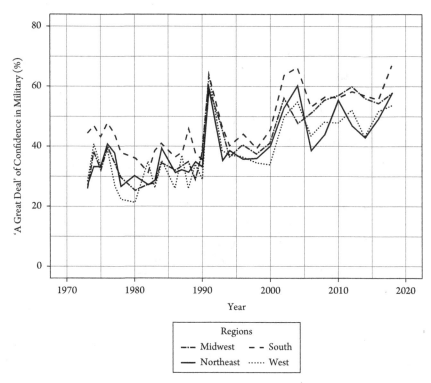

Figure 2.5 Public Confidence in the Military over Time by Region of Respondent (General Social Survey, % a great deal of confidence)

less than the party gap. In 1974, confidence in the military among conservatives (47%) was already 16 points higher than confidence among liberals (31%). This ideology gap shrank slightly to just a 9-point difference during the Carter administration, but it has persisted as the largest demographic gap related to confidence in the military consistently for the last five decades.[3]

The convergence between the party gap and the ideology gap suggests that partisan sorting—rather than a growing divergence in public attitudes about the military—has played a major role in driving these partisan differences. Partisan sorting refers to a broader phenomenon in American politics where parties gradually became more ideologically homogeneous within and more sharply separated on ideology across parties. As a result, citizens are better able to place themselves in the "correct" party based on their ideological preferences (Fiorina and Abrams 2008; Fiorina 2016; Druckman and Levendusky 2019; McCarty

---

[3] Only in 1986, at the height of the Iran-Contra scandal, did conservative confidence in the military (30%) briefly plummet and fall below liberal confidence (33%) before again rebounding to a nine-point gap in 1988.

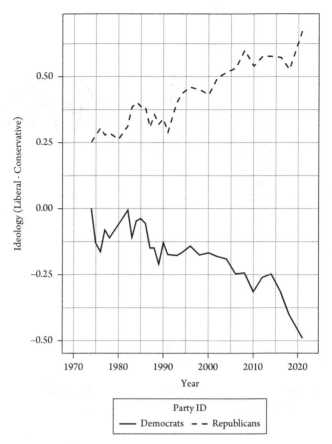

Figure 2.6 Changes in Mean Self-Reporting by Party ID of Respondent (General Social Survey, % a great deal of confidence)

et al. 2006; McCarty 2019).[4] Conservatives stopped identifying with the Democratic Party and liberals stopped identifying with the Republican Party; everyone went "home" to be with other like-minded partisans. In other words, the differences in confidence in the military have not arisen because Republicans suddenly like the military more and Democrats like the military less; rather, the gap has grown because conservatives with already higher confidence in the military have become more likely to identify themselves as Republicans, while liberals with lower confidence have increasingly become Democrats. Figure 2.6 depicts changes in the mean self-professed ideology of both Democrats and Republicans, and Table 2.1 shows changes in the ideological composition of the

---

[4] As Golby (2011) showed, partisan sorting has also driven changes in the senior ranks of the US officer corps. Although the number of conservatives in the military has remained roughly constant since the 1970s, officers are now more willing to identify themselves with the Republican Party.

Table 2.1 **Changes in the Ideological Composition of the Parties from 1974 to 2021 (General Social Survey, %-point change)**

	Liberal	*Moderate*	*Conservative*
Democrat	+26	−10	−16
Independent	−17	+19	−1
Republican	−16	−15	+31
Overall	+3	−5	+2

parties between 1974 and 2021. Although the aggregate number of liberals and conservatives in the US public has hardly changed, the mean ideology of each party has shifted significantly as liberals and conservatives sorted themselves into the correct parties.

This interpretation challenges both Liebert and Golby (2017) and Robinson (2018), which suggest that increased partisanship in the ranks of the military has driven greater affinity among Republicans. If that is happening, perhaps it is happening on the margins, but a simpler process is doing most of the work: people who do not have high confidence in the military simply do not find the Republican Party a congenial home and they leave for the other party, where support for the military is present, but not at such levels of intensity. While attitudes about the military are certainly not the only factor driving this partisan sorting, they may be at least part of the story. And, as discussed in Chapter 3, variations in the ways partisanship and education interact differently among Democrats and Republicans could also contribute to this divergence. Of course, support for the military is not the only—nor even the primary—factor driving these changes in the political parties, but it is one additional reason for conservatives to feel more at home in the Republican Party and liberals to feel more comfortable in the Democratic Party.

Although partisan sorting explains much of the divergence in attitudes, it cannot alone explain why public confidence in the military has increased overall. Confidence among both Democrats and Republicans has increased over the last five decades (and particularly after 9/11), though increases among Republicans clearly have been more rapid. The steplike increase from the 1980s to the 1990s, and from the 1990s to the post-9/11 era, remains evident despite a temporary drop to pre-9/11 levels among Democrats at the height of the Iraqi civil war and just before the blue-wave congressional election results of 2006.

It is possible that improved military performance on the battlefield—or at least public perceptions of improved performance—has helped drive aggregate public confidence (King and Karabell 2003). As suggested in Chapter 1, performance might be thought of as the null hypothesis: perhaps the public expresses greater confidence in the US military now than it did in the aftermath of the Vietnam War because the military did not perform well during the Vietnam War or during the Eagle Claw operation, but beginning with the Reagan-era defense buildup and Goldwater-Nichols reforms, the military dramatically improved its operational performance. The spike in confidence associated with Desert Storm in 1991, during which the US military rapidly defeated the fourth largest army in the world—with much lower than expected US casualties—illustrates this explanation vividly. Perhaps the military gained the confidence the old-fashioned Smith Barney way—by earning it.

Burbach (2017), however, claims that public confidence in the military cannot be explained by performance because, as the title of his article provocatively argues, the US military has been "losing" the wars in Iraq and Afghanistan without a corresponding loss in public confidence. At the summary level, Burbach has a compelling point. When asked to judge the wars in hindsight, the American public expresses quite a negative view on both Afghanistan and Iraq—in early 2020, a Chicago Council on Global Affairs survey showed that 65% of Americans said that the war in Afghanistan has "not been worth fighting," and a similar 67% said the war in Iraq was "not worth fighting" (Smeltz and Kafura 2020).[5] Burbach is right that it would be reasonable to expect that such negative evaluations of the war would undermine public confidence in the military—and yet it did not show up in the 2019 and 2020 surveys conducted for this book. This suggests that either public assessments of war performance are more nuanced than these summary poll questions about the wars capture, or that public confidence in the military is not as dependent on war outcomes as one might expect—or both.

Of course, after the disastrous collapse of the Afghan state within weeks of the pullout of all but a tiny residual force of American troops to protect the embassy in the summer of 2021, the Afghan war was well and truly lost. Polling done in the aftermath of that debacle confirmed that a clear majority (69%) of Americans believed the United States "mostly failed in achieving its goals in Afghanistan" (Green and Doherty 2021). Furthermore, at least one poll—the Reagan National Defense Survey (2021) conducted in the months right after the Afghanistan collapse—seemed to suggest a drop in public confidence; in February 2021 56% of the respondents reported "great confidence" in the military and in November that number had dropped to 45%. The drop from the results of a poll by the same group conducted in November 2018 is even more

---

[5] Data from Chicago Council Surveys. January 10–12, 2020. N = 1,019 adults. Both accessed at https://www.thechicagocouncil.org/research/public-opinion-survey/american-public-support-us-troops-middle-east-has-grown.

pronounced—from 70% to 45%, though the 2018 poll was conducted over Veterans Day weekend and so is perhaps an artificially high baseline. Moreover, combining the top two response categories—"great confidence" and "some confidence"—shows a much smaller drop, 83% in February 2021 to 78% in November. The Reagan survey does not use the same Gallup wording for confidence used in this book, so it is hard to do a direct comparison with the new analyses presented here, but it seems likely that there was some drop-off. The Pew Research Center also asks a different version of the question—their question is "How much confidence, if any, do you have in each of the following to act in the best interests of the public? A great deal of confidence, a fair amount of confidence, not too much confidence, no confidence at all." The Pew survey (Kennedy, Tyson, and Funk 2022) found that in December 2021 the percentage of respondents who reported "a great deal of confidence" was only 25%, a 14-point drop from where it had been in November 2020; combining the two top responses shows a slightly smaller but still marked drop—from 83% to 74%.

However, there are other data suggesting that the drop may not be quite so dramatic. Morning Consult (2022), which uses yet another question that asks respondents about their level of trust in the military ("a lot" or "some"), surveyed about three times a month from October 2020 through December 2021, and the aggregate number ranged from a high of 80% in November 2020 to a low of 73% in December 2021. The Gallup confidence data released in July 2022 showed a similar drop (Gallup 2022). Confidence in every institution decreased from 2021 levels and the military was no exception, dropping from 69% in 2021 to 64% in 2022. This drop was less than the drop in confidence in other institutions, suggesting that the military may have fared comparatively well in a tough environment. Future polling will be needed to unpack how the unambiguous outcome in Afghanistan has impacted public confidence in the military.

That said, the ebb and flow of battlefield performance has not been neat or entirely negative. The US military initially prevailed in Afghanistan in a way that stunned critics—toppling the Taliban even as some prominent voices were claiming the Afghan regime was impervious to military pressure (Apple 2001; Mearsheimer 2001). Two years later, the US military toppled Saddam Hussein in a similarly surprising and low-cost way. To be sure, in both wars, the United States proved unable to consolidate the military gains into a stable postwar order, and within five years the US military was fighting a rearguard action to avoid defeat. Yet even there, the narrative is more complex than Burbach allows. In Iraq, President Bush's 2007 surge decision put the war on a dramatically improved trajectory (much to the surprise of the critics) until the military's departure in 2011 and re-emerging fissures in Iraqi domestic politics opened the door for another decline. US fortunes in Afghanistan improved somewhat after President Obama's own surge decision of 2009, though here the results were more mixed. In other

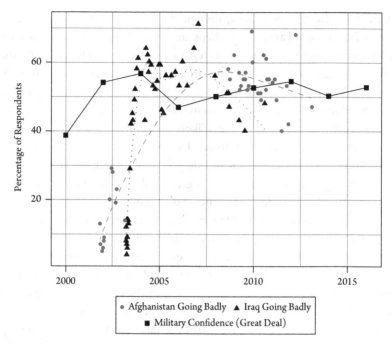

Figure 2.7 Public Confidence in the Military and Public Assessments of Whether Wars are "Going Badly" (Gallup)

words, a close follower of the wars might find ample reasons to credit the US military for its battlefield performance and ample nonmilitary scapegoats to blame for adverse developments. Indeed, Burbach himself notes that three times as many respondents in a 2013 Hoover Institution poll blame the outcome on "civilian policy decisions" as believe that "our military hasn't figured out how to win them."[6]

Figure 2.7 suggests that public confidence might, on the margins, be influenced at least partly by perceptions of battlefield performance. Public confidence in the military jumped markedly in the aftermath of the 9/11 attacks and during the phase when the military surprisingly succeeded in toppling Afghanistan's Taliban and Iraq's Saddam Hussein despite the logistical challenges. Then it dropped back down, losing half of its gain as public assessments of the Iraq war trended dramatically negative in 2004–2006. As the public began to see the positive results of the Iraq surge in 2007–2009, public confidence in the military crept back up a bit.

Burbach also treats performance and partisanship as separate rather than intertwined explanations. Gaines et al. (2007) show that evaluations of

---

[6] Burbach (2017, 163) cites the online database of Hoover Warriors and Citizens Project (https://www.hoover.org/warriors-and-citizens-crosstabs-1). The project eventually culminated in a book, Kori Schake and Jim Mattis, *Warriors & Citizens: Americans View of Our Military* (2016b).

battlefield performance are shaped by partisan filters and media bubbles, and that partisans often draw different conclusions about the military's success even when observing the same objective facts. Nevertheless, Burbach is right that there is at some fundamental level an anomaly between the public's persistently high confidence and now well-entrenched ambivalence about the wars the military has fought.

Although some of the evidence in Figures 2.7 and 2.8 is consistent with Burbach's (2017, 2018) claim that partisans assess the military more favorably when a president from their own party occupies the White House, a closer look at when these partisan changes occur suggests that they may not be purely tribal reactions. Partisans also appear to make largely rational assessments of military policy and performance, though they sometimes may interpret the same facts in different ways based on their underlying values and policy preferences (Gaines et al. 2007). However, consistent with the main thrust of Burbach's argument,

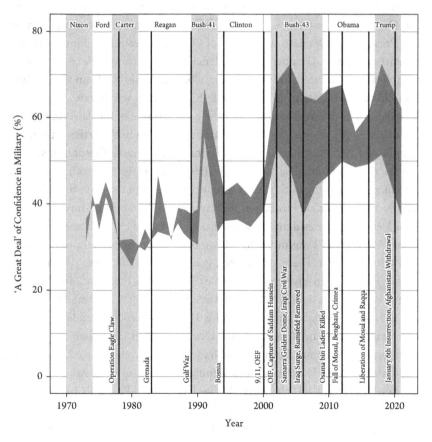

Figure 2.8 Public Confidence in the Military Tracked against War Events by Party (General Social Survey, % a great deal of confidence)

partisan assessments of poor performance seem to be more severe when the opposing party controls the White House and more muted when someone from one's own party occupies the Oval Office. The opposite pattern holds for good news from the battlefield.

The vertical markings in Figure 2.8 note the last GSS poll prior to a number of major events involving the US military. Prior to 9/11, confidence fell among members of both parties following evidence of poor military performance—such as during the "Hollow Force" period of the Carter administration and after the Iran-Contra scandal in the Reagan administration—and rose after more positive military events—including the US invasion of Grenada, the Gulf War, and the NATO intervention in Bosnia in 1996.

Partisan changes after 9/11 are both more complicated and more interesting. Although it is impossible to differentiate clearly between military performance and rally effects using these data alone, confidence among both Democrats and Republicans spiked after 9/11, and elevated confidence in the military has endured ever since. Republican confidence did rise more quickly than Democratic confidence, but these differences became even more apparent after President Bush ordered the start of Operation Iraqi Freedom. Following the start of the war, Democratic confidence dropped from 50% to 46%, while Republican confidence continued to rise, albeit more slowly, from 68% to 70%. After US casualties began to mount and the Iraqi civil war began to deepen in the wake of a bombing that destroyed the golden dome of the Al-Askari Shrine in Samarra, confidence in the military dropped among both parties—though it dropped almost twice as much among Democrats as among Republicans.

After the operational success of the Iraq troop surge in 2007, confidence again increased among both parties, and it continued on the news that US Navy Seals had killed Osama bin Laden in May 2011. By that point, however, there was a Democratic president, Barack Obama, and the Democratic increase between 2008 and 2012 was more than 8 points compared to just a 2 point increase among Republicans. These asymmetric gains inverted following a coordinated attack against two US government facilities in Benghazi, the fall of Mosul to ISIS, and the Russian invasion of Crimea. Between 2012 and 2014, confidence in the military among Republicans crashed by 10 points, while confidence among Democrats dropped by 3 points. As the Obama administration launched a campaign to retake territory from ISIS in Iraq and Syria, confidence began to increase among both Democrats and Republicans. These increases accelerated after local Iraqi and Kurdish forces liberated Mosul and Raqqa in 2017 with the support of US equipment, advisers, and air support. Once again, however, with a Republican president in office as of January 2017, gains among Republicans surged as Democratic confidence increased at a more moderate pace. By 2021, with both outgoing president Trump and incoming president Biden signaling a desire to withdraw from Afghanistan regardless of the conditions on the ground, confidence began to decline again.

On the whole, then, detailed analysis of longitudinal data from the General Social Survey reveals several important insights while leaving other important questions unanswered. First, confidence in the military has increased across virtually every demographic group over the last five decades. Some subgroups—such as conservatives, men, whites, and southerners, in particular—have persistently expressed higher levels of confidence than others, but no single subgroup holds the key to understanding the military's rise in public esteem. King and Karabell's argument that high public confidence was driven by a millennial "generation of trust" no longer holds as a sufficient explanation, if it ever did. Although confidence among millennials did rise meteorically from 40% in 1998 to 66% in 2004, it dropped to 54% by 2018—even as aggregate public confidence rose to its highest recorded level of 61%. And confidence in the military among the younger generations is clearly declining relative to older generations.

Second, increases in confidence have not been gradual and steady; rather, they have proceeded in step changes across decades, with the first significant uptick coming in the wake of the 1991 Gulf War and the second—much larger—increase beginning immediately following the terrorist attacks on September 11, 2001. Indeed, the US military's engagement in a war overseas is more highly correlated with aggregate public confidence than any other variable.

Finally, Americans do appear to make somewhat rational assessments of military performance, but partisanship also plays a major factor in explaining changes in public confidence over time. Confidence among Republicans clearly has grown more rapidly than confidence among Democrats over the last five decades; however, even confidence among Democrats has nearly doubled, from a low of 29% in 1982 to more than 52% in 2018. Perhaps just as importantly, assessments of military performance increasingly are tempered or magnified by partisan filters. Partisans are more willing to give the military credit for good performance when a president from their party controls the White House and more likely to punish the military for bad performance when a president from the other party is in the Oval Office. (The linkage between perceived battlefield performance, partisanship, and confidence in the military is explored in much greater detail in Chapters 5 and 10).

A Close-Up Picture of Public Confidence in the Military: Disaggregating Respondent Type

Although detailed analysis of the GSS data does provide better understanding of which groups moved and when, these surveys were not designed to probe public attitudes about the military in detail, nor to explore why attitudes may have changed when they did, nor to understand what exactly Americans mean when they say they have confidence in the US military. To answer these and other questions, this project designed two original survey instruments by drawing on a variety of sources, including, of course, the standard demographic questions and the well-established Gallup questions exploring public confidence in institutions and leaders of institutions.[7] The new instrument also included questions from the Triangle Institute for Security Studies (TISS) Study on the Gap between the Military and Society from the late 1990s, itself an extension of the decades-long surveys conducted by Ole Holsti (Holsti 1996; Holsti 2001; Feaver and Kohn 2001). As explained in greater detail in the technical appendix (available here: https://dataverse.harvard.edu/dataverse/pfeaver), the National Opinion Research Center (NORC) administered these roughly 15-minute surveys over the internet in two waves: to 4,576 adult Americans from June 18, 2019, through July 8, 2019, and to 4,510 adult Americans from September 10, 2020, through October 14, 2020. In both waves, NORC arranged for a sampling design that would provide an oversample of roughly 900 veterans—more than would normally show up even in a survey administered to this many Americans—to facilitate comparisons across civilian and military divides.[8]

Table 2.2 provides the topline results for the core Gallup question and the 10-point confidence scale, with both broken down by party identification.[9] In the aggregate, 41% of respondents state they have a "great deal" of confidence in the US military, and 75% reported either a "great deal" or "quite a lot" of confidence in 2019; in 2020, those numbers dropped a bit, with 34% reporting "great deal" and 69% reporting the combined level, which we consider "high confidence."

---

[7] In addition to the standard Gallup confidence question, Wave 1 also asked respondents to report their confidence in the military on a 10-point scale. Unless otherwise stated, analyses in this chapter relied on the Gallup question. Analysis using the 10-point scale only substantially alters one of the primary findings, as reported in Chapter 7; in all other cases, the 10-point scale seems to function in about the same way as the standard Gallup question.

[8] The oversample of veterans allows more precise estimates of the veteran population for comparison with the civilian population. The analyses in this chapter did not make use of the veterans oversample.

[9] Note that these are the results only for the 619 of respondents in Wave 1 and the 555 respondents in Wave 2 who received the control in the survey experiment (explained in Chapter 5), i.e., were not prompted with information designed to boost or depress confidence. Also reported are the percentages broken down by the respondents' self-report of partisan identification. Respondents were asked, "Do you consider yourself a Democrat, a Republican, an Independent or none of these?" Respondents who indicated "Independent" were further asked whether they "leaned Democrat" or "leaned Republican." Following a common practice, leaners were grouped along with those who originally identified with a party. See, for example, the Pew Center's explanation for why leaners should be included with other party identifiers (Pew Research Center 2015).

Table 2.2 **Public Confidence in the Military by Party Identification**

	Overall	Strong Dem	Mod Dem	Lean Dem	Ind	Lean Rep	Mod Rep	Strong Rep
Confidence in military (great deal, 2019)	41% (256)	34% (41)	29% (32)	44% (31)	32% (38)	53% (19)	44% (41)	76% (54)
	41% (256)		35% (104)		32% (38)		57% (114)	
Confidence in military (great deal, 2020)	34% (182)	30% (32)	19% (15)	30% (17)	17% (14)	37% (23)	41% (34)	68% (47)
	34% (182)		27% (64)		17% (14)		49% (104)	
Confidence in military (great deal + quite a lot, 2019)	75% (464)	63% (75)	76% (84)	76% (54)	61% (73)	97% (35)	82% (76)	95% (67)
	75% (464)		71% (213)		61% (73)		90% (178)	
Confidence in military (great deal + quite a lot, 2020)	69% (369)	61% (65)	56% (43)	63% (36)	60% (50)	77% (49)	77% (63)	92% (64)
	69% (369)		60% (144)		60% (50)		82% (175)	
10-pt scale (mean, 2019)	7.7 (616)	7.0 (116)	7.7 (107)	8.0 (60)	7.0 (109)	8.8 (46)	7.9 (96)	8.7 (82)
	7.7 (616)		7.5 (283)		7.0 (109)		8.3 (224)	

Note: Numbers in parentheses indicate the number of respondents.

The mean response on the 10-point scale is 7.7, and responses on this scale are strongly correlated (.73) with responses to the Gallup question. A large partisan gap exists, regardless of which measure we use, but this difference is especially striking when comparing "strong Republicans" to "strong Democrats," with the gaps between those who report a "great deal" of confidence and those who report either "a great deal" or "quite a lot" of confidence at 42 and 32 points, respectively, in 2019, and 38 and 31 points, respectively, in 2020.

Table 2.3 instead shows the topline results by ideology and demonstrates just how much partisan identification and ideology have converged. Partisan differences between Republicans and Democrats are virtually identical, with roughly 20-point gaps in 2019 and roughly 30-point gaps in 2020 regardless of which Gallup measure one uses. However, one does see a slight increase in the difference in means using the 10-point confidence scale from 0.8 for party to 1.5

Table 2.3 Public Confidence in the Military by Ideology

	Overall	Ext Liberal	Liberal	Slightly Liberal	Mod	Slightly Cons	Cons	Ext Cons	None
Confidence in military (great deal, 2019)	43% (240)	27% (11)	41% (40)	26% (15)	42% (78)	34% (18)	56% (41)	73% (36)	34% (35)
	43% (240)		34% (67)		42% (78)	54% (95)			34% (35)
Confidence in military (great deal, 2020)	34% (181)	30% (14)	16% (12)	21% (8)	32% (50)	50% (20)	49% (43)	63% (21)	21% (13)
	34% (181)		21% (34)		32% (50)	52% (84)			21% (13)
Confidence in military (great deal + quite a lot, 2019)	75% (464)	43% (16)	74% (67)	74% (40)	77% (132)	82% (41)	88% (59)	93% (42)	65% (67)
	75% (464)		67% (123)		77% (132)	87% (142)			65% (67)
Confidence in military (great deal + quite a lot, 2020)	68% (367)	57% (27)	54% (41)	49% (17)	68% (106)	86% (34)	78% (69)	85% (28)	73% (43)
	68% (367)		54% (86)		68% (106)	81% (131)			73% (43)
10-pt scale (mean, 2019)	7.7 (616)	5.0 (57)	7.7 (83)	7.0 (67)	7.8 (157)	7.6 (68)	8.3 (84)	9.6 (43)	7.4 (57)
	7.7 (616)		6.9 (207)		7.8 (157)	8.4 (195)			7.4 (57)

for ideology. As shown earlier in Figure 2.6, this convergence between party and ideology should be relatively unsurprising because of increased partisan sorting over time. Indeed, our survey confirms an extremely high level of sorting, with 79% of liberals and 80% of conservatives "correctly" sorting into the Democratic and Republican Parties, respectively.

Just as high confidence in the aggregate masks important variation across partisan and ideological subgroups, so too are there interesting variations in confidence by the other main demographic markers that distinguish Americans from each other. Table 2.4 reports the wildly different confidence levels expressed by different demographic subgroups.

To better understand how each demographic factor might be contributing to an individual's overall reported level of confidence in the military, a multivariate regression model shows the correlation of each factor with confidence while

Table 2.4 Percentage of American Public with "A Great Deal" or "Quite a Lot" of Confidence in the Military by Demographics (2020)

	Quite a Lot	A Great Deal	Total (Quite a lot + a Great Deal)
Generation Z (age: 23 & down)	31	32	63
Millennials (age: 23–38)	27	30	57
Generation X (age: 39–54)	39	36	75
Baby Boomers (age: 55–73)	36	40	76
Silent Generation (age: 74 & up)	61	13	74
Male	32	40	72
Female	38	28	66
Active-duty military	18	78	96
Veteran	29	57	84
Nonveteran	35	32	67
Family in military	36	39	75
Social contact with military	29	48	77
White	37	36	73
Black	31	27	58
Hispanic	28	33	61
High school or less	29	36	65
College degree	38	33	71
Graduate degree	35	32	67
Urban	38	30	68
Suburban	31	33	64
Rural	38	45	83

controlling for all of the other factors. (See the technical appendix for full regression model.) Figure 2.9 displays the results of this analysis in a series of predicted probabilities that a respondent from a specific demographic group will report a great deal of confidence in the military, controlling for other factors. Consistent with previous research, the analysis finds large differences across parties and ideology, with conservatives and Republicans nearly 20 points higher than both liberals and Democrats (Liebert and Golby 2017; Burbach 2018). It also finds large gender and racial differences, with men and whites much more likely to

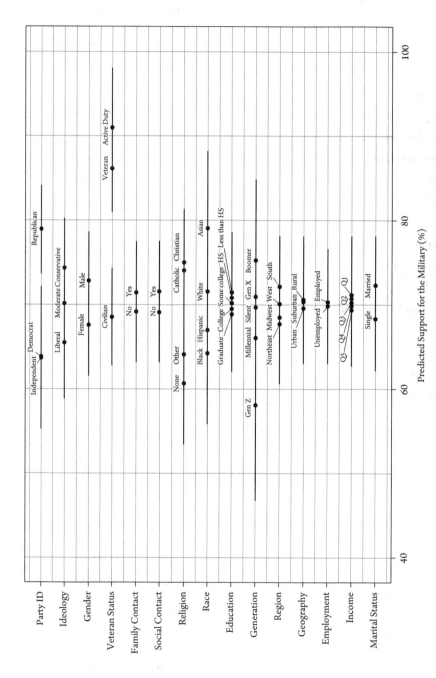

Figure 2.9 Predicting Confidence in the Military by Demographic Features of Respondents (2020)

have a great deal of confidence in the military than women and minorities. African Americans, in particular, express much less confidence in the military than respondents from other racial groups. As in prior studies, self-identified Christians (Protestants and Roman Catholics) express levels of confidence about 10 points higher than those with another or no religious preference. Married respondents and respondents living in urban areas also expressed less confidence than single respondents or those living in suburban or rural areas, respectively. And, consistent with Gronke and Feaver (2001), those who report greater levels of connection to the military—either through social contact, family connections, or personal service—also consistently have higher levels of confidence in the military, a topic explored in greater detail in Chapter 3. Similarly, the differences between active-duty service members and nonveteran civilians are nearly as large as the gap between partisans.

These new surveys also discovered several important demographic changes from previous studies, though they are largely consistent with our longitudinal analysis earlier in this chapter. Contra Karabell and King (2003), millennials, at 57%, are now significantly less likely to express high confidence in the military than are members of other generations, with baby boomers much more likely, at 76%. Also breaking with previous research suggesting that public confidence in the military is a function of southern culture, this survey found that esteem for the military among Americans from the Midwest and Northeast has nearly caught up to that expressed by southerners. Southern confidence did not decline; the other regions caught up. The income reversal noted earlier in the GSS data also holds true in this survey, with wealthier Americans now expressing more confidence in the military than their poorer counterparts, with the poorest Americans significantly less confident than respondents in the other quintiles. The same dynamic held up with respect to employment status, with unemployed Americans expressing less confidence in the military than those holding jobs. Controlling for other factors, differences in respondents' educational attainment are not statistically significant. As explored in Chapter 3, however, the interaction between partisanship and education has changed rapidly in recent years, though it is unclear whether these changes will persist beyond the Trump administration.

The impact that demographic factors play in shaping confidence levels becomes even more apparent when looking at the additive effects of different demographic factors. As a way of capturing this dynamic, one can construct a number of demographic profiles that recur across the American public and show the likely level of confidence a "typical" member who fits that profile might express. The results are displayed in Figure 2.10 (see the technical appendix for

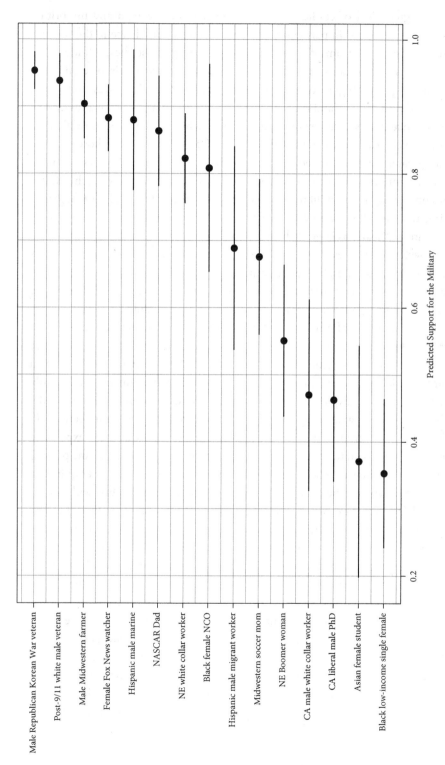

Figure 2.10 Predicting Confidence in the Military by Combined Demographic Profile (2020)

a full breakdown of demographic profiles and the logistic regression model).[10] Although these profiles are not intended to represent the universe of potential subgroups, they do provide a flavor of the variation in confidence levels that exist across America.

Although most descriptions of public confidence in the military emphasize high levels of support, these rough groupings demonstrate that confidence varies significantly across various demographic subgroups of the population. Americans' confidence in the military is hardly uniform. People with different life experiences and from different communities can and do relate to—and therefore perceive of—the military very differently. Depending on the salience of particular issues or the subgroups impacted by certain policies, different portions of the population can be activated in policy debates involving the military. Uniform admiration for those in uniform is by no means guaranteed.

A Close-Up Picture of Public Confidence in the Military: Disaggregating Type of Military

The standard Gallup question just asks about confidence in the "military" without defining what is meant by the military. Most commentary on the Gallup confidence question treats the term as referring to the military as a whole—as an institution comprised of officers and enlisted, with a human element and a weapons element—all of which can function more or less as a unit. That is how the analyses here treat the term, unless otherwise noted. But the confidence question could be thought of as referring to other dimensions of the military. For instance, it could be referring to the topmost leaders who are featured in news commentary about military affairs—the chairman of the Joint Chiefs of Staff, the other service chiefs, and high-profile combatant commanders like those who led the war effort in Iraq and Afghanistan. Or it could be referring to prominent retired military leaders, some of whom speak out often on public affairs and have high-profile perches as talking heads on television and so might be even more salient in the public mind than the active-duty force. Finally, it could also be taken to refer to members of the military whom the individual respondents know personally—colleagues, friends, and loved ones—who stand in for the military as a whole.

---

[10] These results come from several regression models making use of the full sample, including controls for experimental treatments and party interactions, using estimates to predict these values while holding other values constant. Full details are in the technical appendix.

These new surveys cannot conclusively determine what respondents are thinking about when asked the standard Gallup question. But they can shed light on the issue in several ways. For starters, the surveys asked respondents to think about the military in these different ways and to register their levels of confidence accordingly. The results suggest that the public can distinguish somewhat between these various conceptions—and that public confidence is highest overall with respect to an abstract idea of the military as a whole. Yet, crucially, distinctions that are so important to civil-military relations theory, such as the distinction between an active-duty and a retired officer, are only dimly perceived by the public. The evidence strongly suggests that the public lumps all of the military together, as the conventional treatment of the Gallup question assumes.

In addition to the normal Gallup question, Wave 2 also asked respondents whether they had confidence in individual services. As reported in Table 2.5, one sees in the aggregate a fairly flat picture—the predicted level of "high confidence" responses range from a low of 73% for the navy to a high of 77% for the Marine Corps. (Note: in order to get a large enough sample size to track differences across services, the analysis used the full sample and then used a logit model to identify the predicted confidence level, controlling for survey treatments and other possible confounders; see the technical appendix for details of the logit model we used to predict by service variation). As with the overall confidence in the military question, however, this masks cross-party variation, with Democrats and independents reporting markedly lower levels of high confidence for each service than do Republicans. There are also some minor patterns hinting at varying levels of partisan affinity for the services; independents and Republicans rank the navy and army near the top of their confidence list, while

Table 2.5 Comparing Predicted Public Confidence across Branches of the Military (2020) (% great deal + % quite a lot)

	Overall	Dem	Ind	Rep
Army	74%	65%	64%	86.5%
	[71%–77%]	[61%–69%]	[58%–70%]	[84%–89%]
Navy	73%	64%	66.5%	86%
	[71%–75%]	[61%–67%]	[61%–72%]	[84%–88%]
Air force	74.5%	68%	63%	86%
	[73%–76%]	[65%–71%]	[57%–69%]	[84%–88%]
Marine Corps	77%	69%	69%	88%
	[74%–80%]	[65%–73%]	[63%–75%]	[86%–90%]

Note: Numbers in brackets depict the lower and upper bounds of the 95% confidence interval for each estimate.

Democrats rank the air force close to the top. Overall, however, the navy ranks at the bottom with both Democrats and Republicans, and the Marine Corps ranks at the top across each partisan group. But one should not overstate these differences because none of them is statistically significant. I infer from this result that respondents do not make large and substantively meaningful distinctions across the various services. To most in the public, a soldier is a sailor is an airman is a marine, though Chapter 5 will discuss one exception.

Likewise, the survey asked respondents to indicate their level of confidence in "Military Leaders" and in "Retired Generals and Admirals." Here the public does appear to be drawing some distinctions, at least bigger distinctions than regarding the services. As reported in Table 2.6 Americans clearly express more confidence in the "military" than they do in military leaders, with only 66% of respondents stating they had a "great deal" or "quite a lot" of confidence in military leaders and 68% saying the same of retired generals and admirals—a drop of seven to nine points from the level of confidence in the military as a whole in the 2019 survey. Once again, large partisan gaps are apparent; however, the independents' assessment of these groups is notable. At 50% confidence, independents have relatively little confidence in military leaders. Independents have markedly more confidence in retired generals and admirals, and, in fact, have more confidence in this group than they do in the military itself, although these differences are not statistically significant. Although there are few data to explore this pattern in greater detail, one possibility is that independents rely

Table 2.6 **Comparing Public Confidence across Types of Military** (% great deal + % quite a lot)

	Overall	Dem	Ind	Rep
Military (2019)	75%	71%	61%	90%
	(464)	(213)	(73)	(178)
Military leaders (2019)	66%	61%	50%	82%
	(404)	(183)	(60)	(164)
Retired generals (2019)	68%	63%	65%	80%
	(422)	(188)	(77)	(158)
Military (2020)	69%	60%	60%	82%
	(381)	(149)	(52)	(181)
Active troops (2020)	74%	70%	62%	84%
	(413)	(174)	(54)	(185)
Veterans (2020)	75%	68%	67%	87%
	(418)	(168)	(58)	(193)

more heavily on retired officers in the media and on cable news, whom they may perceive as being able to more candidly share their views, to provide information that can help them assess foreign policy decisions.

When directed to think about the military in terms of retired generals, respondents show a seven-point decline in confidence; still high, but distinctly lower than what they say for the military as a whole. When directed to think about active-duty troops or veterans, the change is in the opposite direction. The public rates troops on active duty and veterans higher—five and six points higher, respectively—than they rate the military as a whole. However, other evidence suggests even these differences may matter less than they seem because the public appears to have a difficult time distinguishing between who is on active duty and who is not.

Wave 1 gave respondents three names each from a list of nine of the most prominent military individuals at the time and asked respondents to identify whether those individuals were on active duty or now retired. One of the individuals, Colin Powell, had been retired for nearly two decades, and others had been retired for nearly a decade; still others were on active duty, including then-chairman of the JCS Joe Dunford and his named successor, Mark Milley. One, Jim Mattis, had prominently served as secretary of defense until just months before the survey and, in that capacity, had to deal with a very public controversy over whether it was appropriate for him to serve in a civilian position like that when he was a recently retired general; another, H. R. McMaster, had served as Trump's national security advisor, and had to deal with a similar controversy of the appropriateness of him serving while still on active duty, only to end up prominently being fired a year before we surveyed.[11]

Despite all of the prominent commentary that focused on distinctions between active or retired military, the results show that the public does not know much about who their generals and admirals are or whether they are still on active duty. Figure 2.11 reports the results, which can be summarized quite pithily: on average, the public has very little idea who is retired and who is not. With the lone exception of Colin Powell, members of the public have very little idea who even the most prominent generals and admirals are. In the aggregate, nearly 75% of respondents responded either "don't know" or "never heard of" when asked whether these generals and admirals were on active duty or whether they had retired.

Wave 2 also asked an additional question designed to probe the extent to which the public draws a sharp distinction between those on active duty and

---

[11] The surveys listed the names in two different ways, one without their military rank assigned and one with their military rank—so Joe Dunford and General Joe Dunford, etc. Note that listing the rank had no statistically significant effect.

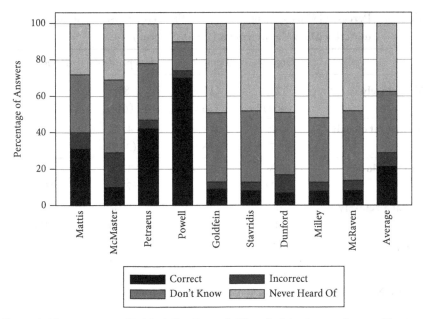

Figure 2.11 Percentage of Public Who Correctly Identified the Serving Status of Senior Military Leaders (2019)

those who formerly served: "How closely do the statements of retired generals and admirals reflect the views of the men and women currently serving on active duty in the U.S. military?" The results in Table 2.7 show that a clear majority (60%) overall think the opinions of retired generals and admirals track with their active-duty counterparts "very or somewhat closely." Interestingly, veterans are even more likely to think this, 69% compared to the 60% as a whole (not reported in the table). The number for the general public is a bit lower than expected and may indicate that the public retains at least some sense of distinction between active and retired voices that are prominent in the media. Nevertheless, this relationship is highly correlated with respondents' assessments of how closely they follow news about the military: 82% and 74% of respondents who say they follow news about the military "very closely" or "somewhat closely"—about half the sample—believe retired generals and admirals reflect the views of those on active duty, while only 30% who say they do not follow news about the military believe the same. In other words, those who are most likely to see retired generals and admirals on the news are precisely the ones who are more likely to think they are speaking for those still on active duty. This evidence is largely consistent with the inference drawn from the preceding two tables: overall the distinction between active and retired generals is not a highly salient one for the public when it comes to what they know about the military.

Table 2.7 **Perceived Closeness of Views of Retired Generals and Admirals to Active-Duty Counterparts (2020, % agree)**

	Overall	Democrats	Independents	Republicans
Very closely	11%	15%	8%	10%
	(464)	(232)	(61)	(171)
Somewhat closely	49%	48%	43%	51%
	(2,177)	(983)	(335)	(859)
Not too closely	30%	27%	32%	31%
	(1,321)	(538)	(253)	(530)
Not at all closely	10%	9%	18%	7%
	(448)	(185)	(138)	(126)
Total	100%	100%	100%	100%
	(4,410)	(1,938)	(787)	(1,685)

Note: Numbers in parentheses indicate the number of respondents.

The public is hard-pressed to say who is and who is not actively serving in the military. And the public draws only faint distinctions between senior military leaders, the rank and file, and the military as a whole—but when it does draw those distinctions, it shows more skepticism about senior military leaders. Collectively, this suggests that the military as a whole is at risk of suffering reputational damage from the deficiencies of only one part—and perhaps that drawing the public's attention to the behavior of prominent individual military members may not be conducive to boosting public confidence in the military. High-profile general and flag officers may be a mixed blessing, from a public relations standpoint.

Conclusion

Topline analysis of the longitudinal GSS data and the new NORC surveys reveals that public confidence persists at elevated levels—a fact generally well known by this point. The analysis here also sheds much more light on the details that are obscured when only the single data point—"how many Americans express a great deal or quite a lot of confidence in the military"—is announced in the media.

The more complex picture presented above is also suggestive of how and why public confidence could decline in the future. In the aggregate, public confidence in the military is highly correlated with whether or not the military is deployed to overseas wars, and—if troop commitments in Iraq and Afghanistan continue to dwindle—America will feel less and less like a nation at war. There is no guarantee current levels of confidence will persist, and a high likelihood they will not, when the nation is no longer on a wartime footing.

Once data are disaggregated, distinct patterns emerge in terms of the type of respondent who might have high confidence in the military. While there are exceptions, of course, on average, high confidence in the military is more a Republican than a Democrat thing, more an old than a young thing, more a male than a female thing, and more a white than a minority thing.

Moreover, when pressed, the public clearly ranks the military as a whole higher than certain prominent military individuals, namely current or retired leaders, but this credit-granting seems to be operating at the margins rather than serving as a major driver of public confidence. This suggests, in turn, that blame-assigning may also only operate at the margins—a topic that will receive more attention in Chapter 10. However, it is also clear that the public does not have a firm grasp on who is actually retired and who is not. I infer that the public likely lumps everyone together, especially if they still use the honorific "General" or "Admiral," as is customary for both retired and active-duty personnel who have reached that high rank. Just as the material benefits of retirement pay and military-funded healthcare extend into retirement, so too do the intangible benefits of association with a high-status organization (a topic explored in greater depth below in Chapter 10).

One difficulty with existing surveys such as the Gallup poll or the General Social Survey is that there is no real way to understand what respondents really mean when they report that they have confidence in the military. In order to explore this issue in detail, the new surveys also asked a number of questions to help better understand different aspects of confidence in the military and to identify different mechanisms that could explain why public confidence may vary. Future chapters explore those data, but first one must dig into a question raised and left hanging by the analyses presented toward the end of this chapter: how do knowledge of and connection to the military shape public confidence in the military?

3

Confidence and the Gaps

Knowledge, Education, Media, and Social Contact

> Whether in your hometown, a park, or a bar, if you end up in a conversation with a stranger and mention that you are or were in the military, someone will make the remarkable confession that he (and it's almost always a he) almost joined the military ... but ...
> —Carl Forsling, USMC (Forsling 2019)

The previous chapter showed that the high confidence the public has in the military in the aggregate masked interesting dynamics that vary with the basic demographic features that shape American public life: our identification with one political party or another, our gender, our age, our race, and so on. This chapter explores the relationship between confidence in the military and another basic identity marker: one's connection to the military. As a general rule (but with important exceptions, as noted below), the intuitive expectation is that the closer one's connection to the military, the more likely one is to have confidence in the military, other things being equal.

"Connection to the military" is measured in four discrete ways. The first looks at subjective self-reports regarding whether respondents think people in the military are just like them. This might be thought of as "connection as identifying with," and one would expect the more you identify with the military, the more you would have confidence in the military. The second looks at more objective measures of knowledge about the military and general education levels. This might be thought of as "connection as knowing about," and here there is not a strong expectation of the relationship since one could come up with a plausible story to account for myriad statistical relationships. Perhaps the more you know, the more you have confidence, in the way that aeronautical engineers might be more immune to fears of flying; or perhaps the more you know, the more you see the problems, in the way that a slaughterhouse

Thanks for Your Service. Peter D. Feaver, Oxford University Press. © Peter Feaver 2023.
DOI: 10.1093/oso/9780197681121.003.0003

inspector might not want to eat sausages. The third way looks at a special dimension of "knowing about," namely the role of the media in shaping what people know about the military; perhaps this could be called "connection as media sourcing," with people learning about the military through different channels and, in the process, developing systematically different viewpoints about the military. Finally, this chapter looks at the personal connections individuals have with those who serve in uniform, either because they socialize with members of the military, work with members of the military, have family members who have served, or have served themselves. This might be thought of as "connection as social ties to," and here the expectation is that the stronger the social link, the higher the level of confidence.

The mirror image of a connection is a disconnect or a gap. This is a chapter about how gaps between the public and the military might shape public confidence. As America shifted to a post–Cold War footing in the 1990s, concerns rose about a growing gap between the military and civilian society. Indeed, an early precursor to this book was the TISS research project designed to explore exactly that gap (Feaver and Kohn 2001). In the late 1990s, it was possible to imagine a future in which the gap between society and the military would grow ever wider. The 9/11 attacks may have changed that trajectory somewhat by producing a large rally round the flag as well as a renewed appreciation for the importance of the military as a provider of national security in a dangerous world. But the underlying demographic and sociocultural trends—the passing of the draft-era generation, the shrinking of the all-volunteer force, the decline of attention to military history and civics in curricula at all levels of education, and the growing diversity of the American experience—continue. Consequently, the gap questions remain as pertinent today as ever.

Connection as Identification with the Military and Public Confidence

When members of the public look at the military, do they think they see something with which they can personally identify, even if they have not themselves served in uniform? And if they do, is such a form of connection related to levels of confidence? Future chapters explore certain dimensions of this kind of identification. Chapter 5 will look at the ethical dimensions—whether the public thinks the military's ethical profile aligns with their own. Chapter 6 will look at the political dimensions—whether the public thinks the military's political profile aligns with their own. This chapter looks at a more basic dimension: what the

Table 3.1 **Whether Most Members of the Military "Look Like Me" by Race (2019, % agree)**

	Overall	White	Black	Hispanic	Asian
Most look like me	12%	14%	9%	7%	18%
	(71)	(48)	(8)	(10)	(5)
Some look like me	30%	33%	24%	29%	11%
	(175)	(112)	(21)	(41)	(3)
A few look like me	18%	18%	14%	21%	27%
	(107)	(60)	(13)	(29)	(7)
Most don't	20%	16%	29%	24%	27%
	(119)	(53)	(26)	(34)	(7)
Don't know	20%	20%	24%	19%	16%
	(119)	(68)	(22)	(26)	(4)
Total	100%	100%	100%	100%	100%
	(591)	(340)	(91)	(140)	(26)

public thinks the demographic makeup of the US military might be and whether individuals in the public think that profile aligns with their own identity.

Wave 1 of the proprietary survey asked respondents how they perceived the demographic makeup of the US military: "As you consider the people serving in the military, do you think they mostly look like you, or do they mostly come from very different demographic backgrounds than you?" The responses were quite evenly distributed across response options: 12% thought that "most look like me," 30% thought "some look like me," 18% thought "a few look like me," 20% thought "most don't look like me," and 20% just said they "don't know."[1] In the aggregate, then, this does not suggest a very high degree of public identification with the military.

Disaggregating respondents by various demographic factors reveals some interesting patterns. Table 3.1 shows there is a noticeable racial component to this identification question: only 33% and 36% minorities of black and Hispanic respondents reporting "most" or "some" members of the military look like me, compared to a solid 47% plurality of white respondents. More strikingly, however, only 30% of Asian respondents state that "most" or "some" members of the military look like me, though this may be due in part to the small sample size. Although not displayed, differences between genders are not statistically

---

[1] This table only reports those who received the control condition on the main experiments, as described in the technical appendix and in Chapters 5 and 6.

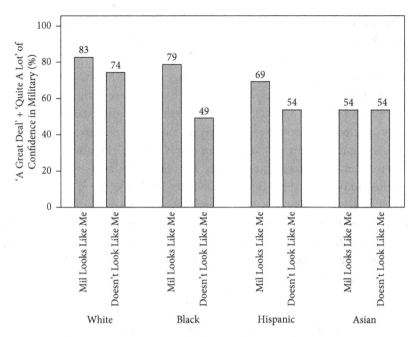

Figure 3.1 Whether Most Military Look Like Me by Race and Confidence Levels (2019)

significant: 44% of men and 41% of women report that "most" or "some" members of the military look like them.

Recall from Chapter 2 that race had a statistically significant impact on one's overall level of confidence in the military. That raises the question of whether race might work in conjunction with this "connection as identification" factor to likewise affect public confidence. Figure 3.1 presents a preliminary cut at this question. In order to have large enough numbers for meaningful comparisons across so many subgroups, the figure here reports the numbers on the full sample. Thus, some of the respondents received prompts designed to nudge up their confidence, while others received prompts designed to nudge down their confidence. As reported in Chapters 5 and 6, these nudges did move confidence a bit up and down, but probably not enough to render this particular analysis invalid.[2] For ease of presentation, this figure combines the confidence responses, so "a great deal" and "quite a lot" are combined into "high confidence," while "some" and "very little" are combined into "low confidence"; likewise, the figure

---

[2] In the technical appendix, there are sensitivity analyses to confirm that the statistical relationship between the "looks like me" question and confidence is statistically and substantively significant in a logistic regression controlling for experimental treatments and all relevant demographic variables used in Chapter 2 and elsewhere in this chapter.

combines the "looks like me" options, so "most" and "some" are combined into "looks like me," while "a few" and "most don't" are combined into "doesn't look like me."

Figure 3.1 conveys the simple intuition that people who think the military looks like them are more likely to express high confidence in the military than are those who think the military does not look like them. Asian respondents are an exception, where there is effectively no movement whatsoever. The drop-off in confidence is more pronounced among black and Hispanic respondents than it is among white respondents. Since, as noted in Table 3.1, whites are more likely than nonwhites to believe that the military "looks like them," the decline in confidence that is associated with the perception that the military does not look like them may be an important part of the overall picture. As Janowitz (1960) would anticipate, one of the benefits of having the military reflect the diversity of civilian society is that such an alignment would prop up overall public confidence in the military.

Connection as Knowledge/Education about the Military and Public Confidence

As reported in the previous chapter, there is much the public does not know about the military. For instance, respondents were not able to identify whether prominent individuals were on active duty or had retired, and this suggested that the public might be lumping everyone together when asked general questions such as the Gallup one on confidence in the military. This section can now dig into this issue more deeply by exploring some of the other measures of knowledge and overall education level.

Wave 1 asked each of the respondents a battery of six other questions designed to tap their basic knowledge about national security matters. In order to avoid having several of the harder questions skew the results, NORC randomly assigned respondents into two groups and gave each group different versions of a few of the questions (with the correct answer **bolded**):

1a. Which of the following is NOT a military service? 1. Army; 2. Air Force; **3. Merchant Marines**; 4. Marine Corps; 5. Navy.

1b. Which military service has the most personnel? 1. Marine Corps; 2. Space Force; 3. Border Security Patrol; **4. Army**; 5. Merchant Marines.

2a. Which of the following ranks from <u>highest to lowest</u> the number of American combat fatalities: Vietnam (1962–1975), Gulf War (1991), Afghanistan (2001–2019), Iraq (2003–2019)? 1. Afghanistan,

Vietnam, Gulf War, Iraq; 2. Gulf War, Vietnam, Afghanistan, Iraq; **3. Vietnam, Iraq, Afghanistan, Gulf War**; 4. Vietnam, Afghanistan, Iraq, Gulf War; 5. Vietnam, Gulf War, Afghanistan, Iraq.

2b. In which of the following countries has a US service member died since the beginning of 2017? Check all that apply. **1. Afghanistan**; **2. Niger**; 3. Yemen; **4. Somalia**; **5. Iraq**.

3. Who is the Commander in Chief of the armed forces? 1. Chairman of the Joint Chiefs of Staff; 2. Army Chief of Staff; **3. President**; 4. Secretary of Defense; 5. Supreme Allied Commander.

4. Are women currently allowed to serve in combat arms units in the US military? **Yes**, No, Don't Know.

5. What does the acronym MRE stand for? 1. Mission Rehearsal Episode; **2. Meal, Ready-to-Eat**; 3. Main Reconnaissance Effort; 4. Mandatory Readiness Exercise; 5. Mars Rover Element.

6. What was the last declaration of war by the United States? 1. after the September 11, 2001, terrorist attacks; 2. after the Soviet Union launched the Sputnik satellite in October 1957; **3. after the attack on Pearl Harbor in December 1941**; 4. during the Cuban Missile Crisis in October 1962; 5. when ISIS captured Mosul in June 2014.

All of the answers are easily available on the internet, and so NORC made a point of asking respondents just to give the answer they could offer on their own without looking up the correct answer.[3]

Table 3.2 presents the topline results of the knowledge quiz. As expected, some of the questions were easy enough that sizable supermajorities knew the correct answer; for instance, nearly everyone knew that the merchant marines were not a military service, and most knew that the army had the most personnel and that the president was commander in chief. Perhaps surprisingly, given prominent commentary about a war-weary public supposedly greatly agitated by the burdens of endless wars, respondents did not seem to be tracking the wars all that closely; the lowest scores were all the questions related to the use of force,

---

[3] As reported in the technical appendix, NORC dropped all respondents who sped through the overall survey as part of their quality assurance process. Although all numbers reported in the text include the full sample, the appendix reports the results of additional robustness checks that exclude any respondents who completed the survey so quickly as to suggest that they were not thinking about the questions. For this battery, there is also a robustness check that dropped respondents who took significantly longer on these questions, suggesting that they were looking up the answers on the internet rather than following directions and answering according to their existing knowledge. Neither approach substantively or statistically altered the reports reported in this chapter, even when both speedsters and slow completers were excluded.

Table 3.2 **Accuracy of Responses to Knowledge Questions (2019)**

Question	% Correct	% Incorrect	Total
Which of the following is <u>not</u> a military service?	93% (2,126)	7% (168)	100% (2,294)
Which service has the most personnel?	81% (1,816)	19% (422)	100% (2,238)
Which of the following ranks from <u>highest to lowest</u> the number of American combat fatalities: Vietnam (1962–1975), Gulf War (1991), Afghanistan (2001–2019), Iraq (2003–2019)?	28% (649)	72% (1,658)	100% (2,307)
In which of the following countries has a US service member died since the beginning of 2017? Check all that apply.	12% (269)	88% (1,974)	100% (2,243)
Who is the commander in chief of the armed forces?	82% (3,710)	18% (828)	100% (4,538)
Are women currently allowed to serve in combat arms units in the US military?	81% (3,712)	19% (850)	100% (4,562)
What does the acronym MRE stand for?	61% (2,790)	39% (1,758)	100% (4,548)
What was the last declaration of war by the United States?	38% (1,711)	62% (2,826)	100% (4,537)
Overall average (knowledge scale)	62%	38%	100% (4,498)

whether there was a declared war, and especially which wars had generated the most US combat fatalities and where US soldiers had died in combat.[4]

The battery forms a simple scale of objective knowledge. As reported in Figure 3.2, the responses follow a standard bell-shaped curve with a few extremely high and low performers and most clustered around the middle. A bell-shaped

---

[4] It is striking that as many as 19% of respondents did not know that Vietnam had the highest US fatality toll, even though Vietnam was 10 times more bloody than Iraq. Likewise, it is striking that as many as 72% of respondents thought the war in Afghanistan had generated higher fatalities than the war in Iraq, even though the death toll was only roughly half as many. A plausible inference is the familiar problem of recency bias, in which respondents overweight recent events in their assessments of risk, combined with the steady drumbeat of negative coverage about the post-9/11 wars in Iraq and Afghanistan, have likely created a general misperception among the public about the true costs of America's wars over the years.

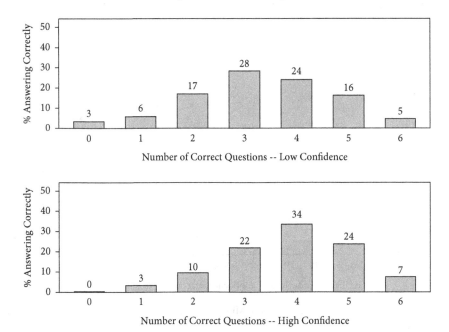

Figure 3.2 The Link between Knowledge about Military Affairs and Public Confidence (2019)

distribution shows up for the portion of our respondents that report high confidence in the military and for the portion that reports low confidence. However, Figure 3.2 also shows that there is a marked knowledge-skew among those with high confidence, meaning that those with high confidence in the military were more likely to score higher on the knowledge test than those with low confidence. To be sure, there is a sizable percentage of the public—as many as 21%—who both know a lot about the military (get all the questions right or miss just one) and who report low confidence in the military; by comparison, 31% of those with high confidence scored that well on the quiz. But the overall pattern is notable: those with high confidence in the military tended to know more about the military than those with low confidence.[5]

One can also probe this issue by using a cruder proxy for knowledge about the military: education level.[6] Recall from Table 2.4 in the previous chapter that education level was positively correlated with higher confidence in the military. Respondents with just a high school education or less had a high

---

[5] As reported in the technical appendix, this pattern is strongly statistically significant when one controls for other predictors of confidence in the military in a multivariate logit model.

[6] The correlation between education-level and knowledge is .32. Even when controlling for other demographic and social factors, this relationship remains statistically significant.

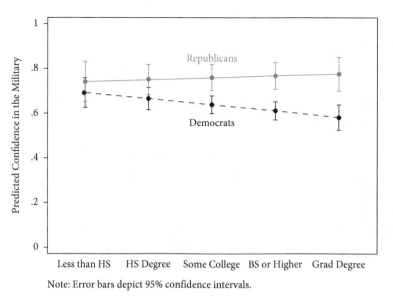

Figure 3.3 Predicted Confidence in the Military by Education and Party ID (2020)

level of confidence overall, 64% in the 2020 survey, but that climbed to 72% for those with a college degree before falling slightly to 67% for those with a graduate degree. However, when one digs deeper, interesting patterns emerge that suggest education's impact on confidence depends in part on one's partisan identification.

First, as depicted in Figure 3.3, the modest positive relationship between education level and confidence in the military seen in the aggregate is present only among Republicans, and it is not statistically significant when controlling for other factors that influence confidence. For independents, there is no such positive relationship; if anything, higher-education independents have a slightly lower level of confidence. Democrats, however, exhibit a negative relationship between confidence and education level: when controlling for other factors in a multivariate logit model, higher-education Democrats show a markedly *lower* level of confidence in the military.[7] Republicans and Democrats with no high school degree both have roughly the same levels of confidence in the military, but confidence in the military diverges as education increases. Democrats with higher levels of education break with the rest of the population to exhibit lower levels of confidence. One must be careful not to overstate this effect. Education is a driver of confidence, but it is notable that it seems to operate one way with Republicans and another way with Democrats. This divergence hints at a

---

[7] A similar result is found in unpublished analyses of surveys run in 2012, as reported in Golby and Feaver (2018)

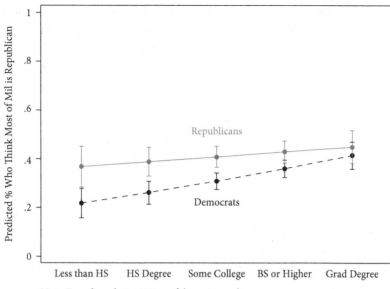

Figure 3.4 Perceptions of the Military's Partisan Makeup by Education Level and Party ID (2020)

pattern to be explored in much greater detail in Chapter 6, namely the partisan underpinnings of confidence in the military.

The differential effect that education level has on Democratic versus Republican respondents shows up in another area, as depicted in Figure 3.4. Education level has no impact on Republican assessments of the partisan makeup of the military; low-educated Republicans give answers that are virtually indistinguishable from highly educated Republicans. But with Democrats, education level seems to have an impact in shaping perceptions. The higher the level of education, the more likely that Democratic respondents will think that the military is Republican, when controlling for other factors.[8]

Combining these two factors—respondents' perceptions of military partisanship and respondents' education level—in a single model predicting the respondents' level of confidence in the military yields the result that perceptions of partisanship do significantly reduce, but do not completely eliminate, the

---

[8] This dynamic is clear with respect to the respondents' perceptions of the partisan makeup of the military. It showed up in the unpublished 2012 data and the 2019 survey wave. It also worth considering whether a similar dynamic obtained with perceptions of other aspects of the military, for instance perceptions of whether the military is educated. In 2012, the more educated a Democratic respondent is, the *less* likely he or she is to think the military is educated. However, that result could not be replicated with the 2019 data. More educated Democrats were slightly less likely to believe members of the military are educated, but this difference was not significant.

effect of one's education level (see the technical appendix for model, available here: https://dataverse.harvard.edu/dataverse/pfeaver). Although not presented, the positive effect of factual knowledge also appears to hold even when conditioning on partisanship; however, greater factual knowledge is a slightly stronger predictor of higher confidence in the military among Republicans than it is among Democrats or independents. This suggests that education may serve to prime or teach partisans what they should think about the military in different ways, though the cross-sectional data in these proprietary surveys are too limited to determine this for sure. It also raises questions about the different roles that factual information and social narratives might play in the education process among partisans.

In sum, the knowledge connection appears related to public confidence in the military. However, the effect of education is at least partly conditioned on partisanship. In the aggregate, people who appear to know more about the military also have higher confidence in the military. And, in the aggregate, people who have higher education levels have higher levels of confidence. But Democrats show a different pattern, one where higher levels of what I am calling a "knowledge connection" produces somewhat lower levels of confidence. In short, Republicans and Democrats both appear to learn about the military as they become more educated, but they may learn different things.

Connection as Media Sourcing: The Channels by Which the Public Learns about the Military

For most Americans, what they know about the military comes through the media, whether the news media or popular media like television and films. The military is quite prominent in the media, especially the popular media, and so even if someone is not a news junkie, it is likely that most American adults have read, heard, or watched things that conveyed ideas about the military. These proprietary surveys make it possible to probe how a respondent's consumption of media might be linked to different perceptions about the military, including different levels of expressed confidence.

First, the survey asked our respondents, "What is the most common way you get political and election news?" Figure 3.5 depicts the results, which track with other studies marking the decline of radio and print journalism and the rise of television and especially new social media (Shearer 2018; Mitchell et al. 2021; Napoli 2011).[9]

---

[9] The results in Figure 3.5 track closely with a Pew Research Center poll conducted in November 2019. The difference for each individual source falls well within the margin of error: https://www.journalism.org/2021/02/22/americans-who-mainly-got-news-via-social-media-knew-less-about-politics-and-current-events-heard-more-about-some-unproven-stories/.

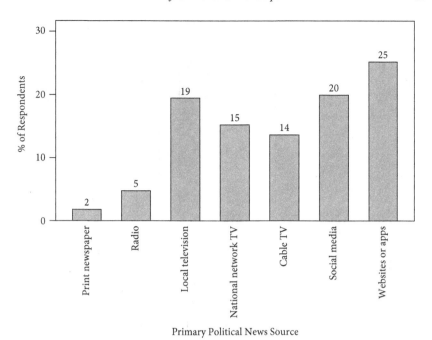

Figure 3.5 Most Common Media Source for Political News (2020, % of respondents who picked each source)

Of greater interest is the link, if any, between the primary source of news and the respondents' level of confidence in the military. Figure 3.6 depicts one cut at that question. There is some variation, ranging from relatively low levels of confidence among those who rely on local television to the relatively high levels of confidence among those who rely on national network television. But no meaningful pattern in this variation seems to emerge. Other studies have shown that those who rely primarily on social media and other forms of "new media" for their political news are less engaged and less knowledgeable (Mitchell et al. 2020, 2021). The findings here do not challenge that view but suggest that, if so, this dynamic is not making them an outlier in terms of public confidence in the military.

A more interesting pattern emerges when exploring how confidence interacts with the respondents' identification of the news sources they trust and distrust, as reported in Table 3.3. Because the survey followed the Pew Research Center's approach (Jurkowitz et al. 2020) and deliberately picked news sources with a pronounced and widely perceived partisan skew, this trust in the media is another way of capturing the partisan dimensions of military confidence. Respondents who claim to trust right-leaning outlets (Rush Limbaugh, Breitbart, Fox, and *Wall St. Journal*) have markedly higher levels of confidence than those who claim to distrust those same outlets. The pattern is less marked and somewhat more

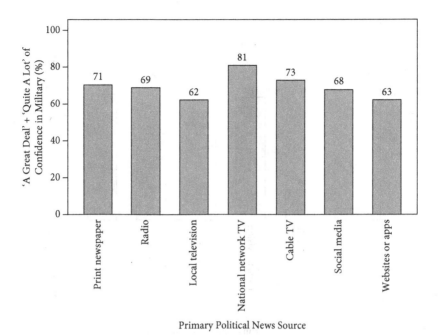

Figure 3.6 Confidence in the Military by Most Common Political News Source (2020)

mixed with respect to the left-leaning outlets. Yet note that for the outlets that received the highest levels of criticism from President Trump and his allies—the *New York Times*, CNN, and the main network television outlets—people who claimed to distrust those outlets had somewhat higher levels of confidence in the military. It is not clear why the pattern does not show up in a similarly left-leaning outlet like NPR, though perhaps it is an artifact of NPR's effort to brand itself as above partisan politics.

The foregoing discussion looked at the media effects through the prism of how respondents report that they get their *political* news. Yet the results are not much different when one homes in on the media effects through the prism of how respondents get their *military* news: "How have you, personally, learned most of what you know about the military?" As depicted in Figure 3.7, by far most of the respondents claim to learn about the military either from regular news sources or from friends and family with military experience. As expected, these sources greatly dwarf personal experience. It is surprising, however, to see how few claim—or perhaps how few admit?—that they mostly learn about the military from entertainment, whether movies or television.

Figure 3.8 shows a meaningful, if muted, pattern for how one's source of learning about the military might shape high confidence in that institution. People who report learning from the military whether directly or through social connections report higher levels of confidence than those who report learning

Table 3.3 **High Confidence in the Military by Trust/Distrust in News Media Sources (2020) (% a great deal or quite a lot of confidence)**

News Source	Trust	Distrust	Neither
Rush Limbaugh Radio Show	87% (83)	63% (153)	66% (100)
Fox News	85% (137)	63% (153)	58% (82)
Breitbart	83% (43)	65% (123)	71% (100)
Wall Street Journal	78% (144)	67% (87)	62% (142)
ABC/NBC/CBS	76% (189)	77% (112)	49% (73)
National Public Radio (NPR)	74% (147)	68% (70)	64% (124)
Huffington Post	73% (83)	72% (93)	67% (165)
New York Times	70% (143)	77% (114)	62% (116)
CNN	70% (132)	79% (158)	56% (86)

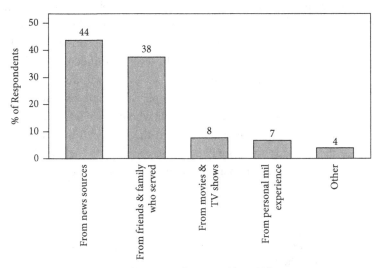

Figure 3.7 Primary Source of What Respondents Learned about Military (2020, % indicating yes)

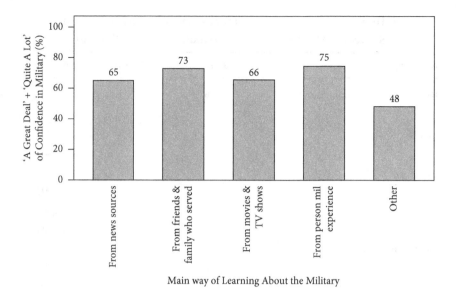

Figure 3.8 High Confidence in Military by Source of Learning about Military (2020, % with high confidence)

about the military from news or entertainment media.[10] The small (4%) percentage of respondents who report learning from some other unspecified source have dramatically lower levels of confidence in the military, but given the small sample size, this finding should not be pushed too hard.

This pattern of the closer one's connection as measured by source of information is seen even more vividly when looking at how closely respondents claim to be following news about the military: "How closely do you follow news related to the military?" As depicted in Figure 3.9, the more closely one claims to be following news about the military, the higher the level of confidence.[11]

In sum, when connection to the military is viewed in terms of one's source of information about the military, intuitively plausible patterns emerge. People who trust conservative-leaning outlets, people who distrust left-leaning outlets, and people who learn what they know about the military from their own experience or their friends are more likely to be people with high levels of confidence in the military. By contrast, people who distrust conservative and trust

---

[10] The differences between both "from friends and family" and "from personal experience" are statistically significant when compared to "from news sources," but not when compared to "from movies and TV shows." The differences between "other" and every other source are also statistically significant.

[11] As shown in the technical appendix, this relationship is significant in a logistic regression when controlling for other variables described in Chapters 2 and 3.

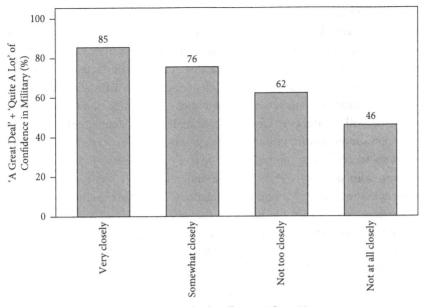

Figure 3.9 Confidence in the Military by How Closely One Follows Military News (2020, % high confidence)

left-leaning outlets, or who learn about the military from a somewhat greater remove, also tend to have somewhat lower levels of confidence.

Connection as Social Ties to the Military and Public Confidence

The finding, reported above, that people who learn about the military from personal experience or from friends and family are different from those who get their military information from the media underscores that social connections to the military are correlated with public confidence in the military. Recall from Table 2.4 that the subgroup with the absolute greatest overall percentage expressing high confidence in the military were those respondents in our sample who were on active duty—fully 96%. Veterans, individuals who had served in the past, were also among the groups showing exceptionally high levels of confidence—in 2020 as high as 84%. Nonveterans in the aggregate still showed high confidence overall—67%—but this is substantially lower than what we find among those who served or are serving.[12]

---

[12] In the 1990s, the effect was dramatically larger when contrasting military and civilian "elites," and I see no reason to believe that pattern has changed even though I cannot measure it with these data. See Gronke and Feaver (2001).

Previous research showed similar results with respect to those who have social connections with the military—friends and loved ones in the military. A larger percentage of those with social ties expressed higher confidence in the military than respondents who reported no such ties. Analyses conducted on the 2013 Hoover Institution data show that confidence among civilians who interact socially with someone who served is about eight percentage points higher than it would be otherwise, even when controlling for other demographic factors.[13] These new surveys confirm this roughly eight-point difference: respondents who report social contact in the military have higher confidence (75%) compared to those who do not (67%), and respondents who report having a family member in the military have more confidence (75%) than those without family connections (65%). Notably, however, the differences based on social contact are not very robust; they disappear when one controls for respondents' own veteran statuses and other basic demographic variables in the 2020 survey.[14]

The degree to which the public has connections with the military is itself subject to debate. It is beyond question that fewer Americans have a direct, personal connection with the military today than, say, at the height of the mass mobilization military in the wake of World War II and while there was still something close to universal military service for males in this country (Pew Research Center 2011). However, the trope of "1% and 99%," as in "1% of America went off to war and 99% went off to the mall," almost surely confuses the issue.[15]

For starters, in 2019, the active and reserve and National Guard military was actually only 0.72% of the total population; the number climbs to 0.99% if one includes civilians who are serving in DoD (US Department of Defense 2019). However, if one includes veterans in the numerator, then the percentage with a direct personal connection to military service was as high as 6.2% in 2018, and climbs to 6.5% if one includes civilians who are serving in the DoD (Defense Manpower Data Center 2018). Moreover, if one says that the proper baseline

---

[13] Although the Hoover YouGov survey did not ask the same confidence question as either Gallup or the General Social Survey, it did ask respondents whether they had "confidence in the ability of the military to perform well in wartime," offering response categories of "Strongly Agree, Agree, Neither Agree nor Disagree, Disagree, and Strongly Disagree." The results held across various ordered logit regression models, with the *Confidence* as the dependent variable and *Social Interaction* as the independent variable, controlling for other standard demographic factors including party, ideology, race, gender, age, education, and religion. These results held with little difference in the models regardless of whether the model used the *Social Interaction* questions for 1, 3, 6, or 12 months. For more see Golby, Cohn, and Feaver (2016).

[14] Differences based on family contact remain strongly significant in all model specifications of the 2019 survey and in most specifications for the 2020 survey.

[15] The "1% and 99%" framing is usually offered as a way of dramatizing the burdens on the military and, perhaps, of reinforcing a sense of guilt or at least obligation among those who have not. For example, see Starbucks' site on its military commitment (Starbucks n.d.) or Egan (2012).

is not the total population, but rather the population greater than 18 years of age (the age at which service in the military usually would begin), then the percentages shift accordingly: the active force is 0.51% of the population, active plus reserve/guard is 0.93%, plus civilians is 1.27%, plus vets is 8.4% (all for 2018, the last year for which I found data).[16]

If one expands the definition of military connection still larger to include those with a family connection, the percentages grow somewhat larger. Here the numbers are harder to pin down, but I estimate that in 2019 another 0.80% of the population (2% of the older-than-18 population) were immediate family members of someone serving in uniform. The Tragedy Assistance Program for Survivors organization, a private organization that serves the families of the fallen, puts the estimate much higher; they assume that as many as 10 family members—parents, spouses, siblings, children, fiancés, grandparents, and cousins—are directly affected by every military fatality. This would take the percentage of "close connectors" to the current force well above 10%.[17]

And if the definition is expanded to include family members of someone who served, then the number climbs to a strong minority of the American public, even today, some 48 years after the draft ended. The 2020 survey included a battery of questions designed to measure whether respondents had a personal connection to the military. The survey asked, "Has a member of your immediate family (parent, spouse, sibling, or child) served, or do they currently serve, in the military?" It then followed up to ask whether the relative was a spouse, parent, sibling, child, grandparent, or other. It also asked whether those relatives served before or during 2001, after 2001, or both. Figure 3.10 depicts the results. As many as 41% of the respondents indicated that they had some family connection to the military. Among veterans, however, family connections were higher, at 61%. Combining all respondents—both civilian and veteran—with a family connection with those veterans or service members who do not have a family connection yields a rough-and-ready estimate of some 44% of the population who have a personal tie to the military—either they or a close family member are serving or have served in the military. As already reported in Chapter 2, these are individuals who are likely to have a higher confidence in the military than individuals in the rest of the population—as high as 96% approval for currently serving, 84% for those who are veterans, and 75% for those with family members. It is notable, however, that the number of respondents who report a family connection to someone who has served in the military since September 11, 2001, is much lower, at only 13%.

---

[16] US Census Bureau (2020a, 2020b); US Department of Defense (2018, 2019).
[17] Author's estimate based on data accessed here: https://www.taps.org/faq.

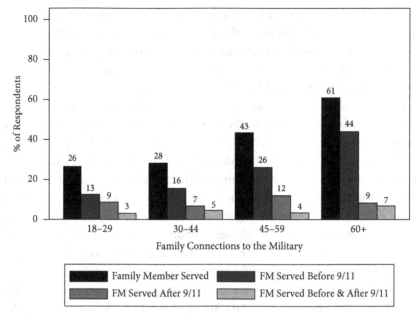

Figure 3.10 Family Connections to the Military by Age Cohort and Dates of Service (2020, % responding yes)

The 2019 survey also asked whether respondents had a social or work connection: "Have you socialized or worked with someone in the military or their spouse in the last 30 days?" and a separate question asking about a longer time frame, "in the last year." In 2019, fully 60% of the respondents indicated that they had some social or work connection in the previous year, and 41% indicated that the connection was as recent as the last 30 days.[18] As already noted, people in this category are more likely to report higher confidence in the military, as much as 77%, than are those in the rest of the population. However, those differences are not statistically significant once one controls for veteran status and other demographic variables. This result suggests that social contact may not play as much of a direct role in elevating public confidence as many previous commentaries, including some of my own earlier work, had argued.

---

[18] These questions show up in the 2020 survey fielded at the height of the pandemic. Responses in 2020 were somewhat deflated compared to the 2019 survey and previous polls: 43% of respondents reported social or work contact in the last year and 25% reported contact during the prior 30 days. Because of the pandemic's dramatic impact on work and social schedules, the 2020 numbers probably overstate the decline and lead to misleading inferences about the long-term picture. The 2019 numbers suffice to show the gradual decline in the opportunities for Americans to interact personally with those who have served.

The 2020 survey probed the influence of personal connections with the military on overall confidence in yet another way. Were individuals who answered the basic Gallup question—"Please tell me how much confidence you, yourself, have in the military"—thinking about the military as a whole when they answered that question, or were they thinking about individuals in the military that they knew personally? Quite late in the survey, the question was put to them directly: "Earlier you indicated that you had [insert response] of confidence in the military. If you were to re-answer that question, but exclude consideration of your co-workers, friends, or family that are in the military and instead think only of the rest of the military, how much confidence would you say you, yourself, have in the military—a great deal, quite a lot, some or very little?" This allows a comparison of the answer they give about confidence in the military when asked in general terms and then the answer they give when asked to ignore the people they know personally and only think about the military institution in the abstract. Figure 3.11 depicts the results.

The results are intriguing and suggestive, but perhaps not dispositive. In the aggregate, asking respondents to exclude their own personal contacts with service members when they assess their confidence in the military actually nudges confidence up slightly—from 73% to 75%, an insignificant difference. Since these surveys are the first to ask the question this way, I would hesitate to push this finding too hard. Moreover, Figure 3.11 shows that updating moves in different directions with respondents' prior confidence levels. This indicates that some people with high confidence seem to *reduce* their confidence when they

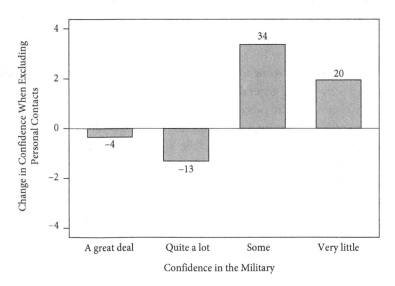

Figure 3.11 Change in Public Confidence in the Military in the Abstract versus as Known by Personal Connection (2020, % with high confidence)

exclude the people they know; that is, for some people, the military as a whole is not as confidence-worthy as the portion they know personally. However, a fairly large number of individuals who have low confidence respond so because they have negative contacts with someone in the military, even though this group is a fairly small portion of the sample (~25%). As discussed at the top, the kind of granular knowledge about the military that comes with close personal connections could produce either high confidence (as in the aerospace engineer without fear of flying) or low confidence (as in the meat inspector eschewing sausage). The data here suggest that both are in evidence, but the former is more abundantly so.

Properly measured, then, the American public still retains a far greater degree of connection to the force than the "1% versus 99%" trope captures, and this connection is indeed a prop undergirding the public's overall high confidence in the military. However, even the substantial connections reported here pale in comparison to the post–World War II days, when virtually everyone served, had a family member who had served, or was friends with someone who had served. Those days are past and, presumably, not going to return, for obvious demographic reasons. A decade ago, for instance, the Pew Research Center estimated that around 61% of Americans had some family connection to a veteran—a significantly higher figure than our current estimate of 41%–44%. Pew estimated that the percentage of younger people with a family connection is much lower, 33% for 18- to 29-year-olds, but this is partly a function of the passing of the World War II generation and partly a life-cycle effect since younger people have by definition lived shorter lives and thus have had fewer opportunities to make connections with anyone, including veterans) (Pew Research Center 2011). The Hoover Institution 2013 poll offered yet another, still more expansive, definition of contact: social contact. The survey asked respondents to report whether they had socialized with someone in the military or their spouse in the last 30 days or last year; among the general population, the percentages ranged from 35% to slightly over 45%. The percentages were even higher among elites, ranging from 45% to 62%, suggesting that significant percentages of both the public and elites have some sort of connection to the military.[19] In the new survey, older Americans report many more "family contacts" in total but not more family contacts with those serving in the post-9/11 wars—that is, with the younger veterans who will still be alive to establish connections and, we theorize, to shape public confidence. In short, the "1%, and 99%" trope overstates the magnitude of the issue, but not the trajectory.

[19] These percentages were calculated by James Golby using source data from the Hoover Institution studies. Data available on request from Golby.

Conclusion

As expected, closer connections to the military, however defined, tend to be associated with higher levels of confidence in the military. However, also as expected, this pattern is not absolute and, in some cases, depending on how it is measured and depending on other conditions like partisanship, a closer connection seems to produce either no change or even a slight decrease in confidence.

Perhaps the vague concept of "connection" needs to be more precisely measured to yield reliable results. The foregoing showed that it is possible to measure connection in four ways. The first is "connection as identifying with the military," as measured by subjective self-reports regarding whether respondents think people in the military are just like them. People who think the military looks like them are more likely to have higher confidence in the military than are people who think the military does not look like them. The drop-off effect is particularly pronounced among black and Hispanic respondents. The logical inference is that diversity concerns are indeed a meaningful contributor (or underminer) of public confidence.

Second is "connection as knowing about" the military, as measured by factual knowledge and by education levels. While there were not strong prior expectations on this approach, an intuitively plausible pattern emerged. In the aggregate, people who appear to know more about the military also have higher confidence in the military. And, in the aggregate, people who have higher education levels have higher levels of confidence. But the effect is conditioned on partisanship since Democrats show a different pattern: higher levels of a "knowledge connection" produce somewhat lower levels of confidence.

Third is "connection as media sourcing"—how respondents know what they think they know about the military. Here the partisan skew in media outlets produces a predictable pattern in confidence. People who trust conservative-leaning outlets, or distrust left-leaning outlets, have higher levels of confidence than people with the opposite media trust profile. Moreover, people who learn about the military from the media have lower levels of confidence than those who learn about the military from first- or secondhand exposure.

Finally, there is "connection as social ties to those who are in uniform," measured by the family connections or work and social connections. As expected, people with a personal connection to the military—either because they themselves served, they have family members who served, or they socialize or work with people with strong military connections—have higher levels of confidence than those without such connections. When pushed to self-examine the extent to which those personal connections were driving their overall level of confidence, respondents indicated that those personal connections might have a slight positive-skewing effect; a small but not-insubstantial minority indicated that their personal exposure actually drove down their confidence in the military, at least somewhat.

Viewed in toto, however, seemingly inexorable demographic trends—the increase in the general population, the decrease in the size of the armed forces, and the passing of generations with larger cohorts of veterans—mean that over time the personal connection prop is likely to diminish. Increasingly, the connections that bind Americans to the military will be heavily mediated by what they can learn through news and entertainment media or perhaps picked up along the way of getting a general education.

This and the preceding chapter showed that one can explain a fair bit of the public's overall confidence in the military just with resort to what might be broadly considered exogenous features of the public—race, gender, party ID, ideology, and various forms of connection to the military. Chapters 5 and 6 will probe the extent to which the public's confidence is driven by perceived qualities of the military—its competence, professionalism, and political makeup. But first, the next chapter will explore how public confidence in the military compares to public confidence in other institutions and whether this comparison, implicit or explicit, might somehow be shaping the way the public views the military.

PART II

WHY DO PEOPLE HAVE CONFIDENCE IN THE MILITARY?

4

Comparing Public Confidence across the Military and Other Institutions

> If they got the order this hour to mobilize and get resources to the places in this country that are suffering, they would give it their all and they have the best logistical capacity of any organization in America . . . he should get the hell out of the way and let the military do its job.
> —Bill de Blasio (Bekiempis 2020)

In early April 2020, just weeks after the nation began its response to the Covid-19 pandemic, former undersecretary of defense—and later to be secretary of the air force—Frank Kendall penned a *Forbes* essay titled "It's Time to Put a Military Officer in Charge of the Fight against Coronavirus." Kendall was only one of many voices to call for the military to play a leading role in the nation's pandemic response or to equate the response to a war, but his essay was notable nonetheless. In it, the former Pentagon acquisition and logistics chief argued that a military officer should be granted the temporary authority to "commandeer resources from any agency," including "HHS, CDC, FDA, DHS, FEMA, and the Departments of Defense, Commerce, and State" (Kendall 2020).

Reflexive calls, like Kendall's, for the military to assume a leadership role in a nonmilitary crisis reflect not only increased public confidence in the US military, but also a severe lack of faith that other government institutions can fulfill the responsibilities they were created to fulfill on behalf of the American people. Why has public confidence in the US military increased over the last three decades while confidence in other government institutions has stagnated or declined?

This chapter explores the determinants of public support for government institutions—not only the military—to assess the strength of competing and complementary explanations for variations in confidence and to understand why

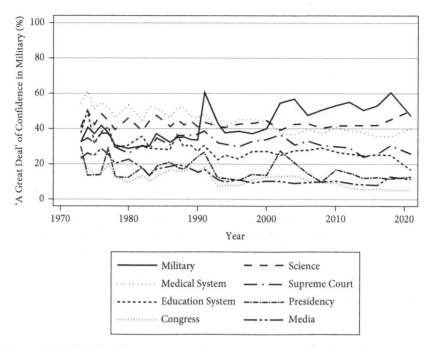

Figure 4.1 Public Confidence in Various Institutions over Time (Gallup, % "A Great Deal")

the military stands so far above the rest.[1] The data show that public perceptions of institutional performance, professional ethics, shared values, and partisanship drive elevated public confidence in the military—as well as confidence in several other professions—and help explain why public assessments of other government institutions have declined. In other words, the average American believes that the military works, and that it works on behalf of most Americans, and that most other government institutions don't.

Changes over Time

The pattern emerges when reexamining longitudinal data from the large trove of polls done by the General Social Survey (conducted by NORC) that were explored in Chapter 2. Figure 4.1 depicts the now-familiar result that over time the military gained separation from other comparable groups to become the standout institution in terms of public confidence. In the immediate aftermath of the Vietnam War, the military was ranked squarely in the middle of the

---

[1] This chapter draws on Golby and Feaver (2020).

pack—slightly above Congress, the executive branch (i.e., the president), and the media; it was basically coequal with the Supreme Court; and it was below education, medicine, and the scientific community. By 2020, it stood almost alone at the top, nearly 20 points above the scientific community, its closest comparative among this group, markedly above medicine, the Supreme Court, and education and at several multiples the level of confidence the public is willing to grant the bottom-feeders: Congress, the executive, and the media.

The same step-change pattern associated with major wars that I noted in Chapter 2 is again obvious here, and it explains not only absolute changes in public confidence in the military, but also changes in the military's relative standing among other institutions. The military maintained its middling position until the Gulf War, when it surpassed the Supreme Court, and assumed its leading position only after September 11, 2001, when it leaped above both medicine and the scientific community. With the exception of the presidency, no other institution appears to receive a wartime rally. And, even in the case of the presidency, such rallies have been short-lived.

Although the numerous lines in Figure 4.1 make the aggregate decline in confidence among other institutions difficult to observe, the next figure shows this trend more clearly. Figure 4.2 displays the percentage of Americans expressing a great deal of confidence in the military versus the average percentage of Americans saying the same of the other institutions that are listed in Figure

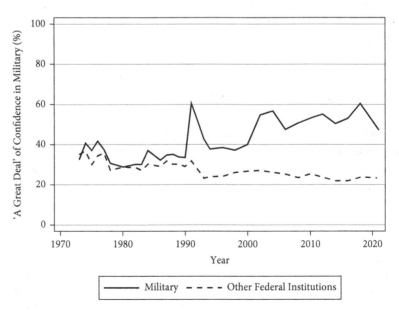

Figure 4.2 Public Confidence in the Military versus Average of Other Institutions over Time (Gallup, % "A Great Deal")

4.1 over the period from 1973 to 2018. In 1973, the percentage expressing a great deal of confidence in the military, at 33%, was slightly below the average for other institutions, at 35%. By 2018, however, confidence in the military had risen 28 points to 61%, while confidence in other institutions dropped nearly half as much, by 12 points, to an average of 23%.

Figure 4.3 displays these trends in a slightly different, but illuminating, way. The curved, dotted line in each of the two charts is the predicted probability that an individual would express a great deal of confidence in the military based on her stated level of confidence in other institutions.[2] The bars at the bottom of the charts are a histogram representing the number of other institutions in which respondents expressed "a great deal" of confidence, scaled from 0 to 1. Taken together, these patterns show that Americans are losing confidence in other institutions and—as they do so—becoming more likely to replace lost confidence in other institutions with confidence in the military. In 1974, only 21% of Americans did not express confidence in at least one other civilian institution, and the likelihood that someone in this group would express confidence in the military was only 10%. By 2018, this group had increased to 31% of the population, but the probability one of these individuals would express a great deal of confidence in the military had soared to 39%. Individuals with a great deal of confidence in all civilian institutions have always been extremely likely to have confidence in the military as well, though even this probability has increased slightly. The real differences today, however, are the high levels of confidence among those with confidence in no or few other civilian institutions and the fact that this subset of the population has expanded.

The post-9/11 increase in Republican esteem for the military discussed in Chapter 2 is again quite apparent in Figure 4.4, where public confidence in institutions is broken down by party. Indeed, no other institution has even come close to holding the same level of confidence among Republicans as the military has over the last two decades, with the percentage of Republicans expressing a great deal of confidence in the scientific community in 2018 more than 31 points lower than the 72% saying the same about the military. Among Democrats, however, 51% of respondents express confidence in both the military and the scientific community.

---

[2] The figure was generated with a simple logistic regression with a binary dependent variable, coded 1 for "a great deal of confidence" in the military and 0 otherwise, regressed against one's confidence in other institutions and the array of demographic characteristics discussed in Chapter 2 for both 1974 and 2018. Confirmatory regressions on the intervening years show that changes in this relationship follow the stepwise increase across decades as discussed in Chapter 2 and above. See the technical appendix for details.

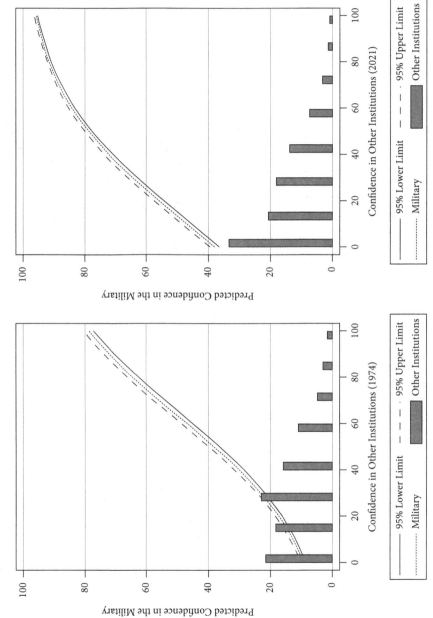

Figure 4.3 Predicted Confidence in the Military against Confidence in Other Institutions

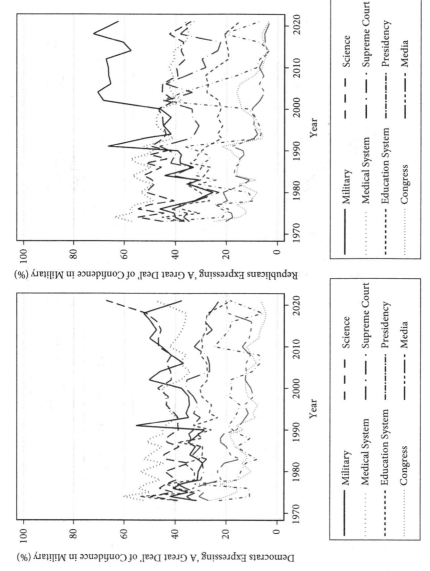

Figure 4.4 Public Confidence in Various Institutions over Time by Party (Gallup, % "A Great Deal")

While not as immediately obvious, the party gap with respect to the military in 2018 is even larger than the party gap for political institutions such as the executive branch, Congress, and the Supreme Court by this measure. In 2018, the number of Republicans expressing confidence in the military was 21 points higher than the number of Democrats, but only 15 and 12 points higher for the executive branch and Supreme Court, respectively, and only 1 point higher for Congress. Among nongovernmental institutions, only the scientific community and the media even approach a double-digit partisan gap, with Democrats 8 points higher for both these institutions.

An important difference between the military and other political institutions, however, is that the direction of the partisan gap does not reverse as it does for both the executive branch and the Supreme Court, and—to a lesser degree—Congress. Republicans, in particular, show large swings in confidence for the executive branch when control of the White House changes and for the Supreme Court when more liberal or conservative justices are confirmed. When Justices Ruth Bader Ginsburg and Stephen Breyer were confirmed in the early 1990s and when Sonia Sotomayor and Elena Kagan were confirmed in 2009-2010, confidence among Republicans dropped significantly. Conversely, when John Roberts and Samuel Alito were confirmed in 2005-2006 and when Neil Gorsuch and Brett Kavanaugh were confirmed in 2017-2018, Republican confidence in the Supreme Court increased. Democratic confidence moved in the opposite direction in response to these appointments, albeit with more moderate changes.[3] As Burbach (2018) has shown, however, changes in the presidency do modestly influence the size of this partisan gap. Even so, confidence in the military among Republicans has remained consistently much higher than confidence among Democrats since at least 2001.

Digging Deeper into Institutional Differences

Although the longitudinal GSS data provide insight into developing trends and suggest the importance of partisan control as an explanation for confidence in some institutions, prior surveys only allowed for limited exploration for why respondents held varying opinions of different institutions. The proprietary surveys were designed to exploit this variation across institutions and to better understand why Americans express confidence in some institutions and not others.

---

[3] For more on how control of the executive branch shapes partisans' views of the military, see Burbach (2018). For more on public confidence in the Supreme Court, see Bartels and Johnston (2013).

To build on the analysis of the military in Chapter 2, the survey also asked respondents about their confidence in other institutions in each of the two survey waves, using Gallup's formulation of the confidence question for both (Gallup 2020a). The first wave asked respondents to assess their confidence in a particular institution, randomly assigned from the following list: the Supreme Court, Congress, the media, and the foreign policy elite. The second wave asked respondents about bureaucratic institutions—such as the Centers for Disease Control (CDC), the State Department, the Internal Revenue Service (IRS), and the US Postal Service (USPS)—and about other professions, including scientists, doctors, police, and teachers. In both cases, in the second wave respondents were randomly assigned to a particular institution and profession.

In addition to asking topline confidence, the survey also asked questions to help reveal what might be underlying these differential rankings. As was asked for the military, the survey asked respondents to register the extent to which they agreed or disagreed (using the standard Likert scale ranging from strongly agree to strongly disagree) with a range of statements about each institution:[4]

A. The [institution] has become too partisan.
B. The [institution] is good at what it does.
C. The [institution] is representative of the demographic diversity of American society.
D. The [institution] maintains the highest standards of professional ethics.
E. The [institution] makes truthful claims.
F. The [institution] shares my values.
G. Most members of American society have confidence in the [institution].
H. The [institution] is knowledgeable about its job.[5]

This list is adapted from previous studies (Robinson 2018; Ohanian 1990; Goldsmith, Lafferty, and Newell 2000; Newell and Goldsmith 2001; Schake and Mattis 2013), and randomized to avoid bias based on question order.

As Table 4.1 shows, Americans continue to express far more confidence in the military than in any other federal institution.[6] Nearly twice as many respondents,

---

[4] In order to ensure grammatical correctness and subject-verb agreement, the survey modified the wording slightly for the questions about members of other professions: scientists, doctors, police, and teachers.

[5] This question was only asked in Wave 2 based on feedback received during presentations at the American Political Science Association, the Inter-University Seminar, the Goldman School of Public Policy, and the Duke University Security Peace, and Conflict lab.

[6] Unless otherwise noted, in this section the percentage of respondents expressing confidence in this section refers to those who stated they had either "a great deal" or "quite a lot" of confidence in a given institution.

Table 4.1 **Percentage Expressing Confidence in Institutions (2019)**

	Military	SCOTUS	Congress	Media	FP Elite
Overall	75	38	13	25	28
Democrats	71	34	12	38	21
Independents	61	34	15	19	23
Republicans	90	45	16	12	41
N	(630)	(1,185)	(1,175)	(1,052)	(1,154)

Table 4.2 **Percentage Expressing Confidence in Departments and Agencies (2020)**

	Military	CDC	State	IRS	USPS
Overall	69%	55%	36%	37%	63%
	(369)	(603)	(427)	(416)	(687)
Democrats	60%	65%	31%	39%	67%
	(144)	(313)	(155)	(193)	(337)
Independents	60%	47%	30%	32%	62%
	(50)	(104)	(60)	(62)	(109)
Republicans	82%	46%	44%	37%	58%
	(175)	(184)	(212)	(161)	(240)
N	538	1105	1180	1125	1094

at 75%, in 2019 reported "a great deal" or "quite a lot" of confidence in the military as they did for the closest competitor, the Supreme Court at 38%. The foreign policy elite, the media, and Congress fare even worse, at 28%, 25%, and 13%, respectively.

The largest party gap emerges on attitudes about the media, with 38% of Democrats expressing confidence in it compared to just 12% of Republicans, a 26-point difference. The foreign policy elite is not far behind with a 20-point party gap, roughly the same as the military's 19-point difference, though in both these cases Republicans express higher esteem than Democrats. Republicans also report more confidence than Democrats when asked about the Supreme Court, where a still-sizable 11-point gap exists. Very few respondents from either party have much confidence in Congress, a rare case of partisan agreement.

Table 4.2 shows that the military retains its edge even when compared to other bureaucratic departments and federal agencies, though the USPS at 63% and the CDC at 55% are much closer competitors. The IRS at 37% and the State

Department at 36% hold about as much public esteem as the Supreme Court, falling more than 30 points behind the military. Similar to the military, the State Department retains a partisan advantage with Republicans. This 13-point gap is just over half the size of the 22-point difference between Republicans and Democrats when they assess the military. Given the extent to which partisans debated the performance of then-secretary of state Mike Pompeo, it would be plausible for the question about the State Department to be capturing partisan views of the Trump administration in general rather than any underlying party difference in views about the functioning of the diplomatic service in the abstract (Rogers 2018; Kelemen 2020). Both the CDC and USPS enjoy relatively more confidence among Democrats than among Republicans, with gaps of 19 and 9 points, respectively. While it is possible that partisans have consistently different views about the CDC and USPS, these differences might also have been affected in hard-to-predict ways by the ongoing controversies about the CDC's role setting guidelines during the pandemic and the USPS's role delivering mail-in ballots during the election (Rothwell and Makridis 2020; Altschuler 2020; Holmes and Cohen 2020; Fandos and Epstein 2020). Neither Democrats nor Republicans express much confidence in the IRS, and independents have consistently low assessments of these bureaucratic departments and agencies across the board.

Table 4.3 shows that the confidence gap between the military and members of other professions is much closer than it is for other federal institutions, however. The public's assessment of doctors and scientists is statistically no different, with both at 68% in 2020, than its assessment of the military, and teachers at 64% and police at 61% are only slightly behind. This result might in part be because "the military" is the wrong comparison group for individual members

Table 4.3 **Percentage Expressing Confidence in Professions (2020)**

	Military	*Scientists*	*Doctors*	*Police*	*Teachers*
Overall	69%	68%	68%	61%	64%
	(369)	(753)	(788)	(642)	(743)
Democrats	60%	81%	72%	45%	77%
	(144)	(395)	(369)	(216)	(379)
Independents	60%	60%	53%	54%	53%
	(50)	(131)	(100)	(89)	(118)
Republicans	82%	56%	69%	82%	55%
	(175)	(225)	(318)	(336)	(246)
N	538	1105	1165	1055	1168

of these professions. As shown in Chapter 2, the public does make somewhat different assessments of confidence in "active duty troops" and "generals and admirals" than they do in the military as an institution. The troops, at 74%, stand clearly above these other professions, while generals and admirals are right in the middle of the pack at 66%. The partisan gaps among these professions are striking, however. Republicans' confidence in police is 37 points higher than such confidence among Democrats, while Democrats' confidence in scientists and teachers is 25 and 22 points higher than it is for Republicans. Only doctors share high levels of cross-partisan esteem, but even here independents are more than 15 points behind the other two parties. Once again, independents' confidence is at or near the bottom of the partisan pecking order for every profession respondents were asked about.

The public also rates the military favorably compared to other institutions and professions across the range of attributes I asked respondents to rate, as Figures 4.5 and 4.6 display. Across all institutions, agencies, and professions, the military is ranked as least partisan, most competent, most representative, and most likely to share respondents' values. The military also ranks near the top of the list for high standards of professional ethics, though even here the public's assessment of the military's ethical standards, at 58%, is statistically no different than 60% for scientists and 59% for doctors. It is only on the issue of truthfulness where the public gives the military a middling rating of 45% in 2019 and 46% in 2020. Although this assessment still looks impressive when compared to Congress, the media, or the foreign policy elite, it is the same as the public's assessment of the Supreme Court's truthfulness, and it falls behind every profession as well as the CDC and USPS. Chapter 5 will dig into the public's assessment of military honesty a bit more, as it is the one attribute about which the public clearly has some doubts.

The public's rating of the military's competence clearly stands out. At 83% in 2019, the military's competence rating almost doubles the public's assessment of the Supreme Court's, and respondents rate the competence of other institutions roughly 50 points lower than they do the military. In 2020, the public's estimation of military competence did drop 8 points, but it still remained higher, at 75%, than the public's ratings of every other profession and agency. All of the professions also received strong competence assessments of around 69%, but among federal agencies only the USPS at 71% came even close to the military's 75%, while the CDC was 14 points behind and the IRS and State Department were 26 and 35 points behind the military, respectively.

Although respondents rate the foreign policy elite as less partisan than the Supreme Court, the Court otherwise consistently comes in second in terms of positive attributes. Nevertheless, a majority of the public never agrees that the Supreme Court exhibits any of the positive attributes. The public's assessment

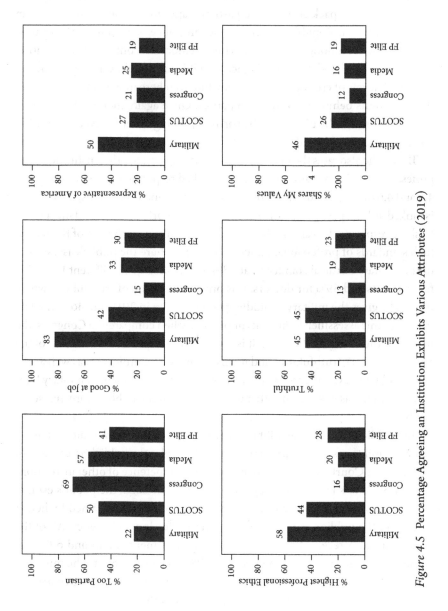

Figure 4.5 Percentage Agreeing an Institution Exhibits Various Attributes (2019)

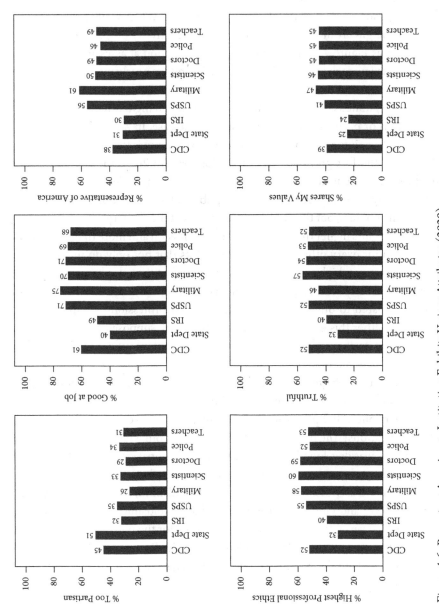

Figure 4.6 Percentage Agreeing an Institution Exhibits Various Attributes (2020)

of Congress remains abysmal on all questions, particularly on the question of whether the institution is "too partisan," where 69% report they agree Congress is. The media and foreign policy elite score quite comparably to one another across the range of attributes, with the public assessing the foreign policy elite as slightly more ethical, truthful, and in line with its values while believing the media is marginally more competent and representative.

Finally, as Figure 4.7 shows, the public is fairly good at assessing how other Americans view each institution, with overall numbers nearly matching those of individual assessments.[7] It is clear in both survey waves that most respondents believe the public's confidence in the military is much higher than it is for other institutions or professions—which is, in fact, the case. In 2019, the military, at 69%, was 29 points ahead of the Supreme Court and more than 44 points above the media, the foreign policy elite, and Congress. In 2020, the perception of public confidence in the military compared to other agencies and professions was even larger than the real difference in public esteem. The USPS was 7 points behind the military, but the public's perception that the military is respected was at least 10 points higher than it was for every profession and more than 17 points larger than for every other agency. This suggests that not only do members of the public express high confidence in the military, but they also know that other members of the public respect the military. Indeed, they overestimate this respect compared to other institutions, agencies, or professions. Chapter 7 will explore whether this expectation that Americans are supposed to "support the troops" may itself explain part of the reason why public confidence in the military has been so high since September 11, 2001.

But, given how highly correlated these measures are across institutions, do differences in these attributes provide additional insight into why the public likes the military and other professions like scientists and doctors more than it likes other institutions? The business research literature from which the modified list of attributes was developed suggests that the institutional credibility of business institutions, such as corporations, typically breaks down into two principal components: trustworthiness and expertise (Goldsmith, Lafferty, and Newell 2000; Lafferty and Goldsmith 1999; Newell and Goldsmith 2001). As Figure 4.8 shows, however, this distinction does not hold for the public institutions we examined in our survey. Although Figure 4.8 only displays information from 2020, the results of the principal component analysis in each wave were nearly identical.

---

[7] The question on confidence and the question assessing others' confidence are highly correlated (.51), but there is enough variation to suggest that respondents separated their own assessments. As discussed in Chapter 7, however, social pressure does play a role in shaping individual assessments of confidence in the military.

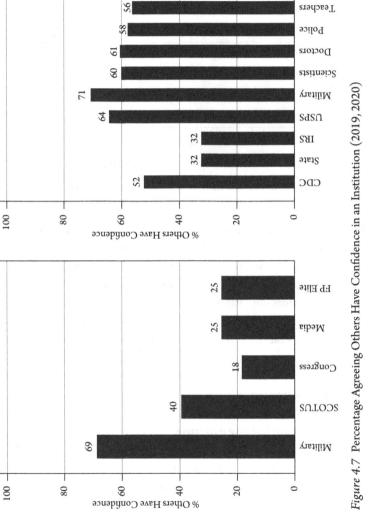

Figure 4.7 Percentage Agreeing Others Have Confidence in an Institution (2019, 2020)

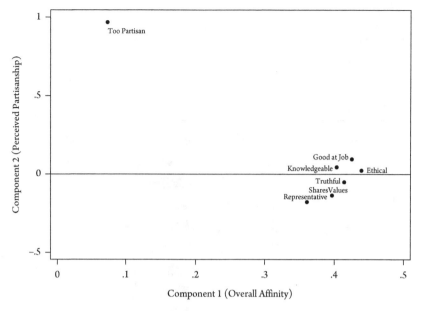

Figure 4.8 Principal Component Analysis of Institutional Attributes (2020)

Principal component analysis is a method that helps find underlying structure in data by looking for the ways the data are dispersed and then identifying which components (individual variables or clusters of variables) most closely covary with the observed patterns.[8] The stronger the covariance between clusters of variables, the more one variable can "explain" the other. For example, you might be able to explain a lot of the variation in the way members of Congress vote using one liberal- to conservative-ideology component. However, there might also be other components—such as whether the members come from northern or southern states or urban or rural districts—that separately help explain other variations in voting behavior. Principal component analysis helps find those types of components and assesses which explain most of the variation by looking for underlying patterns in the data. When depicted graphically, as in Figure 4.8, each axis shows how heavily each variable is weighted for each component. The farther away from 0 a variable is on a given axis, the more it matters for that component; the closer to 0 a variable is on a given axis, the less it matters.

The principal component analysis presented below includes the answers respondents gave about the military, the agencies, and the professions for all the institutional attribute questions discussed earlier. This analysis identified two main

---

[8] For additional details on the principal component analysis, see the technical appendix.

components, regardless of which wave analyzed.[9] The first component, Component 1 (along the horizontal axis in Figure 4.8), consists of a relatively equal weighting (approximately .4 for all but "too partisan") across variables, indicating that these variables may together be picking up an underlying affect or admiration for an institution. The other component, Component 2 (along the vertical axis), is based almost entirely on an individual's assessment of whether or not a given institution is "too partisan."[10] The weighting for "too partisan" is close to 1, while all the weighting for all the other variables is clustered around 0, meaning they are not important for this component. Component 1, which may be thought of as institutional affect, is the most important, accounting for more than 65% of the variance in an individual's confidence. Component 2, the "perceived partisanship" component, explains only about 15% of the variance in an individual's confidence; however, it is notable that respondents' assessments of an institution's partisan leanings pick up some variation that the other variables together simply do not. Nevertheless, even changes in these other attributes do provide additional insight into why the public has more confidence in some institutions than it does in others, as explored below.

In sum, Figure 4.8 suggests that when the public looks across the array of public institutions and decides what level of confidence to put in each one, the public is engaged in a two-step thought process. One step involves taking an overall affect measure of the institution—how well it functions, with what level of perceived ethics, and with what level of connection (through shared values and representativeness) to the American people; step 2 involves assessing the perceived level of partisanship that the institution displays. Together, these two steps lead to collective rankings of institutions, with those ranking high on overall affect and low on perceived partisanship coming out on top.

Exploring the Predictors of Confidence across Institutions

As shown in Chapter 2, there is significant variation across demographic subgroups of the American public that affect confidence in the military, and

---

[9] To simplify interpretation, the sign of the "too partisan" variable is reversed. Doing so does not substantively alter the results. It only shifts the position of "too partisan" from approximately −.1 on the horizontal axis to around .1 on the horizontal axis. All future regression analysis reverts to the normal coding of the "too partisan" variable.

[10] Principal component analysis of Wave 2 data revealed two primary components, with a 4.02 Eigenvalue for Component 1 and 1.01 Eigenvalue for Component 2. Analysis of Wave 1 data also revealed two components, with a 4.63 Eigenvalue for Component 1 and a 0.72 Eigenvalue for Component 2, narrowly meeting the criteria under the average variance extraction rule (Fornell and Larcker 1981).

the same is likely true of other institutions. Consequently, it is important to explore the extent to which the relationships between these underlying attributes ("good at job," "truthful," "shares my values," etc.) and the variation in public confidence in an institution that we described in the previous section holds up when controlling for demographic factors.

Figure 4.9 visually displays the results of three separate logistic regression models—one each for institutions (2019), agencies (2020), and professions (2020).[11] The dependent variable is a binary measure of confidence in a given institution, where respondents reporting "a great deal" or "quite a lot" of confidence in an institution are coded as a 1 and 0 otherwise, following the standard Gallup reporting method for public confidence.[12] Since the survey asked every respondent questions about the military as well as about one other institution (or two, in Wave 2), one can compare how their assessment of an institution's attributes varies with their confidence in each institution. Each of the attributes is scaled from 0 to 1, with 0 representing a "strongly disagree" response and 1 signifying a "strongly agree" response. Demographic variables are coded as previously discussed in Chapter 2. Recall that respondents in Wave 1 were randomly assigned to be asked about a particular institution, and in Wave 2 about both an agency and profession. Thus, each respondent is in a pooled data set once in Wave 1 (for the institution the survey asked them about, e.g., Congress or the media); twice for Wave 2 (once for the level of confidence in an agency and once for the level of confidence in a profession). In addition, the respondents from the original control groups—the ones from the main experiments that tried to nudge respondents' confidence up or down, as discussed later in Chapters 5 and 6—are included one more time in each wave: once for their confidence in the randomly assigned institution in Wave 1, or once for the additional agency and once for their confidence in the additional profession in Wave 2, and then one additional time for each wave for their untreated confidence in the military.

The first panel in Figure 4.9 on the left provides the results for the institutions (2019), the center panel for the agencies (2020), and the third panel for the professions (2020). When looking at the model, the reader should compare the dot and the associated horizontal error bar—a 95% confidence interval—for

---

[11] For additional details and model specifications, see the technical appendix.

[12] These results are robust to other modeling choices and coding methods. This analysis used an ordered logit model with a 4-point dependent variable as well as standard OLS models using both the 4-point scale as well as the 11-point (0–10) scale. In some of these cases, the relative size of the coefficients changes, causing "ethical standards" or "shares my values" to become relatively more impactful than "good at what it does." In no specification did any of the attributes identified as significant in Model 3 fail to achieve statistical significance, however, though use of the 10-point scale for the dependent variable caused correlations with "representative" and "truthful" to also achieve significance.

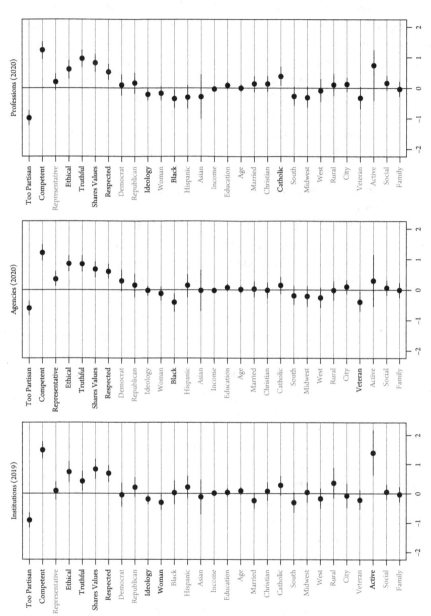

Figure 4.9 Predictors of Overall Confidence in Institutions, Agencies, and Professions (2019, 2020)

each variable to the vertical line at 0. If the error bar overlaps with 0, it means that one cannot statistically distinguish the effect of that variable from 0; if the bar does not overlap, we can be confident there is a statistical relationship. Dots to the right of the vertical line mean that a given variable is positively correlated with a respondent's confidence in an institution, while dots to the left mean the relationship is negative. The results across each model in Figure 4.9 are strikingly similar, especially for the key variables of interest—the attributes. It is clear that overall these attributes, with the exception of perceived representativeness of the country, are strongly related to respondents' confidence in an institution. In fact, running these models without including the attribute variables yields the result that demographic characteristics could only explain about 2% of the variation (what's called the model's pseudo R-squared value) in respondents' confidence in a given institution. After including the attributes in the models along with the demographic variables, the models can instead explain a hefty 40% of the variation.

Figure 4.9 vividly depicts those factors that are significantly linked to institutional confidence and those that are not. Across the board, whether or not a respondent believes an institution is competent—or good at its job—is the single best predictor of confidence in an institution, an agency, or a profession. Holding all other variables at their means, these models predict that shifting competence from its lowest value to its highest value would correspond with an expected 30%–35% change in a respondent's expressed confidence in a particular institution. The perception that an institution is too partisan is the second-strongest predictor of confidence, but it has a negative effect that corresponds with a predicted 20%–25% drop in confidence when one adjusts the too-partisan variable from its minimum to its maximum. The perceptions that an institution shares one's values or that it has high ethical standards are both strong predictors as well, and both are associated with a 15%–20% change from their minimum values to their maximum. The belief that others have confidence in an institution corresponds with about a 13%–17% confidence shift. The perception that an institution is truthful also has a positive relationship, but the strength of this relationship varied quite a bit from 2019 to 2020. In Wave 1, a shift from minimum to maximum perceived truthfulness predicts just an 11% increase in confidence compared to 22% and 23% for the agency and profession models in Wave 2. There is no obvious explanation for this change from 2019 to 2020, but it might be related to the difference between the types of institutions asked about across the two waves. Recall from Figures 4.5 and 4.6 that none of the institutions the survey inquired about in 2019 received particularly positive assessments of their truthfulness. In fact, the military was at the top of the list in 2019, but in 2020 the military ranked just seventh out of the nine institutions included. The only perceived attribute included that is not strongly related with confidence in an institution is the belief that an institution is representative of the American public. This variable was only significant in the agencies model, and it had very small predictive value compared to the other perceived attributes.

After including the attribute variables, few of the demographic variables are statistically significant, and almost none of them correspond with large shifts in confidence. The two possible exceptions are whether a respondent is on active duty in the military and a respondent's political ideology. In the first wave, the model would predict that someone on active duty would be roughly 25 points more confident in our randomly assigned institution than someone who was not in the military, all else equal. Since this relationship does not show up in the second wave, it is possible that this result is a feature of the institutions included in the first wave. There are plausible reasons to think members of the military would be more confident in formal institutions like Congress and the Supreme Court or even with the foreign policy elite. Given that this result does not carry over to veterans, however, it is also possible that members of the military feel some pressure to express confidence in formal government institutions and that pressure might become less intense after they leave the military. Ideology does appear to matter as well, at least in two of three models. Here the predicted decrease in confidence of 15%–20% points if a respondent's ideology were to change from liberal to conservative seems plausible given general conservative skepticism about government institutions.

Although not depicted in Figure 4.9 (see technical appendix, available here: https://dataverse.harvard.edu/dataverse/pfeaver), demographic variables operate in largely intuitive ways when the one removes the perceived attribute variables from the model. As shown in the 2018 GSS data earlier in this chapter, Republicans and conservatives are more likely to express confidence in institutions, perhaps driven in part by their strong affect for the military and in part by their party's control of the Senate and perhaps even a slight perceived partisan advantage in the Supreme Court. Americans with larger incomes also express more confidence in institutions than poorer respondents, consistent with previous research suggesting that policymakers tend to be more responsive to wealthier constituents (Erikson 2015). In general, women are less likely to express confidence in institutions, as are younger Americans and minorities. Despite the high confidence in the military observed in Chapter 2, being from the South or the West is correlated with lower confidence in institutions overall. There are no statistically significant correlations based on education levels, social or family contact with the military, or population density (rural). As discussed earlier, however, models for confidence in institutions based on demographic variables alone are extremely inefficient—especially when compared to those including the perceived attribute variables. In those models, perceived competence and perceived partisanship dominate although beliefs about other attributes also play a role in predicting confidence in various institutions.

Conclusion

Until this chapter, the analyses in this book had taken at face value the Gallup poll question asking respondents to indicate "how much confidence" they have in the military and other institutions. Drawing on both tracked changes in confidence in the military over time and an exploration of which attributes presently explain confidence in the military and in other institutions, it is possible to develop a much better understanding of what the public might mean when they express confidence in the military. The results from the June 2019 and October 2020 surveys demonstrate that people who have confidence in the military also perceive that the military works better than other institutions, and that it does so more competently and ethically than other US institutions. Americans are also less likely to express confidence—at least in general—in an institution they believe is too partisan, and they are more likely to express confidence in an institution when they believe other citizens also have confidence in it. Since neither Gallup nor NORC nor anyone else has been asking these detailed questions consistently for the last five decades, however, they only provide a snapshot of what Americans believe today. There is still no definitive understanding of whether those factors—performance, professional ethics, partisanship, and pressure—have been driving changes in confidence in the military over the last five decades or whether they might spur future changes, either up or down.

Some important questions remain. Have military partisanship, performance, professional ethics, or social pressure caused large numbers of Americans to put increasing confidence in the military at the same time they have been losing confidence in civilian institutions? And, if so, why have these perceptions changed, and changed unevenly across groups like Republicans and Democrats? In order to answer these questions, one needs to explore whether and how new information about the military causes Americans to update their confidence in, and beliefs about, the military. The next chapters turn to these questions.

5

Performance, Professional Ethics, and Public Confidence in the Military

> "Maybe if I knew what it would take to screw it up, I could avoid it."
> Chairman of the Joint Chiefs of Staff Martin Dempsey, in response to a question about why the public has such high confidence in the military.
> —Ricks and Gourley 2014

A key motivation for this book is the recognition that everyone seems to know *that* the public holds the military in high regard, but no one is exactly sure *why*. Perhaps public confidence is based on judgments about the military's competence in war and other assignments, or perhaps it is based on its reputation for high professional ethics, or perhaps even its status as an apolitical oasis in our polarized partisan environment. Or perhaps the public is socially squeezed by peer pressure. There are many more plausible explanations than there have been rigorous tests (King and Karabell 2003; Burbach 2017; Robinson 2018). Chapter 2 already found support for one of the pillars: the idea that the public rallies to the military in times of war, even a lingering quasi-war as has been waged over the past two decades since the 9/11 attacks. Chapter 4 showed that when you compare public confidence in the military to other agencies, institutions, and professions, a pattern emerges—perceived competence is positively correlated with confidence, and perceived high partisanship is negatively correlated with confidence.

This chapter builds on these findings to test more precisely two of the more prominent alternative (or complementary) hypotheses—the idea that the military is respected because it is competent and the idea that the military is respected because it is highly ethical.[1] Later, Chapter 6 explores a third, namely the idea that the military enjoys confidence because it soars above sordid partisan

---

[1] Earlier versions of this chapter were presented as Golby (2019) and Golby and Feaver (2019b).

politics. Survey experiments make it possible to isolate the causal impact of new information regarding competence, ethics, and partisanship to more concretely identify the causal impact, if any, of these factors.

This chapter finds that public confidence in the military moves in mostly, but not entirely, intuitive ways. For instance, when primed with negative information about the military's performance or ethical behavior, confidence decreases. When presented with positive information on these topics, however, the confidence question does not move as much, and in some cases may actually decrease. These movements operate along mostly intuitive causal pathways, but in some cases priming respondents with information about the performance or ethics of the military seems to also change the public's views of other, seemingly more distant qualities of the military.

This chapter relies almost exclusively on the proprietary survey data collected by the National Opinion Research Center (NORC) in two waves, one in early summer 2019 and the other in early fall 2020. As introduced in Chapter 2 and discussed in greater detail in the technical appendix (available here: https://dataverse.harvard.edu/dataverse/pfeaver), each wave consisted of a detailed survey of roughly 4,500 adult Americans. Of course, each survey asked the basic Gallup question regarding confidence in the military: "Please tell me how much confidence you, yourself, have in the military—a great deal, quite a lot, some or very little." The analyses that follow explore the determinants of this basic response with two main lines of analysis, each entailing additional questions. First, the survey asked respondents about the degree to which they hold other positive or negative attitudes about the military—for instance, whether they thought the military was competent or truthful or shared the values of the respondent—to see how those views covary with a respondent's overall assessment of confidence in the military.[2]

Second, the survey used a battery of experiments to explore how the public responds to both positive and negative priming that taps into the causal logic inherent in alternative explanations for why the public holds the military in high esteem. Survey experiments are a well-established method allowing analysts to isolate what might be driving attitudes of interest. Respondents are randomly assigned to groups, with one group receiving the "control," a neutrally worded question. In this case, the respondents in the control group (619 in Wave 1, 556 in Wave 2) were asked: "We are interested in how well information about the US

---

[2] This list was adapted from previous studies (Robinson 2018; Ohanian 1990; Goldsmith, Lafferty, and Newell 2000; Newell and Goldsmith 2001; Schake and Mattis 2013). NORC randomized the list to avoid question-ordering effects and varied whether agreeing was associated with a positive value or a negative value to catch respondents who are simply providing straight-line responses in order to speed through the survey.

military can reach the public. The length of the 'war on terror' and associated US military activities have created a large amount of information that can be hard to follow. We want to ask you some questions about the US military. Please tell me how much confidence you, yourself, have in the military—a great deal, quite a lot, some or very little?"[3]

Respondents in the treatment groups received this same basic question, but with additional information added that might in theory nudge their confidence level up or down. Since the respondents are randomly assigned to various treatment groups, the null hypothesis would expect that there should be no difference between those who described their level of confidence in the military after receiving the control and those who described their level of confidence in the military after receiving one of the prompts. The actual difference in the average responses between those who received the control versus those who received these additional primes is considered the treatment effect.

Is Public Confidence in the Military a Question of Competence?

Perhaps the public trusts the military because the military is good at what it does. When asked to perform a mission, the military carries out that assignment with a high level of competence that wins over the public. For scholars looking at public confidence early in the post–Cold War era, this seemed like a very plausible explanation (Gronke and Feaver 2001; King and Karabell 2003). For scholars looking at confidence after several decades of uncertain outcomes in the global war on terror, this seemed less plausible (Burbach 2017). However, as noted above in Chapter 2, Burbach (2017) may be overstating the degree to which the public views these wars as failures that can be laid at the feet of the military that waged them. Indeed, as Burbach (2018) also notes, a partisan filter might provide one way that the military escapes blame for operational setbacks and thus retains a reputation for competence even in the presence of ambivalent results on the battlefield (and I will explore still other dynamics along these lines in Chapter 10). Chapter 2 presented some evidence consistent with this view: responses to major military news stories moved in intuitive ways, but they were often magnified or muted based on party. None of this previous work, however, constituted a direct test of the intuition that public confidence equates to

---

[3] Following Robinson (2018), Wave 1 also asked respondents to answer the same question using a 1–10 point thermometer. Except where noted in the text, this version did not yield different results—certainly not substantively different and probably not more usefully precise answers.

Table 5.1 **Public Attitudes on Military Competence Attributes by Party Identification (% agree with statement)**

	Overall	Dem	Ind	Rep
Good at what it does (2019)	83%	79%	77%	93%
	(513)	(239)	(92)	(182)
Good at what it does (2020)	75%	70%	61%	86%
	(416)	(174)	(52)	(190)
Usually wins wars (2019)	60%	59%	42%	72%
	(372)	(178)	(50)	(144)
Knowledgeable about job (2020)	75%	71%	59%	85%
	(413)	(177)	(50)	(186)
Total N (2019)	(617)	(300)	(119)	(198)
Total N (2020)	(555)	(248)	(86)	(221)

public estimations of military competence. The analyses here provide such a test, by examining how public responses vary when the public is given different information about three of the high-profile missions that have been assigned to the military in recent years: waging war in Afghanistan, assisting public health authorities in the response to the coronavirus pandemic, and assisting law enforcement in response to the public protests about police violence.

Before exploring the results of the survey experiment, it is important to establish a baseline by reporting the results when NORC put the question to our respondents directly. The survey asked them to register the extent to which they agreed or disagreed (using the standard Likert scale ranging from strongly agree to strongly disagree) with a range of statements, each a claim that the military has a particular positive or negative quality, specifically, whether they agreed with (A) The military is good at what it does; and (B) The military usually wins the wars it fights.[4]

Table 5.1 displays the percentage of those respondents who agree with the sentiment expressed.[5] Several things stand out. First, consistent with the

---

[4] Wave 1 asked this battery *after* conducting the experiment designed to move public confidence up or down. This allows one to use the battery for causal mediation analysis of the pathways along which the experimental nudge might be moving public attitudes. In order to address other analytical priorities, the battery came *before* the experiment in Wave 2, so it is not usable for causal mediation purposes.

[5] Note that the results are only for those respondents who received the control condition, since the questions were asked after the survey experiment.

partisan gap in the overall confidence question, as reported in Chapter 2, partisan gaps of at least 13 points persist across the attributes, with Republicans providing much more favorable responses than either Democrats or independents on every question.

Second, although topline confidence among independents is relatively high (as reported in Chapter 2), independents give markedly lower assessments than partisans on these key military attributes. Gronke and Feaver (2001) observed a similar phenomenon, which they described as "brittle confidence" because topline confidence numbers obscured the fact that some respondents' confidence is not propped up with equally strong judgments about the attributes thought to undergird that confidence in the military. Finally, as observed in Chapter 4, respondents' assessments of whether or not the military is competent appear to be rather important in shaping their overall confidence levels. In other words, when Americans say they are confident in the military, what they are really saying is that they believe the military is good at what it does and that it does its job without getting too caught up in partisan politics. Respondents' perceptions of military competence, in particular, are strongly correlated (.55 in Wave 1 and .60 in Wave 2) with responses to the Gallup confidence question.

The survey experiments make it possible to isolate the causal impact of military performance on overall confidence more precisely. The experiments are built around certain high-profile military missions that were unlikely to have escaped public notice. In Wave 1, a randomly assigned group of 574 respondents received a question carefully designed to underscore the idea that the military was operationally *effective* by painting the war in Afghanistan as a success (with the treatment shown here *in italics*, but not emphasized that way in the actual survey):

> We are interested in how well information about the US military can reach the public. The length of the "war on terror" and associated US military activities have created a large amount of information that can be hard to follow.
>
> *For instance, did you know that the United States military has been fighting continuously in Afghanistan since shortly after the terrorist attacks on the Pentagon and World Trade Center that occurred on September 11, 2001? The United States military has achieved its most important strategic goals in Afghanistan. There have been no large-scale terrorist attacks on US soil since 2001 and a peace settlement is now within reach. The Taliban has signaled it may be willing to come to the negotiating table, and the United States may soon be able to declare victory in Afghanistan.*

> In light of that, we want to ask you some questions about the US military. Please tell me how much confidence you, yourself, have in the military—a great deal, quite a lot, some or very little?[6]

A randomly assigned group of 584 respondents in Wave 1 received a differently worded question, one designed to underscore the idea that the military was operationally *ineffective* by painting the war in Afghanistan as a failure (with the treatment *in italics*):

> We are interested in how well information about the US military can reach the public. The length of the 'war on terror' and associated US military activities have created a large amount of information that can be hard to follow.
>
> *For instance, did you know that the United States military has been fighting continuously in Afghanistan since shortly after the terrorist attacks on the Pentagon and World Trade Center that occurred on September 11, 2001? The United States military has failed to achieve any of its most important strategic goals and it has become mired in the longest conflict in American history, with no end in sight. The Taliban continues to gain strength and still conducts mass-casualty attacks around the country. It is undeniable that the United States military has lost the war in Afghanistan.*
>
> In light of that, we want to ask you some questions about the US military. Please tell me how much confidence you, yourself, have in the military—a great deal, quite a lot, some or very little?"

Of course, political leaders often ask the military to conduct missions other than war, and it is also worth investigating whether the military's performance in those areas can drive public confidence up or down. Accordingly, in Wave 2, some 576 respondents received this *positive* prompt before being asked the standard confidence question:

> More than 50,000 troops from the National Guard and active duty military have recently participated in the domestic response to the coronavirus outbreak. Overall, the military's involvement helped produce far fewer deaths than there might otherwise have been and many people believe the military response has been a great success. In light of that, we want to ask you some questions about the US military. Please tell me

---

[6] In this and the subsequent treatments, respondents were then asked the two follow up questions regarding "the generals and admirals leading the United States military" and the generals and admirals who have retired from the United States military."

how much confidence you, yourself, have in the military—a great deal, quite a lot, some, or very little?

Some 541 respondents received this *negative* prompt:

> More than 50,000 troops from the National Guard and active duty military have recently participated in the domestic response to the coronavirus outbreak. Overall, the military's involvement did not produce any discernible effect on the death rate from the virus and many people believe the military response has been a great failure. In light of that, we want to ask you some questions about the US military. Please tell me how much confidence you, yourself, have in the military—a great deal, quite a lot, some, or very little?"

Potentially even more controversially, political leaders also ask military units to assist law enforcement in times of great social upheaval. In May and June 2020, the country erupted with wide-scale protests regarding policing and race relations. In some locales, the National Guard was deployed to help maintain law and order, and the Trump administration conducted an internal debate that quickly became widely known in public about whether to go further and invoke the Insurrection Act to mobilize active-duty forces (Neuman 2020; Brooks 2020; Filkins 2020). Accordingly, Wave 2 tested how public confidence in the military might shift in response to nudges about how effective the military had been in those assignments. Some 566 respondents received this *positive* prompt before being asked the standard confidence question (with the treatment *in italics*):

> In the face of widespread protests, political authorities recently mobilized the National Guard and put other active duty military units on alert to be ready to intervene. *Overall, the military's involvement seemed to help tamp down violence and restore order, reminding the public that the use of the troops in domestic conflict has always been an important and traditional military mission.* In light of that, we want to ask you some questions about the US military. Please tell me how much confidence you, yourself, have in the military—a great deal, quite a lot, some, or very little?

Some 593 respondents received this *negative* prompt (shown here *in italics*):

> In the face of widespread protests, political authorities recently mobilized the National Guard and put other active duty military units on alert to be ready to intervene. *Overall, the military's involvement seemed to do little*

to tamp down violence and restore order while inflaming tensions, reminding the public why the use of the troops in domestic conflict has always been controversial. In light of that, we want to ask you some questions about the US military. Please tell me how much confidence you, yourself, have in the military—a great deal, quite a lot, some, or very little?

Figure 5.1 reports the results from this core experiment as a difference in means between the treatment and the control—in other words, between the average response to the question with a prompt designed to move opinion in one direction or another minus the average response to the straight Gallup question. The higher the dot above the horizontal line, the more the treatment *increased* average levels of high confidence in the military among our respondents; the lower the dot below the horizontal line, the more the treatment *decreased* average levels of high confidence. For instance, Figure 5.1 shows that telling respondents that the military has lost the Afghanistan war decreases the percentage of respondents who report high confidence in the military by nine points, while telling them that the military won increases the percentage by two points.

Contrary to Burbach (2017), these results provide at least some evidence that public confidence is linked to public views about the effectiveness of the

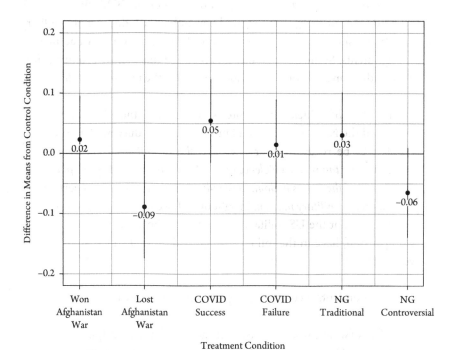

Figure 5.1 Treatment Effects for Public Confidence in the Military (2019, 2020)

military. Confidence went up slightly when the question prompt included the idea that "the United States military has achieved its most important strategic goals in Afghanistan . . . and the United States may soon be able to declare victory in Afghanistan." The increase was very slight and not statistically significant, suggesting that—as shown in Chapter 4 and earlier in this chapter—overall public confidence already has baked in the idea that the military is good at what it does. But being told that the military had failed in the Afghanistan war had a substantively and statistically significant negative effect on confidence of nine points. The results for the domestic missions mostly followed the intuitive pattern, though none of the results reached statistical significance at the 95% confidence level. The results for the Covid experiment suggest that in late September and early October 2020 there still might have been a halo effect around the military's role as a first responder during the pandemic; being told the military had done well seemed to move support up by as much as five points (though not quite statistically significant at even the 90% level). The other treatment, which was intended to convey the idea that the military had not dealt effectively with the pandemic, had no negative impact at all—there was even a slight, but not statistically significant, upward nudge. The case of the military's role in domestic protests produced a result strikingly similar to the Afghan war result; the positive framing had a slight, but not statistically significant, upward effect, and the negative framing had a larger six-point downward effect that was statistically significant at the 90% confidence level (though not the 95% level).

However, consistent with Burbach (2018), interesting patterns emerge when respondents are disaggregated by their partisanship, as presented in Figure 5.2. Figure 5.2 breaks down the core experiment according to whether the respondents self-identify as Democrats, Republicans, or independents. The figure is read in the same way as Figure 5.1: a higher position above the zero line indicates a bigger treatment effect that increases public levels of high confidence and vice versa. The dots reflect the treatment effects just for respondents who self-identify as Democrats, as independents, or as Republicans.

Contra Robinson (2018), there is little evidence that Republican confidence in the military is resistant to negative information about military wartime performance or ethical failures. To be sure, Democrats move the most in response to the military effectiveness prompt on Afghanistan, dropping 14 percentage points when told the military lost; yet Republicans also drop 11 points when receiving the same prompt, which is statistically significant at the 90% level. Independents actually move up slightly by 2 points, though this move is not statistically significant. Telling respondents the United States won in Afghanistan does not move Democrat or Republican respondents much; there is a statistically insignificant shift downward in Republican confidence in response to this positive news prompt, but that may simply reflect a ceiling effect—Republicans

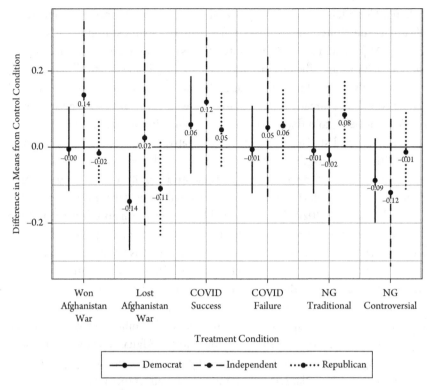

Figure 5.2 Treatment Effects for Public Confidence in the Military Conditioned on Partisan Status of Respondents (2019, 2020)

already have such high base confidence that any increase would seem unlikely. It does, however, move independents by a considerable amount, as much as 14 percentage points. The obvious inference: partisans are somewhat inured to good news about military effectiveness though still receptive and movable by bad news from the battlefront. In other words, partisan confidence in the military has already baked in high estimations of effectiveness. Independents, by contrast, have baked in lower estimates of military effectiveness and so are receptive to good news that seems to challenge this view, but not really to bad news, which merely seems to confirm it.

Partisanship seems to matter a great deal in shaping how the public responds to nudges about military effectiveness in domestic missions as well. Consistent with Robinson (2018), Republicans seem unmovable on the Covid issue; reminding Republican respondents of the military role in Covid response, whether framed in a positive or negative way, has the same modest effect of nudging support up. Democrats respond to the upward nudge but only barely to the downward nudge, and in no case is it statistically significant at the 95% level. Independents seem to move the most in response to positive framing about the Covid mission, but then also move up when given negative framing; because of the small sample size, however, none of these effects is statistically significant. The role of the military in responding to the protests seems to generate the most pronounced partisan effects. Republicans move their confidence up by a statistically significant amount when given a positive framing, and only barely nudge downward with a negative framing. Democrats and independents both move down slightly even with the positive framing, and more dramatically down with the negative framing, although it only reaches statistical significance for Democrats and only at the 90% level. These partisan breakdowns intuitively align with the polarized partisan way the protests were debated in the broader political space; Republican leaders mostly cast the protests in extremely negative terms, calling for a vigorous response from police and other security forces to restore order, whereas Democratic leaders mostly cast the protests as understandable and even laudable expressions of a demand for justice and civil rights and called for a peaceful response from law enforcement (Phillips 2020; Tesler 2020; Heyward 2021). It is natural, then, that Republicans would be receptive to positive news about the performance of the National Guard in this security enforcement role while being resistant to negative news—and that Democrats would have the opposite predilections.

Since the survey asked respondents their views about individual military services in 2020, it is also possible to estimate the effects treatments have on confidence in individual branches. In almost all cases, the military and individual service variables moved in similar ways—with one notable exception. When respondents are primed with the negative protest response framing, confidence in the army dropped from 71% to 59%, a statistically significant result at the 90% level. This shift was roughly twice as large for the army, at 12 percentage points, as it was for the military in the aggregate, at 6 percentage points. None of the other services moved in response to this treatment: respondents expressed 73% and 71% confidence in the navy and the air force, respectively, while confidence in the Marine Corps dropped just 1 point, from 68% to 67%. Perceptions about the army also differed significantly along partisan lines. Confidence in the army among Democrats and independents dropped 14 and 22 percentage points, respectively, while confidence among Republicans only dropped 6 points. While the results in Chapter 2 show that the public does not make fine distinctions between the services, this result suggests that the public does believe that the army plays a different role in response to protests than the other services do. Even here, however, it is largely the Army National Guard and not active-duty army personnel who would likely be called on for this type of domestic mission.[7]

---

[7] The existing literature does not have strong evidence that the public draws a sharp distinction between the Army National Guard and the active-duty army. Of course, the National Guard is the

Pulling this all together, it is clear that competence does matter, but the perception of competence is itself shaped not merely by the framing given to it exogenously—artificially, in this survey experiment, or naturally by media coverage in the real world—but also by a separate partisan frame that such missions enjoy. At the time of these surveys, Democrats and independents were skeptical about using the military in domestic protest settings (see the further discussion of this in Chapter 9), while Republicans were not, and this partisan prism refracted the way respondents moved in response to nudges about competence. It would have been interesting to redo this experiment shortly after the January 6, 2021, assault on the US Capitol, which likely had the opposite partisan refraction; many Republicans may not have wanted the military to suppress the assault, while Democrats likely would have supported it. As it happened, the slowness of the military response may have yielded different dynamics among partisan respondents.

Is Public Confidence in the Military a Question of High Ethical Standards?

An alternative explanation, which might be complementary with the competence story, concerns public views of the military as an institution that retains a high degree of ethical purity in a fashion that might be unusual in the sausage factory of government. In other words, perhaps the public has confidence in the military because the public perceives the military to be living up to the highest ethical standards. King and Karabell (2003) identified perceived high levels of professionalism of the military, including the strides the military had made over several painful decades to promote racial equality within the ranks and to confront the drug abuse problem that bedeviled the force at the depths of the Vietnam War debacle, as a major driver of public confidence. Likewise, Hill, Wong, and Gerras (2015), writing at a time when the military was beset with several high-profile scandals of inappropriate behavior by senior officers,

---

component that most often deploys in a domestic setting and is the one with the greatest local ties because it is the most geographically dispersed. Moreover, the debate within the Trump administration over whether to rely on the Guard or to invoke the Insurrection Act so as to mobilize and deploy active-duty units broke into the public and hinged crucially on fears that public attitudes to the military might turn on this distinction—accepting the Guard in this role but repudiating the active-duty force for engaging in it. However, beyond the survey data presented here and in Chapter 9, I do not know of studies that directly test this proposition. I flag it as a matter worth investigating in follow-on work.

Table 5.2 Public Attitudes on Military Ethics Attributes by Party Identification (2019, 2020, % agree with statement)

	Overall	Dem	Ind	Rep
Professional ethics (2019)	58%	57%	41%	71%
	(367)	(170)	(48)	(139)
Professional ethics (2020)	58%	50%	48%	72%
	(325)	(125)	(41)	(159)
Makes truthful claims (2019)	45%	43%	30%	57%
	(278)	(130)	(35)	(113)
Makes truthful claims (2020)	46%	40%	38%	54%
	(252)	(100)	(33)	(119)
Shares my values (2019)	46%	35%	38%	68%
	(281)	(106)	(44)	(131)
Shares my values (2020)	47%	37%	33%	65%
	(261)	(91)	(28)	(142)
Total (2019)	(617)	(300)	(119)	(198)
Total (2020)	(555)	(248)	(86)	(221)

reinforced this judgment and warned that the scandals could undermine public confidence in the military.

As shown in Chapter 4, the public's perception of the military's ethical behavior and honesty does stand out when compared to other federal institutions like the Supreme Court, Congress, or the presidency. However, the military's professional ethics do not look so exceptional to the public compared to those of agencies like the CDC or the Post Office or to those of professions like doctors or scientists. And the public's assessment of the military's honesty when compared to other agencies and professions is middling at best, and perhaps even lacking. Table 5.2 offers a more detailed assessment of the public's perception of the military's professional ethics, recording the percentage of respondents, broken down by partisan ID, who agreed with the following statements: "A. The military maintains the highest standards of professional ethics; B. The military makes truthful claims; C. The military shares my values."[8]

Note that a clear majority of respondents (58% in both waves) think the military maintains high ethical standards, though there is weaker agreement overall as to whether the military is truthful and shares the values of the respondent

---

[8] Note these results report only those who received the control condition in the main survey experiment conducted in each wave.

(however, this last question could be interpreted by the respondents to be asking about political values rather than ethical/moral ones). There are some partisan differences, and the partisan breakdown on the ethical question is very similar to the partisan breakdown in the overall confidence question. As reported in Chapter 2, Democrats reported confidence in the military just a bit below the level shown by the public in the aggregate, while Republicans reported confidence at much higher levels and independents at much lower levels. That same pattern shows up in levels of agreement with the idea that the military maintains the highest level of professional ethics. Note also that the partisan gap is most marked on the question of whether the military "shares my values," where 65% of Republicans agreed, compared to only 37% of Democrats. For the most part, the results are rather durable between the two waves, as befits an underlying attitude that is relatively well entrenched in the public mind. However, there is a notable movement among Democrats on one question—a seven-point decline in Democrats who say the military maintains high professional ethics from 2019 to 2020; since Wave 2 came at the height of a bitter presidential campaign, it is possible that partisan intensity played a role here.

Survey experiments make it possible to better isolate the causal impact of military ethics on public confidence. The test of the ethics hypothesis follows a design similar to the foregoing analysis of the competence issue—comparing the mean responses of randomly assigned groups receiving nudges about the ethics of the military to a control who were only asked the standard Gallup confidence question. A randomly assigned group of 597 respondents in Wave 1 received a special prompt, one designed to underscore the idea that the military *lives up* to high ethical professional standards (with the treatment highlighted here *in italics*):

> We are interested in how well information about the US military can reach the public. The length of the "war on terror" and associated US military activities have created a large amount of information that can be hard to follow.
>
> *For instance, did you know that the United States military increasingly come from a smaller percentage of the population? As a result, the United States military embodies the best values of American society. During the course of the wars in Afghanistan and Iraq, the United States military has minimized civilian casualties and treated civilians on the battlefield with respect and dignity. By and large, American military officers exhibit the best qualities of leadership and character the nation has to offer. According to figures released in 2018 by the Department of Defense Inspector General, only a small percentage of generals and admirals on active duty had committed moral or ethical offenses ranging from sexual assault, misuse of government*

funds, gambling scandals, and inappropriate statements about members of Congress between 2013 and 2017.

In light of that, we want to ask you some questions about the US military. Please tell me how much confidence you, yourself, have in the military—a great deal, quite a lot, some or very little?

A randomly assigned group of 581 respondents received what was intended as the opposite prompt, one designed to underscore the idea that the military *does not live up* to high ethical professional standards (treatment *in italics*):

We are interested in how well information about the US military can reach the public. The length of the "war on terror" and associated US military activities have created a large amount of information that can be hard to follow.

For instance, did you know that the United States military increasingly come from a smaller percentage of the population? As a result, the United States military has become disconnected from the best values of American society. During the course of the wars in Afghanistan and Iraq, the United States military has caused a large number of civilian casualties and at times has mocked civilians on the battlefield over cultural differences. By and large, American generals and admirals have not been held accountable for their moral and ethical failings. According to figures released in 2018 by the Department of Defense Inspector General, generals and admirals on active duty had committed more than 300 separate moral or ethical offenses ranging from sexual assault, misuse of government funds, gambling scandals, and inappropriate statements about members of Congress between 2013 and 2017.

In light of that, we want to ask you some questions about the US military. Please tell me how much confidence you, yourself, have in the military—a great deal, quite a lot, some or very little?

Figure 5.3 shows the results of the ethical prompt in the aggregate, and it can be interpreted in the same way as the competence figures presented above. It is readily apparent that public confidence in the military did not move in immediately obvious ways in response to prompts about the degree to which the military lived up to its putative high ethical standards.

The expectation of the survey experiment was that public support would increase (perhaps only marginally, given the ceiling effect of already high levels of confidence) when told that only "a small percentage" of senior military officers have been caught in clear ethical scandals such as "sexual assault, misuse of government funds, gambling scandals, and inappropriate statements

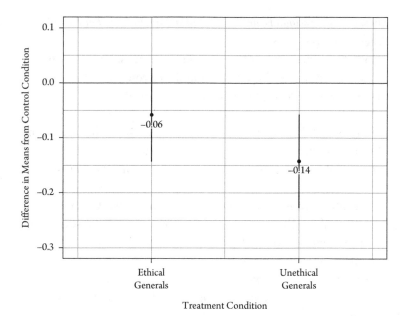

Figure 5.3 Treatment Effects for Ethics Prompt in the Aggregate (2019)

about members of Congress." Likewise, public support would decrease (perhaps more markedly) when told that "more than 300" senior officers have been caught. That is not what happened in this experiment. The prompt expected to decrease public support did have a substantively significant effect, moving support down by 14 percentage points; however, the prompt expected increase public confidence actually *decreased* it by 6 percentage points in the aggregate. Of course, the prompts are two ways of describing the same underlying data and one cannot rule out the possibility that many respondents found "a small percentage" to be too high, though not as alarming as "more than 300." To be sure, the downward movement in response to what was intended as a positive frame just misses statistical significance at the 90% level. Perhaps merely raising the ethics frame brought latent concerns about military misbehavior to the surface for our respondents in the aggregate. In either case, the inference is that public confidence in the military may indeed have baked into it a strong assessment of the military as living up to its high ethical standards. Thus, prompting the public to think about ethical problems does drive down public confidence somewhat.

As with the somewhat surprising results on ethics in the aggregate, party conditionality moves in rather unusual ways, as shown in Figure 5.4.

Independents are the only group that respond as expected, moving up 5 points when prompted with information intended to convey the idea that the military is highly ethical and moving down 9 points when prompted with information intended to convey the opposite idea (though the movement is not

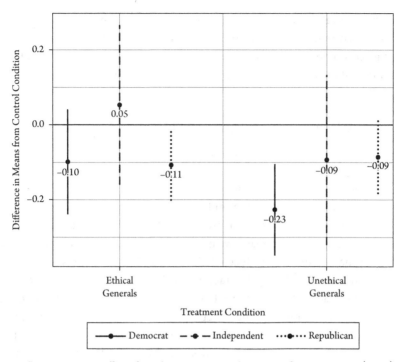

Figure 5.4 Treatment Effects for Ethics Prompt Broken Down by Partisan ID (2019)

statistically significant at the 95% confidence level). Democrats move a moderate amount in response to the supposedly positive information, 10 points, but they move in the "wrong" direction and just miss statistical significance at the 90% confidence level. They move quite a lot, down 23 points—the largest statistically significant movement across all of the partisan subgroups in response to any treatment—when prompted with the negative information about generals and admirals behaving badly. Republicans move down 9 percentage points (statistically significant at the 90% confidence level) in response to the negative information, as expected, but move 11 percentage points down in response to the supposedly positive information. The provisional inference is that partisans—respondents who identify with one party or the other (including, as explained before, partisans who self-identify only as "leaners") and start out with much higher levels of confidence—have markedly different expectations about military ethics than do independents, who start out with much lower levels of confidence.

One should not push these findings too far, given the limits to statistical power because of the sample size. It is worth replicating this approach in future work, and with larger sample sizes to better measure the effect. Nevertheless, the results are suggestive that the high level of public confidence expressed by

Democrats and Republicans assumes a separate confidence in ethical standards that is shaken when prompted to think about ethics; for independents, their lower level of confidence may likewise assume a lower confidence in ethical standards that moves in intuitive ways in response to new information.

By What Causal Pathways Did these Treatment Effects Travel?

The foregoing covers the treatment effect of prompts that in theory might move public confidence in the military up or down. The very modest treatment—basically a sentence or two of additional information in a survey question—produced a comparably modest result. The results are not always indistinguishable from a null effect—from the conclusion that this information does not, in fact, have much of a statistically significant impact on confidence in the military, at least not at the relatively high bar of a 95% confidence interval. Nevertheless, more of the effects are significant at a less-exacting 90% confidence level, and most move in a way consistent with theoretical expectations. The analysis so far, however, has only looked at the direct treatment effect, raising the question of whether the treatment effect, to the extent one exists, might operate indirectly by changing other attitudes about the military. One way to gain some purchase on this question is through causal mediation analysis, and one of the standard approaches to causal mediation is useful as a first-cut exploration.

Recall from Tables 5.1 and 5.2 that the survey also asked respondents to give their assessment of the military along a number of dimensions beyond the simple Gallup question of overall confidence. In addition to the five assessments already noted above—"good at job," "wins wars," "is ethical," "is truthful," and "shares my values"—the survey also asked whether respondents considered the military to be too partisan. The next chapter digs more deeply into the "too partisan" dimension, but here it is useful to assess whether the treatment effects might be mediated through these intermediate assessments—whether, for instance, telling respondents that the military had underperformed in Afghanistan changed the average response regarding the military's truthfulness or its partisan nature. Of course, the primary expectation is that the competence prompts would have the biggest effect on the directly related values of "good at job" and "wins at war," and that the ethical prompt would have the biggest effect on the three ethical values of "ethical," "truthful," and "shares values." However, it is at least possible that there might be unexpected causal pathways, and the effect on "too partisan" is intrinsically interesting whatever the result.

This approach to causal mediation begins by showing the cross-tabbed results by treatment category in Table 5.3. This is an admittedly busy table that reports the results of respondent agreement with the various statements asserting that the military has a certain quality or not—is too partisan, is good at what it does, shares my values, and so on.

The table shows the results broken down both by experimental condition—the control group or the various treatment groups—and by party. Table 5.3 shows that a large majority of respondents believe the military is "good at what it does" and that the military "wins the wars it fights." However, this rosy assessment is not immutable.

Recall from Figures 5.1 and 5.2 that priming respondents to believe that the military has not achieved its goals on the battlefield by telling them that "the United States military has failed to achieve any of its most important strategic goals and it has become mired in the longest conflict in American history, with no end in sight" and that "it is undeniable that the United States military has lost the war in Afghanistan" had the intuitively expected result of moving overall confidence downward, for both Democrats and Republicans. Telling them that the military won in Afghanistan moved confidence up much less, and that modest effect was almost entirely driven by movement in independents. Table 5.3 now helps explain that movement better, since it shows that the "lost in Afghanistan" prompt has the intuitively expected negative impact on public assessments of those values most closely associated with competence, whether the military is good at what it does or wins the wars it fights. The "won in Afghanistan" treatment had less of an effect, moving respondents eight points on the narrow issue of whether or not the military wins the wars it fights while also modestly dropping perceptions that the military is too partisan and increasing perceptions that the military shares respondents' values.

Similarly, the positive ethical prompt had very little impact across any of the attribute questions. The negative ethical treatment has some intuitively expected effects on the values most closely linked to ethics, but it also damaged assessments of military competence, partisanship, and shared values—these latter are traits of the military that are, at first glance, more distantly connected in theory to the matter of military professional ethics. As noted earlier, respondents start with relatively high assessments of the ethical nature of the military, but views are more mixed on whether the military is truthful—and downright divided on whether the military shares the values of the respondent. From that baseline, being told about high levels of unethical behavior had dramatically negative effects on respondents' assessments regarding how ethical and truthful the military is—just as it had the markedly negative effect on overall public confidence in the military, as reported in Figure 5.3. It is notable, however, that priming the

Table 5.3 **Public Agreement with Other Military Attributes by Experimental and Party Conditions (2019, 2020) (% agree or strongly agree)**

Treatment (2019)	Too Partisan	Good at Job	Wins Wars	Ethical	Truthful	Shares Values
Control	22%	84%	60%	58%	46%	46%
Won war	17% (−5%)	83% (−1%)	68% (+8%)**	59% (+1%)	46% (0%)	52% (+6%)
Lost war	20% (−2%)	77% (−7%)*	50% (−10%)**	54% (−4%)	37% (−9%)**	39% (−7%)*
Good ethics	21% (−1%)	80% (−4%)	61% (+1%)	61% (+3%)	46% (0%)	51% (+5%)
Bad ethics	26% (+5%)	72% (−12%)***	51% (−9%)**	43% (−15%)***	35% (−11%)***	40% (−6%)

Treatment (2020)	Too Partisan	Good at Job	Knowledgeable	Ethical	Truthful	Shares Values
Control	26%	75%	75%	58%	46%	47%
COVID success	24% (−2%)	78% (+3%)	80% (+5%)	61% (+3%)	51% (+5%)	50% (+3%)
COVID fail	25% (−1%)	75% (0%)	77% (+2%)	62% (+4%)	52% (+6%)	50% (+3%)
Restored order	28% (+2%)	77% (+2%)	80% (+5%)	61% (+3%)	47% (+1%)	50% (+3%)
Inflamed tensions	28% (+2%)	75% (0%)	78% (+2%)	61% (+3%)	**54% (+8%)****	49% (+2%)

*** = p < .01; ** = p < .05; * = p < .1 for one-tailed tests.

public with information suggesting that members of the military are unethical drives assessments of the military down across the board.

Recall from Figures 5.3 and 5.4 that the prompt designed to suggest that the military was ethical did not have the expected effect on respondents, with confidence levels among both Democrats and Republicans dropping despite being told information that was expected to make them think the military was more ethical. Although not presented here (see the technical appendix for details), analysis of these effects by party hints at why the overall confidence level among Democrats may not have responded to the "ethical generals" prompt as expected. Telling Democrats that the military has a comparatively low level of unethical behavior among its senior ranks had the paradoxical effect of making Democrats less likely to think the military was truthful, with a drop of as many as 12 points. Table 5.3 shows that Republicans did respond to that prompt as expected when one drills down on subsidiary questions—being given the "ethical generals" prompt did make Republicans slightly more likely to assess the military as ethical and truthful. Thus, the decline in overall confidence among Republicans after receiving the "ethical generals" prompt was *not* because it made Republicans somehow think the military was less ethical or truthful. Something else must be going on, but given the limits of the data one can only speculate as to what it might be.

Even mentioning the military's role in the Covid response—whether framed positively or negatively—had a favorable impact on public assessments, though only modestly so. As discussed earlier, it seems that the recent positive experience that many Americans had with the National Guard during the early stages of the pandemic may have muted what was intended to be a negative framing. Shifts related to the treatments related to the protests led to modest and somewhat counterintuitive effects, at least in the aggregate. Although the positive framing—in which the military helped restore order in response to protests—led to favorable shifts across most of the attributes, so did the negative framing. In fact, the negative framing caused the largest positive shift, with more respondents agreeing that the military is "truthful." This change was almost entirely the result of an uptick among Republicans, who increased 16 points from 54% to 70%. Republicans also saw a large 10-point bounce on the ethical standards question.

These results were not expected, and so there is no ready theory to explain them. They are surprising enough even to defy efforts at a convincing post hoc explanation. It is possible that something like the quasi-tribal own-partisan effect that Robinson (2018) identified—where Republicans rally to an institution they deem "one of their tribe" when it is criticized in the media—is operating, but why it would be so much stronger in this relatively modest treatment than others is hard to say. Perhaps the fact that Democrats made criticizing Trump's use of the military as a law enforcement tool—a tool, Democrats claimed,

Trump deployed for crass partisan propaganda value—so prominent in their line of critique in the run-up to the 2020 election made that issue hyperprimed for partisan response (Glueck and Ember 2020; Herman 2020; Sanders 2020).

There are some tantalizing data from outside this study that point in this direction. If the foregoing is right, then one would expect public opinion to move more dramatically—and more markedly in a partisan-contingent fashion—when the military gets caught up in an issue that has significant campaign salience. Precisely that happened with the January 6, 2021, insurrection attempt, when supporters of President Trump stormed the Capitol to delay the certification of President-elect Biden. The event itself and the military response to the event quickly became enmeshed in competing partisan narratives. Thus one would expect a survey conducted in the aftermath of the January 6 events, while partisan emotions were still running high, to reflect a drop in public confidence and positive affect toward the military. That is, indeed, what the Reagan Institute found in its survey conducted barely a month after the event (Ronald Reagan Institute 2021). Both public confidence and public trust in the military dropped, and the drop was bigger among Democrats, the group that would be most dismayed by how the security forces performed in defending the Capitol.[9]

Table 5.4 sheds more light on these issues by reporting the results of a statistical analysis of the causal mediation effects designed to measure both direct and indirect pathways. The direct pathway is the one from the treatment directly to confidence, where telling respondents that the military lost the war in Afghanistan lowers their overall confidence in the military. While the attributes most closely related to the treatments (e.g., losing the war in Afghanistan and losing wars or unethical behavior leading to assessments that the military has low ethical standards) are likely to drive changes in confidence, it is also logically possible that these prompts would lower confidence in the military not merely because of the direct effect but also through other pathways. For example, you might believe the military lost the war because the military is bad at its job or you might believe the military is competent but that its decisions became too influenced by partisan factors. Since Table 5.3 showed that the survey

---

[9] However, one should not push this too far since several features of their survey design make it a less than ideal test of this idea. First, respondents were not offered the standard Gallup question but one with the following response options: "a great deal," "some," "not much," and "a little." The drop is mostly a decline in the percentage that gave the top-most "a great deal" response. If one combines the two top categories, the drop is pretty small. But these two top categories do not map cleanly onto the one used in this book, so it makes comparisons difficult. Moreover, their 2018 survey was conducted over Veterans Day weekend—a time when one might expect an artificial boost in promilitary affect—and the results were out of step with the other surveys that year. That said, it seems plausible that here has been some decline from 2019 to 2021, as the survey indicates, and that is consistent with the interpretation presented in the text above.

Table 5.4 Average Causal Mediation Effects (2019, 2020)

Treatment	Too Partisan % Mediated	p	Competent % Mediated	p	Ethical % Mediated	p	Truthful % Mediated	p	Shares Values % Mediated	p	Total (Decrease) % Mediated	p
Lost war (2019)	–4%	0.27	40%***	0.00	4%	0.34	–9%*	0.09	28%**	0.04	(–9) 60%***	0.01
Good ethics (2019)	1%	0.6	52%*	0.08	–19%	0.27	2%	0.72	–25%	0.24	(–6) 11%	0.85
Bad ethics (2019)	1%***	0.01	28%***	0.00	19%	0.00	1%***	0.00	14%**	0.05	(–14) 63%***	0.00
NG inflamed (2020)	0%	0.99	6%	0.76	–3%	0.69	–9%*	0.07	3%	0.84	(–6) –3%	0.94

*** = p < .01; ** = p < .05; * = p < .1 for one-tailed tests.

treatments did affect other assessments of the military, this analysis allows us to sort out which changes were most closely linked to changes in confidence. Table 5.4 shows how much of the overall treatment effect might be attributed to these indirect effects for the four treatments involving the largest aggregate shifts.[10] In layman's terms, the "percentage mediated" refers to the proportion of the treatment effect a given variable causes. For example, the total "Lost War" treatment effect is roughly −9 points (in parentheses under the "Total" column). The mediator variables in our model collectively explain about 60% of that total, or around 5.4 points of the total 9-point drop.[11]

Overall, the most significant driver of changes in public confidence across these experiments was a decreased perception that the military is good at its job, *even* for questions related to ethics. The change in perceived confidence explains more than one-third of the variation in confidence for the "Lost in Afghanistan" and "Bad Ethics" treatments and shows similar levels for three other positive treatments not depicted (but those three fall well short of statistical significance). Although not displayed in the table (see the technical appendix for details), a perceived decrease in competence also drove 52% of the curious result where confidence among Republicans dropped when they received the "Good Ethics" treatment.

Decreased perceptions of low ethical standards and truthfulness do explain part of the change in confidence resulting from the "Bad Ethics" treatment, but these proportions—19% and 1%, respectively—are much smaller than those operating through the competence pathway. It is intuitive that failure in a foreign war or a domestic mission would influence confidence because it changed public perceptions about military competence. However, these results suggest that respondents lose confidence in the military when they hear about ethical

---

[10] Table 5.4 used the product of coefficients method for multiple mediators to estimate the indirect effect of our experimental treatments on public confidence through each potential mediator (MacKinnon, Fairchild, and Fritz 2007; Preacher and Hayes 2008; Golby, Feaver, and Dropp 2017). Responses to questions about whether or not the military is "good at what it does" and whether the military "wins the wars it fights" are highly correlated (.63). Table 5.4 reports competence based on the question about the military is "good at what it does," but replacing this variable with "wins the wars it fights" does not significantly impact our results.

[11] Negative mediation effects are the least intuitive to interpret. In general, the simplest way to understand them for present purposes is to assume that the experimental treatment caused the mediator variable to move in the opposite direction of the overall treatment effect, while the mediator variable itself remained positively correlated (or negatively for "too partisan") with public confidence in the military. For example, a negative percentage for the "truthful" mediator under the "Lost War" treatment means that priming respondents with information that the military lost the war in Afghanistan actually led respondents to become more likely to say the military is truthful—even as overall confidence in the military decreased.

scandals not primarily because they care about the ethical behavior itself, but rather because it causes them to doubt the military's competence.

We also observe statistically significant mediation effects driven by lower assessments of military truthfulness that accounts for small, but statistically significant, changes in confidence. One possible explanation for this result for the "Lost War" treatment is that news of a loss causes the public to question military honesty and candor in light of 18 years of optimistic statements by senior military officers.[12]

In fact, the public's relatively low assessment of military truthfulness in Wave 1—combined with the nine-point drop in truthfulness in response to the "Lost War" treatment—is striking. So is the response to this question: "Senior military leaders, like generals and admirals, have told the American people the truth about the war in Afghanistan." Only a paltry 24% of respondents agreed or strongly agreed with that statement, with relatively modest partisan differences. Among Republicans, 31% agreed, compared to 21% of Democrats and 18% of independents. This appraisal seemed at least somewhat out of step with the public assessment of military honesty and professional ethics presented earlier in this chapter.

Consequently, Wave 2 probed around the edges with statements designed to tease out why respondents were skeptical about what military leaders were saying about operations in Afghanistan. One explanation for the disconnect between higher assessments of honesty and lower assessments related to Afghanistan is simply that positive statements about the military are harder to justify when applied to a very specific context such as the nation's longest war. While the *Washington Post*'s "Afghanistan Papers" revealed very little new information of which close observers of the war were not already aware, it did promote this narrative of dishonesty to the broader public (Whitlock 2021). But wartime secrecy requirements and political pressure to distort the truth also provide justifiable, or at least understandable, reasons why military leaders might be less than forthcoming when dealing with the public.

In order to explore these dynamics, Wave 2 randomly divided the sample into thirds and asked each group one of the following variants of this question: "A. Senior military leaders, like generals and admirals, have told the American people the truth about the war in Afghanistan. B. Senior military leaders, like generals and admirals, have told the American people the truth about the war in Afghanistan to the extent possible given wartime requirements for secrecy. C. Senior military leaders, like generals and admirals, have told the American

---

[12] The optimism and consistency of statements by senior military leaders has become something of a meme. See, for example, "'We're making real progress,' say last 17 commanders in Afghanistan..." @DuffelBlog on Twitter, August 22, 2017; DuffelBlog 2020a.

Table 5.5 **Views on Candor of Senior Military Leaders by Level of Confidence (2020)**

		Overall Agree	Not Confident in Military	Confident in Military
Senior leaders have been telling the truth	Democratic respondents	31% (671)	24% (264)	36% (407)
	Republican respondents	34% (537)	33% (93)	34% (444)
Senior leaders have been telling the truth given wartime secrecy requirements	Democratic respondents	29% (720)	15% (310)	40% (410)
	Republican respondents	51% (554)	33% (103)	55% (451)
Senior leaders have been telling the truth given political pressure	Democratic respondents	40% (667)	25% (264)	51% (403)
	Republican respondents	36% (563)	25% (109)	39% (454)

people the truth about the war in Afghanistan to the extent possible given pressure by political leaders to distort the facts on the ground." Table 5.5 reports the level of respondent agreement with statements about truth-telling regarding the war, again broken down by level of confidence in the military.

The results provide a more positive, though still somewhat mixed, perception of senior military leaders' truthfulness about operations in Afghanistan. Overall, 31% of respondents report they believe military leaders have been telling the truth about the war, a modest 7-point increase from 2019 to 2020. Republicans are more likely than Democrats to credit the military with candor in the control group, though less so than they were in 2019. When accounting for operational restrictions and wartime secrecy requirements, this gap widens considerably. Republicans increase 17 points from 34% to 51%, while Democrats remain mostly unchanged. Moreover, Republican respondents with high confidence in the military—and to a lesser degree, Democratic respondents—are even more likely to credit the military in this fashion than are respondents with low confidence. On the other hand, Democrats are more likely than Republicans to believe that the military's truth-telling has been shaded by political pressure, and this is especially the case for Democrats with high confidence in the military. Overall, Democrats increase 9 points, while "high confidence" Democrats increase 15 points, from 36% to 51%. Since this experiment came at the height of the 2020 presidential campaign, it seems likely that partisan considerations might be driving at least some of this Democratic response.

Conclusion

Although public confidence in the military has been quite resilient over the last two or three decades, these experiments help shed some light on General Dempsey's desire to know what might screw up public confidence in the military. The findings suggest that poor operational performance and prominent ethical missteps could eventually lead to an erosion of public confidence, largely because both appear to make the public less confident that the military can do its job well.

The treatments are quite modest—essentially a few sentences in a prompt. In the real world, there could be a steady drumbeat of criticism (or praise), and so it is likely this would have a bigger impact. At the same time, particularly for ambiguous cases, the drums might be beating in opposite ways, producing just a cacophony of cross-cutting praise and criticism, so the net effect might be closer to what these results estimate. Either way, it seems clear that these dynamics would be refracted through the lens of partisanship, with Republicans and Democrats hearing—and therefore responding—in slightly different ways.

While the survey experiment is an effective way of precisely measuring *whether* there is a causal effect, and causal mediation sheds some light into *how* it is happening, the experiment leaves hanging the question of *why* the effect is happening in this way.[13] Perhaps the new information is particularly salient and useful for the respondent, or perhaps the new information is actually surprising to the respondent. And perhaps it may simply be that the new information just gets respondents to think of something connected to the military in a way they would not without the prime. To catch the distinctions, imagine airplane passengers listening to an announcement about safety ratings over the public address system and then being asked how confident they are in the ride. If the information is, "We have a 95% safety rating," that might be salient and useful; if the announcement is, "We have only a 50% safety rating," that might be surprising (and alarming!); and perhaps just mentioning the safety rating primes thoughts about problems that the passenger had hitherto blissfully disregarded. It may even be that the new information activates some social desirability bias—where the respondent feels pressured to think one way or the other—and thus the treatment changes how honest the respondent is; as will be discussed later in Chapter 7, public confidence in the military is indeed shaped by such dynamics in the aggregate, and perhaps the treatments in this chapter are interacting with that in ways I have not fully anticipated. Unfortunately, the analyses presented in this chapter are not able to fully adjudicate between these

---

[13] I am indebted to David Burbach for suggesting this way of thinking about the issue.

different explanations. For my money, simple priming—getting the respondent to think about something—may well be the most likely explanation, but perhaps for some respondents surprise or even social desirability may be at work. Future work could unpack this.

The next chapter digs into another prominent explanation for public confidence: the idea that the public sees the military as operating outside of, and above, the partisan politics that divides the country. The results presented thus far already raise important questions about this hypothesis, with ample evidence that the partisanship of respondents shapes their attitudes regarding military competence and professional ethics.

6

Politics, Politicization, and Public Confidence

> Pentagon Insists U.S. Military Will Only Intervene in Foreign Elections.
> —Duffelblog.com, 2021

One thread traces through the previous chapters and merits closer scrutiny now: it is apparent that partisan Americans see things differently when it comes to civil-military affairs. The partisanship issue is not always the dominant nor the most important divide, but it is a persistent one. Most obviously, a majority of Republicans and Democrats concur in holding the military in high esteem, but that concurrence masks significant divides below the surface. And, as table after table in preceding chapters attest, it is all too easy to find Republicans and Democrats offering markedly different perspectives when pressed on the nitty-gritty of civil-military affairs. The pattern raises a hoary question, one that has concerned scholars for decades (Huntington 1957; Janowitz 1960; Holsti 1998–99; Feaver and Kohn 2001; Golby 2011; Robinson 2018): are relations between the military and civilian society hopelessly entangled in partisan politics? This chapter digs into this question, leveraging the new proprietary data to show how partisan considerations both shape confidence in the military and how confidence in the military might shape the political roles the public is willing to see its military play.[1]

The political question is central to civil-military relations theory. A bedrock principle of democratic civil-military relations is that the military's role in politics must be carefully circumscribed (Huntington 1957; Janowitz 1960). In a healthy democracy, the military plays a critical role in *defending* the polity, but only a marginal (if any) role in *governing* the polity. The business of politics—of

---

[1] Portions of this chapter were presented as Golby (2019), Golby and Feaver (2019b), and Golby and Feaver (2021b).

determining who gets what, when, where, how and, crucially, of determining how those decisions will be made—is the province of the civilian. At most, the military has an advisory role beyond the obvious one of protecting the polity against external or domestic threats that would themselves impose their will on the rightful political order. Because it is so fundamental to democracy, determining the conditions under which the military stays within its proper political boundaries accounts for the lion's share of the scholarship on American civil-military relations (Huntington 1957; Feaver 1996, 1999, 2003; Desch 1999; Brooks 2019).

But the military still must operate within a political context, and decisions that military leaders and service members make can have political implications. Over the past several decades, the question of military politics has only grown in importance as scholars have raised warnings that the US military was becoming politicized (Feaver and Kohn 2001; Golby 2011, 2020; Robinson 2018; Barno and Bensahel 2019; Golby and Karlin 2020; Brooks 2020, 2021). Brooks (2020), for example, argues that Huntingtonian professional norms paradoxically increase politicized behaviors. In a similar vein, Golby and Karlin (2020) suggest that the term "apolitical" is too vague to provide practical guidance, suggesting instead that normative theory should focus on prohibitions against partisan behavior, the use of institutional credibility to advance personal policy preferences, and electoral involvement, or "PIE." The PIE framework for politicization covers at least three distinct issues:

- (i) *Partisanship*: the possibility that the military, as an institution, is taking on something of a partisan identity, either because a disproportionate percentage come from one party (Feaver and Kohn 2001; Holsti 1998–99; Ricks 1997; Dempsey 2009; Golby 2011), or because members are increasingly willing to openly espouse views that hitherto might have been held in private (Urben 2013, 2014, 2021), or because the rest of the body politic views the military as "captured" by one of the parties (Robinson 2018) and thus attitudes toward the military reduce to just one more manifestation of American partisan polarization (Golby 2011)—or some combination of all three.
- (ii) *Use of institutional credibility*: an increasingly prominent role is being played by military voices—especially retired military—in public debates over policies, including policies far from areas of core military concern (Brooks 2009; Dunlap 1994); high levels of military prestige also increase incentives for presidents to use the appointment process to identify military leaders aligned with their own policy preferences and to use these officers to shape domestic public opinion (Golby 2011; Golby, Feaver, and Dropp 2017).
- (iii) *Electoral interventions*: an increasingly prominent partisan role played by military voices—primarily retired military—during political campaigns

(Golby, Dropp, and Feaver 2012; Griffiths and Simon 2021) as well as the prevalent use of uniformed military personnel and martial imagery by congressional candidates on the campaign trail.

Of course, the military, as a large and powerful institution, has always had an irreducibly political role in the bureaucratic politics of policymaking and policy implementation. But traditional normative theories of civilian control in the United States, whether in the Huntingtonian or Janowitzean traditions, have always emphasized the importance of keeping the military out of partisan politics. This has been reinforced by norms, such as the one against senior military voting—or at least acknowledging their votes publicly—that General George C. Marshall made famous (Cavanaugh 2016). And it has been reinforced by law and policy, with tight restrictions in the Uniform Code of Military Justice against the military publicly expressing political views.[2]

Politicization shows up as a concern when considering both what might drive public confidence in the military as well as why we might care about the public's level of confidence. On the one hand, a prominent explanation for why the public might retain high confidence in the military while confidence in other governmental institutions has declined concerns the military's reputation as being above and outside of partisan politics (Gronke and Feaver 2001; King and Karabell 2003; Hill, Wong, and Gerras 2013). On the other hand, this high public esteem might give the military special influence in partisan politics and thus create the opportunity for mischief that might ultimately undermine the military's standing. On either hand, it may be the case that the high levels of political polarization in contemporary America mean that public attitudes toward the military are hopelessly politicized, just because the public itself has been so polarized along partisan lines (McCarty et al. 2006; McCarty 2019). This chapter explores all sides of the question and finds enough support to validate all of these concerns.

While these two hypothesized relationships—low politicization leads to high confidence versus high confidence leads to high politicization—are somewhat in tension, both could be operating at the same time. It is possible that the public's high confidence in the military derives from a belief in the military's historical status as transcending partisanship but this high confidence then leads to temptations that place that very status in jeopardy. By analogy, a person's high reputation for virtue could be the very thing that places that individual

---

[2] Urben (2021), however, makes a compelling case that the corpus of laws and regulations urgently needs to be updated to address new challenges created by the advent of social media. And the norm is murky because of the strenuous effort to get the military to vote (Inbody 2015).

in situations where that virtue is sorely tested—perhaps tested to the breaking point.[3]

The Partisan Thread from Previous Chapters

Before digging into the matter more deeply, recall some of the basic findings related to partisanship from previous chapters. First, as noted in Chapter 2, public confidence in the military in the aggregate masks an underlying partisan dimension. Yes, the public as a whole has high confidence in the military, but that result is driven by Republicans who express exceptionally high levels of confidence; Democrats on average show markedly lower levels of confidence. In the 2020 wave, less than a quarter of Democrats show the highest level of confidence ("a great deal") but roughly half (49%) of Republicans do; and when one groups the high-confidence responses ("a great deal" and "quite a lot"), the strong majority of Democrats (60%) expressing this view is eclipsed by the overwhelming supermajority (82%) of Republicans.

Second, as shown in Chapter 3, partisans' attitudes about the military diverge as their level of education increases. This divergence appears to be primarily driven by changes on the Democratic side. Democrats with lower levels of education are far less likely to think that most members of the military are Republican and noticeably more confident in the military than are more highly educated Democrats. However, attitudes among Republicans stay relatively flat on both issues. Highly educated members of both parties are about equally likely to believe that most members of the military are Republicans, but this assessment of military partisanship leads more educated Democrats to hold the military in lower esteem than their Republican counterparts do.

Third, as reported in Chapter 4, the partisan dimension of confidence in other institutions appears to be at least partly driving public confidence in the military. It is an inverse relationship with Republicans—Republicans flock to express confidence in the military as their confidence in other institutions declines. But it is a positive correlation for Democrats—Democrats who have high confidence in other institutions also tend to have higher confidence in the military.

Fourth, as shown in Chapter 5, partisanship shapes how the public responds to other determinants of confidence. Consistently, Democrats responded more dramatically to the cues designed to push confidence in the military down, though partisan responses appear to be heightened among all groups during the

---

[3] Eliot Cohen (2004) has likened this to generals engaging in a second career as pole-dancers in Las Vegas, and Jason Dempsey (2009) has called this the "paradox of prestige."

second wave of the survey, which was conducted only weeks before the 2020 presidential election.

Fifth, as will be seen later in Chapter 10, there is an important partisan dimension to the blame game that arises as the public assesses the performance of both civilian officials and the military in wartime. The public seems to insulate the military from blame, as much as—if not more than—it insulates its own copartisan civilian leaders, while it lays the fault of any poor wartime performance squarely on the backs of civilian leaders from the opposite party.

Since the public's own partisanship shapes the way it views military affairs, one would therefore expect to see interesting partisan patterns emerge when the public is asked to assess the partisan profile of the military itself—and when one probes how those partisan dimensions might further shape public confidence in the military. This chapter proceeds by exploring five questions, each answerable in fresh ways by leveraging the data in the 2019 and 2020 surveys of public opinion: (1) Does the public perceive the military to have a partisan identity? (2) Do primes about military partisan identity move public confidence in the military? (3) Does the public respond to military cues on vote choice? (4) Does the public respond to military cues on the most politicized uses of the military? (5) Does confidence in the military make the public receptive to politicized roles for the military?

The new surveys provide a wealth of information on these questions but it must be acknowledged that the surveys came during a time of high partisan polarization. The second wave, in particular, came at the height of the 2020 election when partisan loyalties (and animosities) were activated to an extraordinary degree. Of course, it may be that partisan polarization will be an enduring feature of the political landscape, at least for a while, and so perhaps these two snapshots are not as idiosyncratic as one might expect. It is striking that where the surveys included questions in both waves most of the partisan findings presented in this chapter hold for both waves. In other words, except where noted, there is not a pronounced "end-of-campaign effect" that leaps out from the results. Of course, these assessments should be replicated in follow-on studies to see whether they dissipate or whether they are part of the new-normal.

1. Does the public perceive the military to have a partisan identity?

Wave 1 asked respondents several questions about how they perceived the partisanship and ideological makeup of the US military. Note that the tables that follow only report the results for respondents in the control group—that is, respondents who were not given the prompts in the survey experiments described earlier in Chapter 5 or a bit later in this chapter. Thus, these respondents were not prompted to think of the military as succeeding or failing in the Afghanistan war, as dealing with ethical challenges, nor as having a particular partisan identity. As Table 6.1 shows, 56% of those respondents report they believe most members of the military affiliate with a political party, down slightly from 58% in 2019. While the percentage of Democrats stating that most members of the military are partisans increased by 5 points to 63% in 2020, the number of independents and Republicans saying the same decreased, with Republicans dropping a statistically significant 12 points from 61% to 49%.

Among the subset of respondents who believe most members of the military affiliate with a political party (Table 6.2), a strong majority states there are "equal numbers" of Republicans and Democrats in the military; those stating "most are Republicans" come in a close second at 38%, with a paltry 7% reporting most are Democrats. Some partisans do seem to project their own beliefs onto the military, with Democrats slightly more likely to state most members of the military are Democrats, Republicans more likely to report most are Republicans, and 73% of independents claiming members of the military are balanced along partisan lines. There is a significant shift among Democrats between the 2019 and 2020 waves, however, with Democrats 20 points more likely at 43% to state most members of the military are Republicans. This shift may, in part, be due

Table 6.1 **Public Beliefs about Whether the Military Has a Political Affiliation by Party Identification of Respondent (% agree)**

	Overall	*Dem*	*Ind*	*Rep*
Most affiliate (2019)	58%	58%	55%	61%
	(362)	(174)	(66)	(122)
Most affiliate (2020)	56%	63%	51%	49%
	(309)	(156)	(44)	(108)
Don't affiliate (2019)	41%	42%	43%	39%
	(255)	(127)	(52)	(77)
Don't affiliate (2020)	44%	37%	47%	50%
	(243)	(91)	(41)	(111)
Don't know (2019)	0%	0%	2%	0%
	(2)	(0)	(2)	(0)
Don't know (2020)	1%	1%	1%	1%
	(4)	(1)	(1)	(2)
Total (2019)	(619)	(300)	(120)	(199)
Total (2020)	(556)	(249)	(86)	(221)

Table 6.2 **Public Beliefs about Which Political Affiliation the Military Has by Party Identification of Respondent (% agree)**

	Overall	Dem	Ind	Rep
Most are Dems (2019)	9%	9%	6%	10%
	(31)	(15)	(4)	(12)
Most are Dems (2020)	7%	11%	5%	3%
	(23)	(17)	(2)	(4)
Most are GOP (2019)	27%	23%	18%	38%
	(96)	(40)	(12)	(45)
Most are GOP (2020)	38%	43%	23%	36%
	(122)	(70)	(11)	(41)
About equal (2019)	64%	68%	75%	52%
	(225)	(114)	(48)	(62)
About equal (2020)	55%	46%	73%	61%
	(178)	(76)	(33)	(69)
Total (2019)	(352)	(169)	(64)	(119)
Total (2020)	(323)	(163)	(46)	(113)

to the military's involvement in a number of controversies related to the Black Lives Matter protests during the summer of 2020. Although Trump ultimately decided not to invoke the Insurrection Act to use active duty troops in support of law enforcement on domestic soil, members of the National Guard backed up federal law enforcement in Washington, DC, on June 1, when they cleared Lafayette Square prior to Trump's photo op with chairman of the Joint Chiefs, General Mark Milley, at St. John's Church (Baker et al. 2020; Gibbons-Neff, Schmitt, and Cooper 2020; Gjelten 2020). Or it may just reflect the greater attention paid in the media to the military's political views as the campaign season progressed (Myers 2020b; Shane 2020a, 2020b).

As Table 6.3 clearly shows, respondents' perceptions about the military's ideology are less ambiguous, with a 31% plurality believing most members of the military are conservative and 30% saying they don't know the ideology of most members of the military. A strong plurality of Republicans and nearly a third of Democrats agree that most members of the military are conservative, with only small minorities asserting the military is liberal. As with the attribute questions reported earlier in Chapter 5 (Tables 5.1 and 5.2), however, independents again stand out in their assessments of the military, with 51% of independents answering "Don't Know" and 27% stating members of the military are moderate.

Table 6.3 **Public Beliefs about Military Political Ideology by Party Identification of Respondent (2019)**

	Overall	Dem	Ind	Rep
Most are liberal	10%	13%	3%	9%
	(62)	(41)	(3)	(18)
Most are moderate	29%	29%	27%	29%
	(177)	(87)	(32)	(58)
Most are conservative	31%	28%	20%	43%
	(194)	(85)	(23)	(86)
Don't know	30%	29%	51%	19%
	(186)	(87)	(61)	(38)
Total	(619)	(300)	(120)	(199)

In fact, in several ways (but not every way), independents are a bit more likely to believe the military is "more like them" politically (e.g., slightly more likely to say the military doesn't affiliate with a political party or consists of political moderates). Note, as reported in Table 6.5, however, that only 38% of independents agreed that the "military shares my values." In other words, when asked directly, "Does the military share your values?" independents expressed some doubt—in contrast to Republicans, who were decidedly (68%) of the view that the military shared Republican values. But when asked indirectly to describe the politics of the military, independents tended to give answers that match their own political profile, presumably their own political values. This pattern is all the more curious because independents are less likely to assign other positive attributes to the military, with the notable exception of competence. Part of this may be because of a potential remove independents feel from the military, as illustrated in Table 6.4, where 27% of independents say they don't know whether the military "looks like" them. However, the 39% of independents who report that either "most" or "some" members of the military "look like me" is not substantially different from the 40% of Democrats or even the 46% of Republicans who did the same. Independents seem to be saying that they are not sure that the military shares their values or personal characteristics, but they do tend to think the military shares their politics.

Of course, it is one thing to describe a certain partisan profile of the military. It is another thing altogether to view that partisan profile as problematic. The survey put the question directly to our respondents, asking them whether they thought the military had become too partisan.

Table 6.4 **Whether the Military "Looks Like Me" by Party Identification (% agree)**

	Overall	Dem	Ind	Rep
Most look like me	13%	13%	11%	12%
	(77)	(39)	(13)	(24)
Some look like me	29%	27%	28%	34%
	(181)	(82)	(33)	(67)
A few look like me	18%	20%	16%	18%
	(114)	(59)	(18)	(36)
Most don't	20%	23%	18%	16%
	(122)	(69)	(21)	(32)
Don't know	20%	17%	27%	20%
	(121)	(50)	(32)	(39)
Total	(615)	(299)	(117)	(198)

Table 6.5 **Public Attitudes on Military Political Attributes by Party Identification (% agree)**

	Overall	Dem	Ind	Rep
Too partisan (2019)	22%	30%	14%	17%
	(138)	(89)	(16)	(33)
Too partisan (2020)	26%	36%	22%	18%
	(146)	(88)	(19)	(39)
Representative of US citizens (2019)	50%	48%	33%	64%
	(310)	(144)	(39)	(127)
Representative of US citizens (2020)	61%	55%	56%	71%
	(341)	(136)	(48)	(157)
Shares my values (2019)	46%	35%	38%	68%
	(281)	(106)	(44)	(131)
Shares My Values (2020)	47%	37%	33%	64%
	(262)	(91)	(28)	(142)
Total (2019)	(729)	(339)	(99)	(291)
Total (2020)	(556)	(249)	(86)	(221)

It is striking that the questions in Table 6.5 themselves reflect a partisan divide. Republicans provide much more favorable responses than either Democrats or independents on almost every question. There is one exception, however: independents were less likely than either Democrats or Republicans to report that the military was "too partisan" in 2019, though independents jumped slightly above Republicans in 2020. Democrats, however, are consistently the most bearish in their assessments of the military's political profile: they are more likely to think the military is too partisan, less likely to think the military is representative of the US citizenry as a whole, and less likely to think the military shares their values. The partisan gap is particularly large on this last question, with both Democrats and independents approximately 30 points less likely to agree that the military shares their values than Republicans.

Wave 2 also asked respondents directly to evaluate the degree of divisive partisanship they perceive within civilian society and within the military:

- If we define partisanship as extreme support for one political party over another (for example, support for Democrats over Republicans or Republicans over Democrats), how divided by partisanship do you think American society is nowadays? 1. Very divided by partisanship; 2. Somewhat divided by partisanship; 3. Only a little divided by partisanship; 4. Not at all divided by partisanship.
- On the whole, would you say that there is about as much partisanship in the military as in American society is, more partisanship than in American society, or less partisanship than in American society? 1. More partisanship in the military than in American society; 2. About as much partisanship in the military as in American society; 3. Less partisanship in the military than in American society.

Table 6.6 reports the responses to these questions broken down by the partisanship of the respondents. In the aggregate, Americans do think civilian society is quite divided—some 62% say "very" and another 23% say "somewhat." Democrats are markedly more likely to think this is the case than Republicans, however, and independents are the least likely. Few Americans, whether in the aggregate or within partisan subgroups, think the military has a bigger problem with partisan divisions than civilian society has. And roughly one-third of American adults think the military is characterized by markedly *less* partisanship than civilian society, though Republicans are 10 points more likely to think this than Democrats.

The data also shed light on the relationship between confidence in the military and partisan perceptions of the military. Table 6.7 displays the results and

Table 6.6 Perceptions of Partisanship in Civilian Society and in the Military by Partisanship of Respondent (Wave 2) (% agree)

	Overall	Dem	Ind	Rep
Very divided by partisanship	62% (344)	70% (174)	45% (39)	59% (131)
Somewhat divided by partisanship	23% (130)	22% (55)	28% (24)	23% (51)
A little divided by partisanship	10% (54)	4% (11)	16% (14)	13% (29)
Not at all divided by partisanship	5% (26)	3% (8)	11% (9)	4% (9)
Total	(556)	(249)	(86)	(221)

	Overall	Dem	Ind	Rep
More partisanship in the military	10% (55)	11% (27)	9% (8)	9% (20)
About as much partisanship	57% (314)	60% (148)	60% (52)	52% (114)
Less partisanship in the military	33% (54)	29% (71)	31% (27)	39% (85)
Total	(556)	(249)	(86)	(221)

supports the more cynical view that members of the public tolerate military partisanship as long as they believe the military shares the respondent's own partisan preferences. The table displays the percentages that report high or low confidence in the military, broken down by their perception of the military's partisan composition. Among Democrats who think that most members of the military are Democrats, 78% have confidence in the military. The same pattern largely repeats itself among independents, with 67% confidence among those who believe there are about equal numbers of partisans in the military and only 36% confidence among those who believe the military consists primarily of either Democrats or Republicans. Only Republicans break the mold. Just over 80% of Republicans have confidence regardless of whether they believe most members of the military are Republicans or whether they believe there is partisan parity. Nevertheless, even so, there is a marked decrease in the percentage with high confidence among the small group of Republicans who believe most members

Table 6.7 **High Confidence in the Military by Party Identification of Respondent and Perceived Political Affiliation of the Military (2020, % agree)**

Confidence Level	Overall	Democrats Low	Democrats High	Independents Low	Independents High	Republicans Low	Republicans High	All Respondents Low	All Respondents High
Most are Democrats	(37)	22% (6)	78% (21)	64% (3)	**36% (1)**	48% (3)	**52% (3)**	31% (12)	69% (25)
About equal	(169)	38% (55)	**62% (92)**	33% (22)	67% (44)	16% (21)	84% (109)	28% (97)	72% (248)
Most are Republicans	(345)	51% (44)	**49% (43)**	64% (10)	**36% (6)**	20% (13)	80% (53)	39% (66)	61% (103)
All respondents	(551)	41% (106)	59% (156)	40% (35)	60% (51)	18% (37)	82% (166)	32% (175)	68% (376)
Total		(262)		(86)		(203)		(551)	
Fisher's (Pr)		.02		.04		.09		.05	

of the military are Democrats.[4] These correlations suggest perceptions of military partisanship are related to public confidence, but they do not by themselves establish that partisan behavior by the military actually causes changes in public confidence.

On the whole, then, the public does seem to recognize some partisanship exists in the military, so public perceptions do not align with the view advanced by most normative theories of American civil-military relations that call for a purely nonpartisan force. But neither do those views align with the perception of a completely politicized force, as warned about in the most alarmist commentary about contemporary civil-military relations. Although there is some awareness of the growing diversity of the military among the public, there also is a correct perception that the military leans slightly conservative and Republican. Partisans themselves do have different perceptions of the military, however, with Republicans consistently more likely to see the military as demographically, politically, and culturally aligned with their party than either Democrats or independents.

---

[4] Reported in the technical appendix are a variety of modeling techniques to further explore whether views about the degree of partisanship in the military varied in interesting ways by the level of confidence the respondent had in the military. There is no significant difference by confidence for Democrats or independents, but Republicans with high confidence were more likely to think the military was less divided by partisanship.

2. Do primes about military partisan identity move public confidence in the military?

The previous chapter showed that public confidence in the military moved in intuitive ways with information about military competence. Public confidence moved in less intuitive ways with information about military ethics, but the analysis suggested two equally plausible but somewhat contradictory explanations for why any mention of ethics seemed to lower confidence: (a) perhaps the public has such a high baked-in estimate of the military's own elevated ethical standards that any priming that causes the public to doubt the military's ethical reputation likewise has an understandable effect in undermining public confidence; or (b) perhaps those primes simply increased the salience of the steady, but quiet drumbeat of news coverage about sexual assaults and ethical scandals in the force over the last decade or so and thus what was designed as a "ethics are high" nudge functioned more as an "ethics are low" nudge. Either way, getting the public to think about the military as not being competent or not being ethical had the expected effect of somewhat driving down confidence in the military.

This chapter explores another possible driver of public confidence, something left hanging by the observation in Chapter 4 that public confidence in the military has remained high while confidence in the other partisan political institutions of the state is quite low. Could it be that the public has high confidence in the military because the public sees the military as different from those other institutions that increasingly look beset by partisan politics? Earlier claims (Gronke and Feaver 2001) led to the expectation that public confidence in the military in the aggregate would *decrease* if the public came to view the military as having a partisan nature. This somewhat altruistic view of the public has received widespread acceptance, especially among military leaders who regularly invoke their standing above partisan politics as a key pillar of public support for the military (Browne 2020; Garamone 2016; NPR Staff 2016; Blitzer 2020). More recent research (Golby 2011; Golby and Liebert 2017; Burbach 2018; Robinson 2018) led to a more nuanced if not cynical expectation. Perhaps it was not overall partisanship that mattered, but whether the military's partisan affinity aligned with—or opposed—their own: partisan respondents might welcome hearing that the military matched their own partisan profile but would be dismayed to hear that the military aligned with the opposite party.

To explore this issue, the survey included a number of experiments, along the lines described in Chapter 5 and the technical appendix (available here: https://dataverse.harvard.edu/dataverse/pfeaver), that varied the partisan identity alleged to have taken root in the US military. In Wave 1, a randomly assigned group of 536 respondents were pushed to believe the military increasingly had a *Republican Party* identity (treatment in italics):

We are interested in how well information about the US military can reach the public. The length of the "war on terror" and associated US military activities have created a large amount of information that can be hard to follow.

For instance, did you know that the United States has become increasingly polarized in recent years, and the American electorate has become divided into rival tribal camps that demonize each other? Despite a longstanding tradition of political neutrality, the United States military has not been immune to these changes. *According to a recent study, a large majority of active duty service members have begun to openly post their support for Republican candidates for political office on their social media accounts. A recent poll showed that nearly 60 percent of all military veterans identified as Republicans and voted for the Republican candidate for president in the last election. Additionally, a large number of retired generals and admirals have openly endorsed the Republican presidential candidates in every presidential election since 2004. If these trends continue, the military will be dominated by Republicans in the coming decades.*

In light of that, we want to ask you some questions about the US military. Please tell me how much confidence you, yourself, have in the military—a great deal, quite a lot, some or very little?"

A randomly assigned group of 526 respondents in Wave 1 were pushed to believe the military increasingly had a *Democratic Party* identity:[5]

We are interested in how well information about the US military can reach the public. The length of the "war on terror" and associated US military activities have created a large amount of information that can be hard to follow.

For instance, did you know that the United States has become increasingly polarized in recent years, and the American electorate has become divided into rival tribal camps that demonize each other? Despite a longstanding tradition of political neutrality, the United States military has not been immune to these changes. *According to a recent study, a large majority of active duty service members have begun to openly post their support for Democratic candidates for political office on their social media accounts. A recent poll showed that nearly 60 percent of all military veterans identified as Democrats and voted for the Democratic candidate for*

---

[5] Note that this question involved mild deception. I do not know of studies that support the claim that a large majority of the military have begun to exhibit partisan Democrat behavior.

President in the last election. Additionally, a large number of retired generals and admirals have openly endorsed the Democratic presidential candidates in every presidential election since 2004. If these trends continue, the military will be dominated by Democrats in the coming decades.

In light of that, we want to ask you some questions about the US military. Please tell me how much confidence you, yourself, have in the military—a great deal, quite a lot, some or very little?"

And, finally, a randomly assigned group of 559 respondents in Wave 1 were pushed to believe the military increasingly had a *polarized partisan identity, more of both Republicans and Democrats*:

We are interested in how well information about the US military can reach the public. The length of the "war on terror" and associated US military activities have created a large amount of information that can be hard to follow.

For instance, did you know that the United States has become increasingly polarized in recent years, and the American electorate has become divided into rival tribal camps that demonize each other? Despite a longstanding tradition of political neutrality, the United States military has not been immune to these changes. *According to a recent study, a large majority of active duty service members have begun to openly post their support for both Democratic and Republican candidates for political office on their social media accounts. A recent poll showed that nearly all military veterans identified as partisans, and veteran voters divided between Republicans and Democrats in the last election. Additionally, a large number of retired generals and admirals have openly endorsed both Democratic and Republican presidential candidates in every presidential election since 2004. If these trends continue, the military will be just as partisan as other political institutions in the coming decades.*

In light of that, we want to ask you some questions about the US military. Please tell me how much confidence you, yourself, have in the military—a great deal, quite a lot, some or very little?"

Early presentations of the results from Wave 1 to scholarly audiences elicited numerous comments about this politicization experiment. Some reviewers thought the wording was too long or awkward. Thus, Wave 2 tweaked the wording somewhat to have a less confusing prompt and reran the same basic test. A control group of 550 respondents received only the public confidence question with no additional information about the military. Some 512 respondents were prompted to think of the military as increasingly Republican:

Did you know that according to a recent study, a growing number of active duty service members have begun to openly post their support for Republican candidates for political office on their social media accounts? Additionally, a large number of retired generals and admirals have openly endorsed the Republican presidential candidates in every presidential election since 2004. If these trends continue, the military will be dominated by Republicans in the coming decades. In light of that, we want to ask you some questions about the US military. Please tell me how much confidence you, yourself, have in the military—a great deal, quite a lot, some, or very little?"

Some 488 respondents were prompted to think of the military as increasingly Democratic:

Did you know that according to a recent study, a growing number of active duty service members have begun to openly post their support for Democratic candidates for political office on their social media accounts? Additionally, a large number of retired generals and admirals have openly endorsed the Democratic presidential candidates in every presidential election since 2004. If these trends continue, the military will be dominated by Democrats in the coming decades. In light of that, we want to ask you some questions about the US military. Please tell me how much confidence you, yourself, have in the military—a great deal, quite a lot, some, or very little?"

And some 567 respondents were prompted to think of the military as increasingly polarized in a partisan way with more open support of both Democrats and Republicans:

Did you know that despite a longstanding tradition of political neutrality, a large majority of active duty service members have begun to openly post their support for either Democratic and Republican candidates for political office on their social media accounts? Additionally, a large number of retired generals and admirals have openly endorsed both Democratic and Republican presidential candidates in every presidential election since 2004. If these trends continue, critics say the military will be fully partisan and no longer live up to its own non-partisan tradition. In light of that, we want to ask you some questions about the US military. Please tell me how much confidence you, yourself, have in the military—a great deal, quite a lot, some, or very little?"

The results are presented in a series of figures, all reporting confidence intervals at the 95% confidence level for a two-tailed t-test of the difference of means, using normal standard errors given the probability and sampling weights assigned by NORC (as explained in the technical appendix).

As shown in Figure 6.1, none of the treatments caused shifts in the aggregate that are statistically significant at the 95% level. In Wave 1, however, respondents did react in the expected direction to the primes about the military having a Republican or a Democratic partisan identity—in both cases, nudging support down a bit. In the aggregate, priming the public to think the military has a Republican cast reduced support slightly by one percentage point. Priming the public to think the military has a Democratic cast reduces support a bit more, moving it down by five points, though it is still indistinguishable from zero. In Wave 2, with a "cleaner" partisan prompt, the results in the aggregate differ somewhat but still are statistically indistinguishable from no effect. This time, the prompt that the military has a Republican cast moved confidence down by five points, whereas the prompt that the military has a Democratic cast nudged it up slightly, by two points.

Where the results are modestly more surprising is how the public responded in Wave 1 to the prompt that the military is polarized with more Republicans *and* more Democrats. The expectation was that priming the public to think the military had become polarized with more openly Republican *and* openly Democratic officers would have a much larger negative effect than either of the two one-party-only prompts. Describing the military as more polarized might make respondents view the military more like the other polarized institutions in society—institutions like Congress, which the public tends to rate quite poorly, or the Supreme Court, which has seen an erosion of public confidence over the last two decades (Thomson-DeVeaux and Roeder 2018). Whether the more altruistic hypothesis that the public hates any partisanship or the more cynical hypothesis that the public hates cross-party partisanship prevailed, regardless the common expectation was that telling the public that the military was mired in polarized partisanship would reduce overall confidence.

On the contrary, in Wave 1 it had the opposite result: it moved support up by six percentage points. While this bump just misses statistical significance at the 95% confidence level, it is the most sizable aggregate move from any of the treatments. The result is probably not an artifact of problems in the execution of the survey. Respondents who received this treatment did not differ from other respondents in terms of how long they took to complete the survey or how often they gave straight line responses to batteries. Respondents who received this treatment also gave intuitively plausible answers to other questions in our survey.

Precisely because Wave 1 was the first survey to ask this question in this way, an obvious question arose: were the surprising results merely an artifact of the question wording? To answer that question, Wave 2 reran the experiment, but

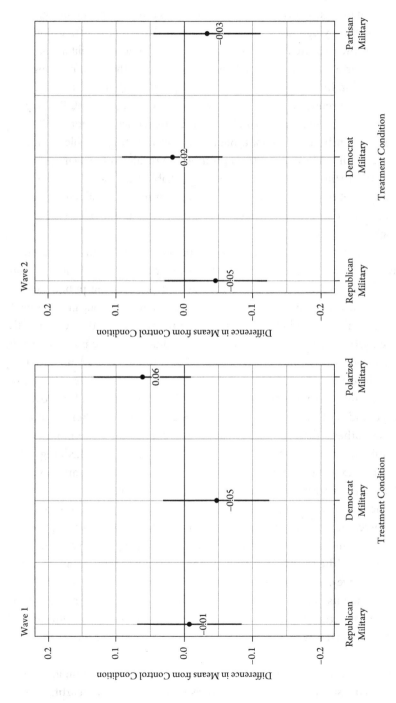

Figure 6.1 Effects of Political Treatment on Public Confidence in the Military

with the differently worded question (as explained earlier). As shown in Figure 6.1, respondents in Wave 2 responded more according to expectations: those who received the prompt that the military was "fully partisan" (with more Democrats and more Republicans) showed a decrease in confidence of three points—more in keeping with prior expectations.

Viewing the results in the aggregate, however, masks what might be the most interesting dynamics in play. Viewing the treatment effects by the partisanship of the respondents revealed several notable patterns, as depicted in Figure 6.2.

These results support the more cynical view (Golby 2011; Golby and Liebert 2017; Burbach 2018; Robinson 2018) rather than the altruistic/traditional view (Gronke and Feaver 2001) that the public expects and wants a nonpartisan military. In Wave 1, telling Democrat respondents that the military was developing a Democratic partisan identity boosted their confidence, albeit very slightly (about 2 percentage points). Telling Republican respondents that the military was developing a Republican partisan identity had the same marginally positive impact. Telling respondents that the military was developing the opposite party identity had a markedly negative effect: dropping confidence among Republican respondents by 13 percentage points and dropping Democrat confidence by 7 points, though the Democrat result is indistinguishable from no effect. Telling independents (which, as explained earlier in Chapter 2, does not include leaners) that the military is Republican *increases* support by 2 percentage points, while telling them the military is Democratic *decreases* support by 6 percentage points, but neither result is significant.

Again from Wave 1, telling respondents that the military is becoming polarized just like civilian society, with more openly Republican officers *and* more openly Democratic officers, produces some evidence of increased confidence.[6] The expectation was that this would decrease confidence in the aggregate—whatever gain in confidence from learning about more openly same-party partisans in the military would be eclipsed by the decline in confidence from learning about more openly opposite-party partisans. On the contrary, confidence in the military went up for those who received the "polarized partisan military" treatment across all three partisan categories of respondents, though none is statistically significant. Moreover, support went up slightly *more* for those who received the "polarized partisan" treatment than it did when respondents were told the military was aligned with their own party. Confidence went up 6 percentage points

---

[6] This result is sensitive to the choice of dependent variable. Using the 10-point confidence scale yields a null result. The analysis above reports the findings using the Gallup scale here because that is the conservative approach—i.e., the results are biased against the prior expectations. Moreover, the Gallup scale is most commonly used in the extant literature. However, in this one instance, it may be that the 10-point scale better captures variation in respondents' attitudes.

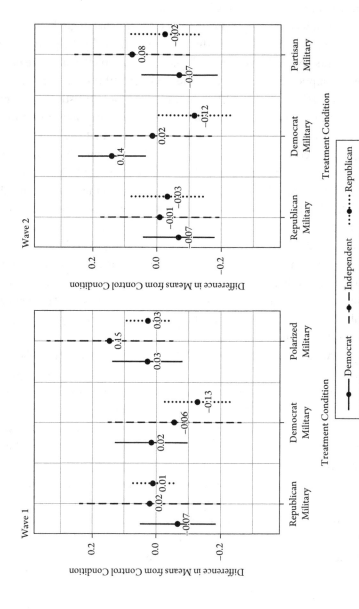

Figure 6.2 Effects of Political Treatment by Respondent Partisanship (2020)

in the aggregate, up 3 points for Democrats (compared to only 2 points when told of same-party alignment), 3 points for Republicans (again compared to only 1 point for same-party alignment), and 15 points for independents.

In Wave 2, it was the Democrats, not the Republicans, who exhibited the most significant movements. The Democrats responded very positively to the prime that the military might have a Democratic partisan identity. Also, this time, consistent with the original expectation that respondents would react negatively to the prime that the military was more partisan in both directions, Democrats saw their confidence decrease markedly. The unexpected response of independents to the "partisan polarization" prime noticeable in Wave 1 is still there in Wave 2, but slightly smaller and still not statistically significant.

Replicating the substantive result with respect to independents in Wave 2 suggests it might be more than a statistical anomaly. Of course, since this study is the first to probe this topic in this way, one cannot rule out the possibility that there is something peculiar in the wording in the "partisan polarization" prompts in both Wave 1 and Wave 2 that causes independent respondents to glean unexpected cues. And it is also possible that Democrats and Republicans only responded in the "expected" way in Wave 2 because by that time (September–October 2020) their partisanship was fully mobilized by the presidential campaign.

Yet it remains an interesting question, and it is possible to construct ad hoc explanations that merit further study. For instance, perhaps the surprising results in Wave 1, though not the less surprising results in Wave 2, align with the traditional "checks and balances" theory. Perhaps some segments of the public see a polarized military in these troubled polarized times as functioning something like another check on the abuse of power by either party. If this were the motivation, one would expect the effect to be the strongest among independents, which it is. Shifting from party to ideology, the effect appears to be driven by respondents at the ideological poles, liberal or conservative, not moderates in the middle. Finally, the effect is stronger among women in the sample than among men. Previous research (Schwartz and Rubel-Lifschitz 2009) has shown that women are more supportive of measures associated with benevolence (preservation and enhancement of the welfare of people with whom one is close), universalism (understanding, appreciation, tolerance, and protection for the welfare of all people and nature), and security (safety, harmony, and stability of society, relationships, and self) values. Perhaps those values extrapolate out to a greater preference for conditions that appear to provide checks and balances in our political system. A greater preference for checks and balances would align with some of the other patterns observed in the data. The effect (in Wave 1) is also strong among men who identify as liberal but does not show up at all among men who identify as moderate or conservative; liberals in 2019 would have a stronger interest in seeing the military as a potential check on the president than would the other categories.

These results also may be evidence of negative partisanship, the tendency of some voters to form their political opinions primarily based on opposition to political parties they dislike (Abramowitz and Webster 2015, 2018; Strickler 2017). Both waves yielded consistent shifts for all the cross-partisan treatments, with 7-point downward shifts among Democrats in both waves and 12- and 13-point decreases among Republicans. Additionally, pooling Democrats and Republicans into "co-partisan" and "cross-partisan" treatments yielded significant cross-partisan treatments in both waves. In Wave 1, the combined treatment effect compared to the control is −8.5 points with a p-value of .03 in a two-tailed t-test. The cross-partisan results in Wave 2 are remarkably consistent with those from the first wave: the combined treatment effect is −8.3 with a p-value of .04 in a two-tailed t-test. While negative partisanship does not account for either the surprising—but statistically insignificant—shifts among independents or the positive movement among Democrats in 2020, it does explain the consistent negative responses seen whenever partisans receive a prime indicating the military is aligned with the opposing party. Ridge (2022) argues that negative partisanship may also account for decreased satisfaction with democracy and lower commitment to democratic norms—an idea to be considered at the end of this chapter through an examination of how partisanship influences support for a key civil-military norm related to the criticism of elected officials by retired generals and admirals.

Whatever the underlying clause, the results as a whole do suggest that Americans do not dislike partisan behavior by the military, unless the behavior is obviously biased against their own party. This means that Americans do not dislike partisan military behavior as much as civil-military relations theory expects they should. If this finding is replicated in future research, that raises troubling questions for how best to police such behavior, as many senior military leaders have sought to do. One reason, but by no means the only reason, to avoid partisanship is that such behavior was thought likely to reduce public confidence in the military. If the public is less attuned to this norm than was previously thought, then the case against partisanship in the ranks has to rest on other, more nuanced planks. Alternatively, it may indicate that the real danger is not partisan activity per se, but rather the perception—or the reality—that the military is becoming too aligned with one party over the other.

As every chapter has shown up to this point, partisans often view the military very differently—even when presented with the same information. And even when they do assess the military in a similar manner, they may do so for very different reasons. Recall from Chapter 5 that both Republicans and Democrats rated the military fairly low on perceived truthfulness, but many Republicans attributed the lack of disclosure about operations in Afghanistan to wartime necessity, while Democrats blamed it on political pressure. To explore these partisan perceptions in greater detail, it is useful to draw on the same approach used in Chapter 5. In addition to asking respondents about their overall confidence in the military, the survey also drilled down with follow-up questions about how they perceive more specific military attributes. This approach permits both an assessment of whether partisan prompts shift public confidence in the military or the perception that the military is becoming "too partisan," and also causal mediation analysis to better understand why partisan activity lowers confidence.

Table 6.8 presents the basic crosstabs between the experimental treatments and these perceived attributes, broken down by party. In the previous chapter, other aspects of military performance—performance on the battlefield and performance as an ethical profession—interacted with partisanship to make Republicans and Democrats interpret the same information differently. The same trend emerges here, perhaps even more clearly, in Table 6.8. Even in the control group, the gaps between the parties range from 13 to 14 points to as much as 33 points. The partisan treatments we presented to respondents only polarized views of the military further. In both 2019 and 2020, priming respondents to believe the military is becoming more Republican caused Democrats to rate the military lower across every category, while Republican assessments stayed roughly the same or inched in the more favorable direction. The percentage of Democrats saying the military is "too partisan" increased by 9 points to 39% in 2019 and 7 points to 42% in 2020. With the exception of "wins wars," however, Democrats' assessments of the other attributes—competence, ethical behavior, honesty, and shared values—actually moved even more, and changes ranged from 8 to 16 points.

These trends mostly operate in reverse among Republicans, but Republicans primed with information suggesting the military's ranks are being filled with Democrats also became much more likely to rate the military as "too partisan." In fact, this treatment reversed the partisan gap in both waves, as Republicans became more likely to be concerned that the military had become "too partisan" than Democrats. The Republican shifts in 2020 were a bit more inconsistent, however, with GOP respondents becoming more likely to agree that the military was knowledgeable and truthful, though neither of these increases were statistically significant. Partisan responses to the general partisan military treatment were more muted. Republicans reading this prompt became more likely to believe the military is "too partisan" and 15 points more likely to believe the military is truthful—though the latter bump only occurred in Wave 2. Democrats instead became more likely to express concerns about the military's ethical standards or honesty, especially in Wave 1, where Democratic assessments dropped 15 and 13 points, respectively.

Table 6.8 Public Agreement with Other Military Attributes by Experimental and Party Conditions (2019–2020, % agree or strongly agree)

Treatment (2019)	Too Partisan Dem	Too Partisan Rep	Good at Job Dem	Good at Job Rep	Wins Wars Dem	Wins Wars Rep	Ethical Dem	Ethical Rep	Truthful Dem	Truthful Rep	Shares Values Dem	Shares Values Rep
Control	30%	14%	79%	93%	59%	72%	57%	69%	43%	59%	35%	68%
Republican mil	**39%** (+9)	16% (+2)	71% (−8)	92% (−1)	54% (−5)	76% (+4)	**42%** (−15)	75% (+6)	**27%** (−16)	59% (0)	**23%** (−12)	72% (+4)
Democratic mil	25% (−5)	**32%** (+16)	77% (−2)	**81%** (−12)	59% (0)	**63%** (−9)	52% (−5)	**58%** (−11)	43% (0)	**44%** (−15)	39% (+4)	**54%** (−14)
Partisan mil	27% (−3)	**23%** (+9%)	79% (0)	94% (+1)	52% (−7)	75% (+3)	**42%** (−15)	75% (+6)	**30%** (−13)	55% (−4)	36% (+1)	68% (0)

Treatment (2020)	Too Partisan Dem	Too Partisan Rep	Good at Job Dem	Good at Job Rep	Knowledgeable Dem	Knowledgeable Rep	Ethical Dem	Ethical Rep	Truthful Dem	Truthful Rep	Shares Values Dem	Shares Values Rep
Control	36%	18%	70%	86%	71%	85%	50%	72%	41%	54%	37%	65%
Republican mil	43% (+7)	24% (+6)	**60%** (−10)	83% (−3)	65% (−6)	84% (−1)	**39%** (−11)	71% (−1)	**33%** (−8)	**65%** (+11)	**28%** (−9)	64% (−1)
Democratic mil	31% (−5)	**34%** (+16)	78% (+8)	85% (−1)	**83%** (+12)	89% (+4)	53% (+3)	70% (−2)	44% (+3)	61% (+7)	40% (+3)	**56%** (−9)
Partisan mil	36% (0)	24% (+6)	70% (0)	86% (0)	71 (0)	78 (−7%)	48% (−2)	78% (+6)	36% (−5)	**69%** (+15)	32% (−5)	63% (−2)

Another clear pattern emerging from Table 6.8 is that treatments that suggest the military is aligning itself with the opposition party (from a respondent's perspective) create much stronger partisan reactions than treatments implying the military is neutral or on the same partisan side as a respondent. Independents are an exception, however. Although the partisan treatment in Wave 1 caused a 16-point increase in independents who perceived the military as "too partisan," it also led to an 11-point bump in those who believed the military "wins wars" as well as a 10-point drop in those who reported that the military is good at what it does. There is no obvious intuitive explanation for why the perception that the military wins wars would *increase* at the same time that the belief that the military is good at what it does would *decrease*. Given the relatively small sample of independents (100 or fewer in each treatment group) and the results of Wave 2, perhaps this contradictory effect is merely a statistical anomaly. That said, one can speculate about another explanation. Although Wave 2 replaced the "wins wars" attribute question with "knowledgeable," the percentage stating the military is "good at what it does," "knowledgeable," and "shares my values" all increased by 21 points among those independents who received the partisan treatment. This group also saw a double-digit uptick among those saying that the military is truthful (10 points) and has high ethical standards (14 points). Perhaps this evidence is at least consistent with the idea that independents seem to believe that a balanced military—even one that is partisan—is more competent and trustworthy than one that is captured by either party. Overall, however, the size of the shifts among all three partisan groups is striking. They strongly suggest that when the public sees military personnel engage in partisan behavior, they do not immediately condemn it. Instead, they pay attention to which partisans that behavior might help or hurt, and they draw their conclusions from there.

Table 6.9 presents the same kind of causal mediation analysis used in Chapter 5. Recall that this method estimates the proportion of the total treatment effect that each attribute causes. For example, the change in "shared values" explains about 25% of the 7-point drop (or roughly 1.7 of 7 points) that occurred among Democrats when we primed them to believe the military was becoming dominated by Republicans. The technical appendix contains the full analysis of the mediation for the treatments in the aggregate and for all treatments by party. Table 6.9 only presents the results for Democrats who received the Republican military prime, for Republicans who received the Democrat military prime, and for independents who received the partisan military prime. In five out of the six cases, a change in shared values is a statistically significant mediator of confidence in the military, explaining between 8% and 38% of the total shifts that result from our experimental treatments. The competence and too-partisan attributes were also statistically significant in three cases each. Despite the fact

Table 6.9 Average Causal Mediation Effects (opposite party and independents)

Treatment	Party	Too Partisan % Mediated	p	Competent % Mediated	p	Ethical % Mediated	p	Truthful % Mediated	p	Shares Values % Mediated	p	Total % Mediated	p
REP mil (2019)	DEM	−15%	0.13	55%	0.21	19%	0.27	−6%***	0.01	25%*	0.1	(−7) 79%	0.18
REP mil (2020)	DEM	6%	0.18	37%**	0.05	24%	0.13	5%	0.16	20%*	0.07	(−7) 93%**	0.03
DEM mil (2019)	REP	9%***	0.00	29%***	0.00	10%*	0.09	−7%**	0.04	8%***	0.01	(−13) 50%***	0.01
DEM mil (2020)	REP	8%***	0.01	8%	0.70	0%	0.25	−6%	0.43	16%*	0.09	(−9) 27%	0.48
Partisan (2019)	IND	22%**	0.02	−21%	0.15	0%	0.99	−5%	0.66	12%	0.84	(+15) 8%	0.91
Partisan (2020)	IND	−7%	0.74	34%*	0.09	5%	0.48	40%	0.14	38%**	0.05	(+8) 100%	0.13

that the treatments expose respondents to information about partisan behavior, perceived competence explains a larger proportion of the treatment effects at roughly 30% in each case. Additionally, when competence is replaced with "wins wars" among independents receiving the partisan treatment in 2019, this variable is statistically significant and explains nearly 70% of the treatment effect.

Overall, the causal mediation analysis presented in Table 6.9 only reinforces the finding that members of the public do not lose confidence in the military simply because they are concerned about the military's nonpartisan norm; rather, they appear more concerned with the military's partisan activity because they believe it shows the military does not share its values or because they are concerned that the military will not be effective if it is too closely aligned with the opposition party. This logic seems broadly consistent with the larger notion of negative partisanship discussed earlier. Even when members of the public assess their own confidence in the military, a large number of them appear to form their opinions based on their dislike of the opposing party instead of on their commitment to affirmative values or policy views. As shown in Chapter 4, the fact that the military has maintained a largely nonpartisan reputation when compared to other federal institutions is a strength that bolsters public confidence. But, as the preceding experiments demonstrate, these perceptions are malleable. Partisan activity by the military—or even broadly publicized narratives that suggest the military is becoming aligned with one party over the other—could have important implications for which Americans trust the military and which do not.

3. Does the public respond to military cues on vote choice?

Chapter 10 will explore whether and how the public responds to cues from the military on matters of public policy—whether to use force against certain threats and whether to make other controversial policy decisions regarding military affairs. The section here explores whether such cueing can operate directly in the area of politics. Earlier work (Golby, Dropp, and Feaver 2012) established that such cueing operates in the matter of the respondents' vote choice, albeit in constrained ways. Surveying during the 2012 campaign showed that key portions of the public responded to cues about presidential endorsements from senior retired military leaders, but only in a very limited way. Military cues did not move vote choice in the aggregate, but being told that senior military leaders endorsed Obama did seem to persuade a small but significant number of independent voters and voters who report low levels of foreign policy interest to favor Obama in the election, as compared with respondents who received no such prompt. Significantly, the Republican nominee, Mitt Romney, did not receive a similar boost, neither in the aggregate nor among those narrower slices of independent and low-attention voters. The natural inference was that the voters already assumed the military, as a conservative institution, would lean toward the Republican candidate, so a pro-Romney cue conveyed no new information; however, a pro-Obama cue would be somewhat surprising and might move voters who were on the margins and not already strongly committed to one candidate or the other.

Wave 2 came in the middle of another presidential campaign, this time between the Republican incumbent Donald Trump and the Democratic challenger Joe Biden.[7] The approach here replicated Golby, Dropp, and Feaver (2012) with a series of survey experiment questions (as described in greater detail in the technical appendix) designed to explore the effect, if any, of a military cue on vote choice.[8] The 847 respondents randomly assigned to the control condition received a basic question about how the respondent intended to vote: "Next, we are going to ask you about the 2020 Presidential election. If the general election for President were held today, for which of the following candidates would you vote? A. Joe Biden, the Democrat. B. Donald Trump, the Republican C. Other, please specify. D. Would not vote." The 934 respondents randomly assigned to the "military support Biden" cues received: "According to recent reports, most members of the military support Joe Biden." Or, for another 921 respondents, "According to recent reports, a large number of retired military generals and admirals support Joe Biden." The 963 respondents randomly assigned to the "military support Trump" cues received: "According to recent reports, most members of the military support Donald Trump." Or, for the final 845 respondents, "According to recent reports, a large number of retired military generals and admirals support Donald Trump." Note that the survey used

---

[7] Polling on 2020 vote choice was fraught, with many after-action reviews concluding that pollsters had systematically underestimated Trump's true support—at least the support that showed up in the electorate (Cohn 2020). This new proprietary poll, conducted from late September to late October 2020, produced an aggregate estimate of Biden 54.3% and Trump 43.3%. At the same time, the RealClearPolitics average of national polls yielded Biden 51.2% and Trump 44%. However, unlike most national polls, this survey was targeted at all Americans and did not create a model to account for likely or registered voters. Of course, the final national result was Biden 51.4% and Trump 46.9%. Since the analytical focus here is on the marginal effects of treatments rather than predicting the actual voting outcome on Election Day, one only needs to worry about a Biden overcount and Trump undercount if there is a reason for believing that the overcounted Biden supporters and uncounted Trump supporters would respond to military cues in a systematically different way from those captured in the analysis. I do not know of any compelling reason to believe this and so have some confidence in the results presented above. If further analysis of the 2020 election identifies a plausible attitude bias in the overcounted Biden and undercounted Trump supporters, then the results above should be viewed more as suggestive than dispositive.

[8] Note that this question came toward the end of the survey, well after all of the other survey experiments.

two different wordings of the prime, one focused on the military as a whole and the other focused on prominent generals and admirals. The expectation was that this would yield the same pattern observed in 2012, with a pro-Democrat cue having some impact and a pro-Republican cue having none.

Figures 6.3 and 6.4 show the results in the aggregate and broken down by the partisan identity of the respondents.

As was the case in 2012, there was some modest (but not statistically significant) movement among respondents who were told that the military as a whole supported Biden but no movement whatsoever among respondents told that the military supported Trump. While Trump was a very unusual Republican, it is possible that in the aggregate the public expected the military to tilt Republican, and thus tilt Trump, and so it was only the "surprising" prompt of military support for Biden that produced any effect at all. Again, as in 2012, it is independents who move the most in response to the cues, though the substantively large shifts just miss statistical significance at the 95% level in both cases. Partisans, by contrast, largely stuck to their guns, regardless of the cue. (Interestingly, there is a slight bump up in the "wrong" direction—with Democrats told that the military supported Biden slightly *increasing* their support for Trump—but this is so small that may well be mere noise in the data.)

As expected, there is no substantive difference between respondents who received the cue worded as "most members of the military" and those who received the cue worded as "a large number of retired military generals and admirals." If there is an effect for one, there is for the other, and vice versa. The obvious inference is that the public does not draw the fine distinctions that some

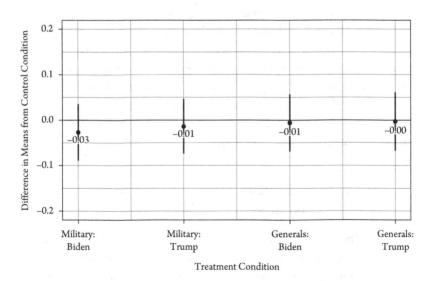

Figure 6.3 Treatment Effect of the Military Cue on Vote Choice (2020)

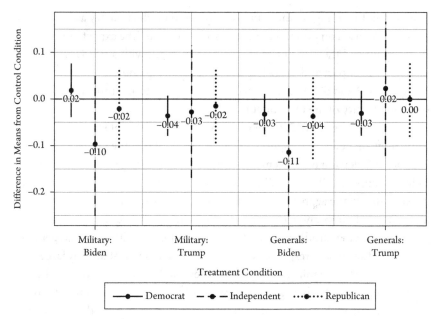

Figure 6.4 Treatment Effect of the Military Cue on Vote Choice by Respondent Partisan ID (2020)

commentators (Gallo 2016; Hicks 2020) draw between active-duty and retired military personnel. While it is obviously true that the latter do not have the legal constraints on their political speech that the former do—and thus, there is in legal and perhaps normative terms a meaningful difference between the two—in practice, the public tends to lump them together. Political campaigns are likely making exactly the same calculation when they recruit retired senior officers to make these endorsements. What is attractive, from the campaign point of view, is not the individual views of a citizen X or Y but the symbolism of endorsements from folk whose first names in polite society remain "General" or "Admiral" long into retirement. From the campaign perspective, the retired military personnel stand for and speak for the active-duty military. These results largely support the inference that the public think that way, too.

4. Does the public respond to military cues on the most politicized uses of the military?

During the Trump administration, military deployments themselves became politicized to a significant extent. In 2018, in the run-up to the midterm elections, President Trump highlighted what he considered to be threats to the southern border of the United States and declared that those threats had reached a crisis point necessitating the deployment of US troops (Youssef and Caldwell 2018). Democrats cried foul and claimed that Trump was manufacturing a threat and a crisis in order to get some sort of rally-round-the-flag effect from the deployment of troops (Daniels 2019; Robinson 2019).

Then, in late spring 2020, as protests over alleged police brutality spread across the country, the question of a politicized use of the military arose again, with even greater intensity. President Trump decried the Black Lives Matter protests as violent and urged governors to deploy National Guard troops to quell them (Neuman 2020). When governors balked at doing so—and when the protests spread to the District of Columbia, where the National Guard unit answered directly to the president (through powers delegated to the secretary of defense and secretary of the army)—President Trump mobilized the DC Guard and openly debated federalizing other National Guard units or even invoking the Insurrection Act, which would allow him to mobilize more capable active-duty units to conduct riot control operations (Brooks 2020). Trump's own military advisers strongly advised against mobilizing the active-duty units but gave what appeared to be grudging support to the mobilization of the DC National Guard (Filkins 2020).

These deployments were controversial in their own right, as is often the case with any potential use of force, but they seemed to take on a peculiarly political tone, with the military being used in the border deployment case to score campaign points for the midterm and then to suppress protests by the president's political opponents in the Insurrection Act case. The previous chapter explored how public confidence in the military shifted in response to primes about whether the military had been successful in dealing with the protests. This chapter looks at a separate question: whether the public support for that mission shifted in response to cues about how the military felt about the mission. Specifically, did the earlier findings (Golby, Dropp, and Feaver 2013, 2017) regarding how the public responds to cues operate when the policy in question had such strong political overtones?

The survey deployed two experiments, both following the design described in Chapter 5 and the technical appendix, to probe this issue. For the border deployment (in Wave 1), the 733 respondents assigned to control received: "Next, we want to know how well certain news stories regarding US national security can reach the public. The media often presents a large amount of information that can be hard to follow. We want to ask you some questions about the southern border. Please indicate to what extent you agree/disagree with these statements. A. I approve of President Trump's declaration of a national emergency along the US-Mexico border. B. I trust the military." The 771 randomly assigned respondents receiving the **military support cue** received this additional piece of information, before being asked about their own attitudes: "According to a recent poll, more than sixty-five percent of active duty military and veterans support the President's decision to send thousands of troops to the southern border to deal with the threat of Central American migrants and believe these actions will keep America safe." The 811 respondents receiving the **military oppose cue** received instead this additional prompt: "According to a recent poll, more than sixty-five percent of active duty military and veterans do not believe Central American immigrants pose a threat to national security."

For the border deployment issue, the survey also explored whether a direct partisan cue—learning that President Trump supported it or learning that Democratic members of Congress had opposed it—moved attitudes in systematic ways. The 763 respondents receiving the **president supports cue** received this additional prompt before being asked to weigh in on the policy: "During a recent speech, the President stated that 'the thousands of troops at the southern border, they understand Central American migrants are a threat and the military knows I am doing what it takes to keep Americans safe.'" And the 728 respondents receiving the **Democratic Congress opposes cue** received this additional prompt: "During a recent speech, a Democratic party leader said that the thousands of troops the President has sent to the southern border do not believe Central American migrants pose a threat and the military knows this stunt will not keep Americans safe."

For the Insurrection Act (in Wave 2), the design was similar. **Control** (1,503 respondents): "As you may know, President Trump recently considered invoking the Insurrection Act, which allows the President to deploy active duty troops within the United States to conduct law enforcement tasks like curfew enforcement and riot control. Do you agree or disagree that active duty troops should be deployed within the United States if protests continue?" **Military support cue** (1,540 respondents): "According to recent reports, the Chairman of the Joint Chiefs of Staff supports using troops in this way." **Military oppose cue** (1,467 respondents): "According to recent reports, the Chairman of the Joint Chiefs of Staff opposes using troops in this way."

Figures 6.5 and 6.6 show the treatment effects as broken down by the partisanship of the respondents. As expected, Democrats overall were strongly opposed to the mobilization of troops for the border and Republicans strongly supported it. There was also an overall partisan gap on the question of mobilizing troops to assist in law enforcement during the protests, though the difference between Democrats and Republicans was somewhat closer. The partisan cues on the border deployment functioned as expected, more or less. As expected, Democrats also responded negatively to the news that Trump invoked the military in his support of the maneuver, and also negatively to the news that Congress opposed, but neither were statistically significant at the 95% level. Republicans responded positively to the prompt that Trump supported the maneuver, but

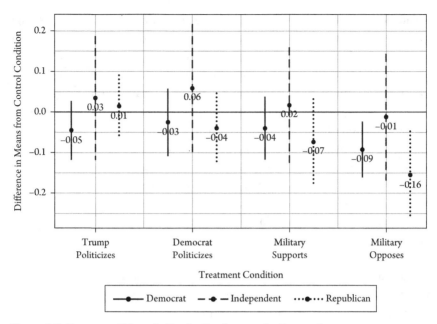

Figure 6.5 Treatment Effects for Border Deployment by Respondent Partisanship (2019)

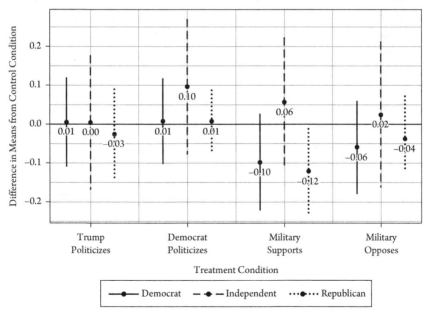

Figure 6.6 Treatment Effects for Trust in the Military by Border Deployment by Respondent Partisanship (2019)

negatively, rather than ignoring or responding in a contrary fashion, to the prompt that Democrats in Congress opposed the maneuver; however, since that prompt also mentioned the views of the military, that may not be the cleanest treatment effect, and neither result was statistically significant. Independents responded positively to Trump's endorsement but, surprisingly, learning that Congress opposed the deployment actually increased support among independents. There is no obvious good explanation for this particular result.

The military cues on the border deployment operated in even more surprising ways across the various partisan subgroups. Based on other research regarding military cues (Golby, Dropp, and Feaver 2017), the expectation was that military support for a deployment (which might be thought of as a "use of force") would have a negligible effect or at most a modest positive effect. A cue that signaled military opposition, however, would have a more marked negative effect. Across none of the partisan subgroups did that exact pattern emerge. To be sure, the military oppose cue did move support down across all three groups—and by statistically significant and substantively significant margins for both Democrats and Republicans. As a practical political matter, knowing that Republican support for the border deployment drops 17 points with a single cue that the military oppose the deployment might give some Republican leaders pause on the policy. (That said, the further discovery that this movement is mostly among self-described Republican moderates may dampen its political impact on a conservative Republican leader.) However, the cue regarding military support paradoxically *reduced* support among both Democrats and Republicans, though not by statistically significant amounts, and it did produce a modest—but still not significant—bump up among independents.

Put another way, attaching the military to the border deployment proposal, whether in support or in opposition, had the marked effect of reducing public support for the policy. Since this is just one experiment with one controversial policy—and one on which there was a marked partisan split to begin with—one must not push this interpretation too far.[9] Yet it is an interesting result, one further bolstered by looking at how these attitudes correlate with public trust in the military, as reported in Figure 6.6. After asking the border deployment question, the survey asked respondents to indicate their agreement with the statement, "I trust the military."[10] As expected, Republicans overall show extremely high levels

---

[9] As reported in the technical appendix, a regression model that controls for demographics and the treatment effects from earlier experiments yields similar results. However, the size of the effect is reduced among Republicans and increased among Democrats who received the "military opposes" cue. Any military involvement, in other words, still had roughly similar results within the parties.

[10] Note, this is not the standard Gallup "confidence in the military" question that is most often used in this book.

of agreement with that sentiment, Democrats show strong but markedly lower, and independents lower still. That level of agreement does not move much in response to cues about the president or Congress invoking the troops in support of their policy positions, nor would we expect it to. Yet, for Democrats and for Republicans, any military cue—positive or negative—produces a marked *negative* effect on their reported "trust in the military," though it only reaches statistical significance for Republicans receiving the military support cue. Paradoxically, the results for independents is in the opposite direction—a slight bump up, regardless of the cue but not significant in any case. The effect on partisans is consistent with the idea that it is corrosive for the military to get dragged into public debates about partisan policy disputes. Overall, the results here do suggest that military involvement in debates over highly politically charged issues does not seem to help advance public support for that policy. It may only serve to politicize the military and drive down public trust in this institution, even among respondents who otherwise might be sympathetic to the policy under consideration.

The results of the military cues for the Insurrection Act experiment, as reported in Figure 6.7, largely reinforce this point. For Democrats, the cues are negligible—in the expected direction, but not statistically significant. For Republicans, the "military support" cue does produce a marked bump up, but it does not reach significance at the 95% level. The "military oppose" cue likewise produces a bump up in support for the policy, albeit a smaller and insignificant one. Given how salient the debate over the Insurrection Act case was—and

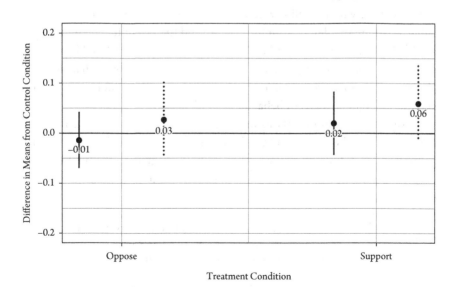

Figure 6.7 Treatment Effects for Insurrection Act by Respondent Partisanship (2020)

in particular how salient was the views of the military, with both Secretary of Defense Mark Esper and chairman of the Joint Chiefs of Staff Mark Milley prominently breaking with President Trump to oppose the policies Trump was considering, and with Trump threatening to fire them as a result (Sheth and Pickrell 2020; Rogin 2020)—it could be that, for some partisan Republicans, the cue of military opposition triggered the memory of that stand-off and caused them to rally to the president and his preferred policy. Although not reported, the overall results are even less impressive. There is no movement for the oppose treatment, and only an insignificant two-point upward shift—from 42% to 44%—for the support condition. In any case, it is hard to make the argument that the military cues here are markedly affecting public opinion of this controversial policy in the aggregate, though there is some upward movement among Republicans who received the support treatment.[11]

5. Does confidence in the military make the public receptive to politicized roles for the military?

As a final cut at the politicization issue, it is fruitful to turn the question on its head: are high levels of confidence in the military contributing to a willingness to give the military roles that politicize them further? Chapter 10 will explore a variety of issues that link up with this under the category of "ideational benefits" that the military enjoys because the public holds it in such high esteem—the privileges, perks, and prerogatives that accrue to those the public is willing to put on a pedestal. Here the focus is on just the aspects of that dynamic that relate most closely to the politicization issue: the degree of political behavior the public is willing to tolerate from the military and the extent to which the public would like to see the military take on political roles that extend well beyond traditional national security concerns. The intuitive expectation is that members of the public who express high levels of confidence in the military are far more likely to welcome this sort of behavior.

Wave 1 asked respondents to indicate their agreement with the following statement: "Members of the military should be allowed to publicly express their political views just like any other citizen."[12] In the aggregate, the public tended to agree that members of the military should be able to offer political opinions,

---

[11] However, as reported elsewhere (Golby and Feaver 2021), the military cue might have a more important effect on one key subgroup: veterans. Among veteran respondents, support from the chairman of the Joint Chiefs also had no significant effect. But opposition from the chairman reduced support among veterans by more than eight points, from 57% to 49%.

[12] As before, the instrument also asked the question with the polarity reversed. The results reported above combine the two sets of responses.

with 52% of respondents agreeing or strongly agreeing with the statement and only 19% disagreeing, strongly or otherwise. Somewhat surprisingly, there are no notable partisan differences, though independents at 57% are somewhat more supportive than Democrats or Republicans. When broken down by levels of confidence, support becomes even stronger among those who express confidence in the military: 57% of respondents with confidence agree that members of the military should be able to express their political views, compared to just 35% among respondents who do not express confidence.

Sharpening the focus by asking respondents whether retired generals and admirals should be allowed to criticize the president of the United States—and then sharpening it still further by identifying a president by name, Obama or Trump – yields even more telling results.[13] First, looking at the issue through the partisan lens in Figure 7.8, one can detect a clear, and somewhat troubling, pattern: partisans are far more willing to say it is appropriate for retired generals and admirals to criticize the opposing party's president than they are when asked about a president from their own party. Democrats, in fact, are more than twice as likely, at 67%, to state it is appropriate for retired officers to break this norm when criticizing President Trump than they are, at 28%, to state it is appropriate when criticizing President Obama. Among Republicans, one can see the same pattern in reverse, though the gap from Trump to Obama is only 15 points. It is possible that the timing of the survey made this dynamic even more salient among Democrats who hoped to vote Trump out of office and slightly less so among Republicans since Obama was a distant memory. In any case, these results suggest support for civil-military norms may be, at least in part, contingent on partisan dynamics. Note that Republicans, as a whole, showed greater reluctance to give approval to violations of the norm that generals should not criticize the president. They were more inclined to accept the norm violation with Obama than with Trump, but even then it was not a full majority. This is probably not evidence that Republicans, as a whole, are more supportive of the norms on which healthy democratic civil-military relations rely. Rather, this is probably because the norm, at the time of the survey, provided protection for the Republican sitting president and so was in their partisan interest. If this cynical view is correct, then Democrats who cheered retired generals serving as the "adults in the room" during the Trump administration will likely have a different perspective during a Democratic administration and begin to show more appreciation of the norms of democratic civil-military relations. And Republicans who castigated retired generals and admirals who spoke out against President

---

[13] Because there are UCMJ restrictions on what active-duty military can say about the president, the survey asked only for the public's views on retired military, who have greater legal latitude.

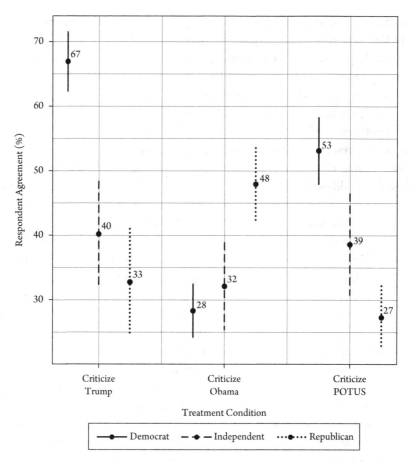

Figure 6.8 Support for Criticizing President by Partisan ID of Respondent (2019)

Trump in the wake of the events in Lafayette Square on June 1, 2020, will likely look more favorably on any retired officers who critique President Biden.

Next, when respondents are clustered by their level of confidence in the military, another picture emerges. Although the same partisan dynamic continues to operate, respondents with greater confidence in the military are also more likely to agree that criticism by retired officers is appropriate than those who don't. In the aggregate, respondents with confidence in the military are nearly 10 points more willing to say it is appropriate for retired generals and admirals to violate this norm, at 43%, than respondents without confidence, at 34%. As shown in Figure 6.9, this result holds even when accounting for respondents' partisanship, with the exception of Democrats, where high-confidence Democrats are less willing to criticize a generic president (who happens to be Trump at the time of the survey) than low confidence. Again, it is possible the timing of the survey heightened the stakes of these partisan dynamics—making Democrats with

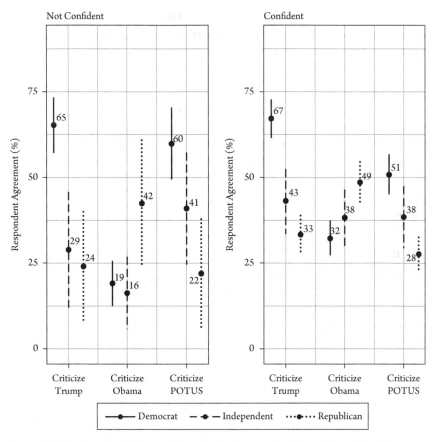

Figure 6.9 Support for Criticizing President by Respondent Party ID and Confidence Level (2019)

confidence more willing to support criticism of Trump but perhaps anticipating that the tables might soon be turned with a Democratic victory and so a bit more wary about the generic president.

The survey also asked respondents to indicate their level of agreement with the following statements: "A. Through leading by example, the military could help American society become more moral. B. The US government would function better if we allowed the military to take over non-military programs, such as tax collection or public education." Respondents were somewhat mixed on the idea that the military might help lead by example, with 44% agreeing or strongly agreeing with that statement. At 53%, Republicans were 12 points more likely than Democrats to express support for military role models, and respondents with confidence in the military, at 48%, were 11 points more likely to support this idea than those without confidence at 37%. The survey found very little support for the proposition that the military might improve governance on nonmilitary functions, such as tax collection or education. Only 12% of respondents agreed or strongly agreed with a statement to that effect, with no significant differences across party or confidence level.

Conclusion

In sum, there is ample reason to be concerned, though perhaps not yet alarmed, about the politicization of civil-military relations in the United States. Somewhat disconcerting patterns emerge across the full range of the PIE frame introduced at the outset—prohibitions against partisan behavior (P), the use of institutional credibility to advance personal policy preferences (I), and electoral involvement (E). While the public does not yet see the military as a hyperpartisan organization, there are indications that many partisans would be willing to encourage the military to assume a more partisan role—as long as it remains on their side.

Partisanship shapes public confidence in the military in interesting ways. The familiar finding about high public confidence in the aggregate masks important underlying divisions. Extremely high confidence levels among self-identified Republican respondents exists in tandem with much lower confidence among Democrats and still weaker confidence among independents. A majority of the public believes that members of the military affiliate with a party, and the plurality view is that those affiliations are evenly divided between Republican and Democrats. However, a sizable minority believes the military leans Republican. Respondents are slightly more likely to believe the military aligns with their own party—Democrats believing the military is Democrat and Republicans believing the military is Republican—but it is not a strong effect. And in Wave 2, conducted during the height of the 2020 campaign, Democrats had lost that tendency with a marked increase in willingness to identify the military as Republican. On the whole, only about one-quarter of the public believes the military is too partisan—an encouragingly low number—but Democrats are twice as likely as Republicans to believe this about the military, suggesting some underlying partisan tension. Likewise, when the issue was pressed in Wave 2, respondents showed clear concerns about the degree of partisanship in civilian society but claimed to be slightly less worried that those problems had seeped into the military.

These views are not set in stone. As the survey experiments suggested, partisan behavior by those in uniform—or even changes in the perception that the military is acting with a partisan bias—can affect public confidence in the military. Overall, public confidence in the military did not derive strongly from a belief that the military was above partisan politics—at least not as strongly as Chapter 5 showed that public confidence in the military derived from public views of how competent the military was. When told that the military has Republican leanings, Republican respondents show a slight increase in confidence, while Democratic respondents show a decrease; when told that the military has Democratic leanings, the opposite result occurs, as expected. In other words, partisans become slightly more confident in the military when they believe it is biased in their favor, and much less confident when they believe it is biased against them. Throughout this chapter, there were multiple indications that the negative partisanship that shapes the views many Americans have about their partisan opponents can also influence their views of the military.

In other words, the public is not policing military partisan behavior, but the public is affected by that behavior. When alerted to possible partisan behavior by the military, individual members of the public appear to take note as to whether those politicized military members are helping or hurting the favored party of the respondent, and then drawing their conclusions accordingly. Members of the public do not lose confidence in the military simply because they are concerned about the military's nonpartisan norm; rather, they appear more concerned with the military's partisan activity because they believe it shows the military does not share its values or because they are concerned that the military will not be effective if it is too closely aligned with the opposition party. Narratives that suggest the military is becoming aligned with one party over the other could, if they take root in the public mind, have implications for which Americans trust the military and which do not.

At the same time, however, partisan politics may also limit the extent of military influence in practice—a theme that Chapter 10 will consider again. Consistent with previous research, military endorsements during a presidential campaign may break through to some independent voters and draw them away from a Republican candidate, but they are not enough to break through the partisan filters of most Democrats or Republicans, who likely will support their party's candidate come what may. While military opposition did drive down support for the controversial border support mission, it had little impact in shaping support for—or opposition to—a potential invocation of the Insurrection Act. While confidence in the military remains high, it is not clear that even that confidence provides enough prestige for the military to fundamentally break through the partisan noise. Yet it may be just enough of a bump that politicians will not be able to refrain from recruiting military endorsers. The analyses in this chapter were not designed to identify why politicians might covet such endorsements but it is not hard to find plausible explanations. Perhaps politicians are hoping the popularity of the military will rub off on them or perhaps they want to pass the "commander in chief" threshold test and believe military endorsements will give them a competency boost on this test. Future research could parse this further as well as measure more precisely the unintended second- and third-order effects of this practice.

Even so, there is ample evidence that many partisans are eager to have those in uniform join the partisan fray, as long as the military is an ally on their side of the partisan divide. Both Democrats and Republicans are far more tolerant of military criticism against their opponents than they are of criticism against their fellow partisans. This theme, perhaps more than any other in this chapter, is a sign of real potential trouble. The willingness of partisans to trade short-term political benefits of co-opting military supporters to their camp, if continued, will do long-term damage to key American norms and the values they are meant to protect. If partisans are only willing to enforce civil-military norms when they are violated by their political opponents, they are no longer norms at all. A more encouraging sign, however, is that despite its lack of confidence in other American institutions, the public does not seem ready to hand normal functions of domestic governance like tax collection or public education over to the military. After seeing the military and National Guard play outsized roles in the Covid response and during the Black Lives Matter protests and the mob attacks on the Capitol, members of the public—even opportunistic partisans—still seem to draw a bright line between national security and domestic governance.

As the final chapter will explore a bit further, the lingering poison of negative polarization—the belief that the greatest threat to the country is the opposite party—intersects with this issue in troubling ways. The problem today is not just that civilians are failing to enforce the norm against military partisan behavior—it is that significant voices are doing all they can to actively politicize the military, and one way they do that is by trying to undermine confidence in the military by accusing the military of being "woke" and threatening more attacks on military professionalism unless the military aligns with a certain partisan agenda.

The analyses thus far have bracketed off an important question: why does it matter what level of confidence the public expresses in the military? The coming chapters engage that question head-on. But first, Chapter 7 explores one underappreciated driver of high levels of public confidence in the military: the belief that a high level of confidence in the military is the politically correct attitude to express.

7

Social Desirability Bias

A Silent Prop Undergirding Public Confidence in the Military

> I have never met anyone who did not support our troops. Sometimes, however, we hear accusations that someone or some group does not support the men and women serving in our Armed Forces. But this is pure demagoguery, and it is intellectually dishonest.
> —Senator Ron Paul (Paul 2007)

> I love a flyover but It was odd to see one over a mostly empty stadium but I am an unwavering patriot that loves this country, has always respected our flag, supported the men and women in the armed forces as well as those in uniform who serve & protect and for anyone to suggest otherwise doesn't know me, my beliefs or what I have stood for my entire life.
> —Tweet from Troy Aikman after a hot-mic picked up his expressing befuddlement that there was a fly-over during an National Football League game even though COVID restrictions kept the stands mostly empty (@TroyAikman, October 20, 2020)

Public confidence in the military has been so strikingly high, and for such a long time now, that it has achieved the status of conventional wisdom. Experts, politicians, and military leaders are aware that the public expresses high levels of confidence in the armed forces. This could not have escaped the notice of the attentive public, the portion that follows current affairs closely in their day-to-day consumption of media. Given the prominence of the military and military symbols in widely attended gatherings like sporting events and national celebrations, even the casual member of the disinterested public would be hard-pressed to have missed the point: it is popular to say good things about the men and women serving in uniform. The new proprietary surveys conducted for this project find strong evidence in support of the conventional wisdom, with some 71% of respondents reporting that "most members of American society have confidence in the military" and only 7% disagreeing with that statement.

Given this shared understanding, then the obverse may also be true: the public believes that it would be unpopular *not* to express confidence in the military. A failure or refusal to express confidence may be tantamount to disrespecting the men and women serving in uniform. Even far more mild expressions of hesitation, as NFL commentator Troy Aikman found out, can result in an awkward moment of social pressure.

A scene in the HBO comedy *Curb Your Enthusiasm* captures the idea perfectly. In the scene, which first aired on October 29, 2017, a group of people are gathering for dinner, one purpose of which is to meet the new boyfriend of one of the characters (David and Schaffer 2017; "Curb Your Enthusiasm" 2017). The boyfriend serves in the military, and as the guests are introduced to him, they each make a point of shaking his hand and saying some variant of "Thank you for your service." The pattern continues until Larry David, the lead character and famous misanthrope, has his turn. Instead of following the custom, he instead gives a hearty handshake and a "Nice to meet you!" greeting. This induces a painfully awkward pause with the boyfriend clearly waiting for a follow-up from David. When none is forthcoming, the boyfriend leaves and the party descends into recriminations of David for not thanking the soldier for his service in uniform. David protests that he didn't see the need since everyone else had just done so, but the hostess throws him out of the house for ruining the dinner party. As he is leaving, David pointedly offers exaggerated thank-yous to everyone else for trivial achievements like "serving hors d'oeuvres."

Such a situation—when there are "politically correct" and "politically incorrect" attitudes that are widely recognized across society—creates the conditions for what political psychologists call "social desirability bias" (Paulhus 1991; Callegaro 2008). Social desirability bias affects poll results, nudging respondents away from offering their true responses to questions about attitudes or behaviors and toward reporting what they believe are the attitudes and behaviors that enjoy high levels of social approval already. Political and social psychologists have found evidence of social desirability bias across a wide range of attitudes and behaviors, including attitudes to race (Sniderman and Carmines 1997; An 2015); attitudes to gender (Sudkämper et al. 2019); attitudes to veterans' benefits (Kleykamp, Hipes, and MacClean 2018); self-reports of personal hygiene behaviors (Moshagen et al. 2010); among many others.

This chapter explores whether social desirability bias is also at work in propping up the high levels of expressed public confidence in the military. Since the vast majority of those responding to these surveys know that the general public holds the military in high esteem, could this drive some to misreport their own views on the military? If so, this would be an obvious manifestation of "hollow confidence"—confidence that does not quite match up to how it looks at first glance. As shown below, there is clear evidence that this is happening. In short, public support for the military is partly due to the belief that one should express support for the military because everyone else is doing so.

How to Detect Social Desirability Bias

The surveys described in the technical appendix (available here: https://dataverse.harvard.edu/dataverse/pfeaver) provide some of the only and best data available to explore the issue of social desirability bias in public confidence in the US military. Both Wave 1 and Wave 2 of the surveys include several experiments designed to reveal whether respondents feel social pressure to report high confidence in the military even when they privately may not share that view.[1]

The first was a simple survey experiment in Wave 1 similar to the ones outlined in Chapter 5. In this case, the survey prompted respondents with information about other people's attitudes regarding the military. Some 109 respondents received the control condition, a simple agree/disagree question: "Do you agree or disagree with the following statement? I have quite a lot of confidence in the US military." Another group of 116 respondents were given the following treatment before being asked the agree/disagree question: "According to recent polls, the US military is by far the most respected institution in America today. An overwhelming majority of Americans believe it is their patriotic duty to 'support the troops.'" A third group of 132 respondents were given a treatment intended to push their attitudes in the opposite direction: "According to recent polls, confidence in the US military decreased by ten points between 2009 and 2017. Fewer Americans now believe it is their patriotic duty to 'support the troops.'" Of course, these treatments were stating the same basic facts—there was no deception in this particular experiment—and the nudge was quite modest. Nevertheless, the expectation was that respondents who received the positive nudge would agree that they have "quite a lot of confidence" in greater numbers than those in the control, whereas those who received the negative nudge would agree in lower numbers.

The second approach to measuring social desirability bias involved a list experiment. Survey list experiments have been useful in tapping into attitudes (racism) and behaviors (corruption) that respondents might feel uncomfortable directly sharing (Kuklinski et al. 1997; Sniderman and Carmines 1997;

---

[1] Measuring social desirability bias through two separate methods makes it possible to check the one against the other as recommended in other studies that rely on list experiments (Aronow et al. 2015; and Ahlquist 2018). Although the experiments were spread across two survey waves, the inclusion of a more traditional survey experiment in Wave 1 experiment provides an additional check on the validity of the list experiment.

Corstange 2009; Blair and Imai 2012; Glynn 2013). Respondents are shown a list of possible attitudes and asked to report the total number they agree with, without indicating which ones probe for misreporting. Wave 2 included such a list experiment.[2]

The list experiment followed the standard form. Very early in the survey, all of the respondents were asked, "Please tell us how many of the statements listed below you agree with," and then a randomly assigned 2,223 respondents were given the control (just the first five items in random order) while a randomly assigned 2,256 respondents were given the treatment (all six items in random order):

1. I have quite a lot of confidence in my local Department of Motor Vehicles (DMV).
2. I have quite a lot of confidence in my closest friends.
3. I have quite a lot of confidence in my dentist.
4. I have quite a lot of confidence in the North Korean leadership.
5. I have quite a lot of confidence in my local mayor.
6. I have quite a lot of confidence in the US military.

At a later point in the survey, after many intervening questions, the survey put the question directly to all our respondents: "Now, we want to ask you about the same topic, but in a slightly different way. Do you agree or disagree with the following statement? I have quite a lot of confidence in the US military."

The difference between responses to the direct question, in which political correctness could be operating, and responses to the indirect question, in which respondents might feel free to reveal any socially incorrect views, provides a measure of social desirability bias. In order to guard against potential floor or ceiling effects that can undermine the reliability of list experiments, the list is designed to contain one question on which previous surveys have shown almost all Americans agree (confidence in one's closest friends) and one on which almost all Americans do not agree (confidence in the North Korean leadership). Care was taken with the wording to ensure the structure of the military item was parallel to other items on the list so that it would not automatically stand out from the rest of the list.

---

[2] Wave 1 included a similar list experiment that suggested a significant amount of desirability bias of roughly 14 percentage points. But based on the small sample size for that experiment and based on feedback received when presenting preliminary analyses of those results, Wave 2 used a significantly adjusted design. In theory, Wave 2 should be the more precise assessment since it incorporated more expert feedback in its design. Wave 2 also allows for more extensive multivariate analyses of the results. For these reasons, the text focuses on Wave 2 even though it yielded even more dramatic results rather than the more conservative, but perhaps more flawed, experiment done in Wave 1.

What the Surveys Found

Figure 7.1 presents the results of the survey experiment from Wave 1 that nudged respondents with prompts about the attitudes of the rest of the public.

The first column shows the responses of those who received no prompting. The second column shows the higher level of confidence reported in the sample of respondents who received the prompt reminding them about high levels of social approval for the military. The third column shows the lower level of confidence reported in the sample of respondents who received a negative prompt suggesting that social approval of the military was declining. Because of the small sample sizes, the confidence intervals are quite large and one cannot rule out the null hypothesis of no effect. Nevertheless, the average responses align with expectations. And given the high levels of confidence already expressed—fully 86% in the control group—it is striking that the numbers still move up or down in response to treatments and in the expected direction.

Table 7.1 presents the results of the list experiment from Wave 2, which explores the same kind of social desirability effects but in a manner designed to reveal attitudes that the respondent might be willing to share but might also feel it could be politically/socially incorrect to do so. Recall that the question asked respondents to review a list of five (control) or six (treatment) "I believe" statements and to report the number of statements they agree with, not which ones they agree with. The first several rows report the responses from

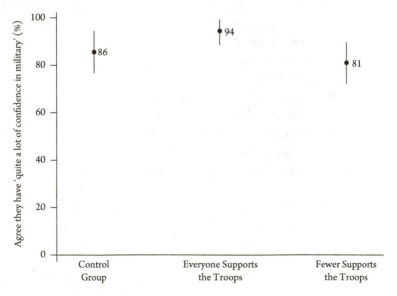

Figure 7.1 Public Confidence in the Military Varied by Pressure to Support the Troops (2019, % agree they have "quite a lot of confidence in military")

Table 7.1 **Public Confidence in the Military as Revealed by the Social Desirability List Experiment (2020)**

Response Value, y	Control N	Control %	Treatment N	Treatment %
0	162	7%	139	6%
1	398	18%	238	11%
2	635	29%	508	23%
3	633	28%	670	30%
4	298	13%	391	17%
5	96	4%	239	11%
6			70	3%
Total	2223	100%	2256	100%
Mean (y)		2.36		2.87
Difference			0.51	
Direct			0.78	
Total effect			**0.27**	

respondents who received the control and the treatment condition, that is, the number of respondents who indicated they agreed with zero of the items on the list, one of the items on the list, two of the items on the list, and so on to the maximum number available. The next row reports the mean number given for the control and treatment conditions. The next row reports the difference, that is, the percentage the number increases when respondents have the added military option on the list. This higher number is considered the "true" percentage, meaning the percentage of the public that would report having "quite a lot of confidence in the military" when asked in a way designed to remove bias. The next row indicates the percentage of respondents who agreed with the question when asked directly, that is, when any social desirability bias, if it exists, should be in operation. The final row shows the difference between those two numbers, between the "true" result revealed by the list experiment and the "direct" result. This difference is the social desirability bias revealed by the survey test; the higher the number, the greater is the social desirability pressure respondents feel to indicate that they have high confidence in the military even though they do not really feel that way.

In this case, confidence in the military seems to be overstated by approximately 27 percentage points when respondents are asked the direct confidence question. Although 78% of respondents state they have "quite a lot" of confidence when asked directly, only 51% reveal that sentiment when asked indirectly. This is quite a large effect. This is the result based on the "direct measure" with the simple binary question: do you agree with the statement "I have quite a lot of confidence in the military." Some 78% of our respondents said they agreed with that statement. If, instead, one uses the more standard Gallup-worded version, which allows respondents to give a range of responses, "A great deal," "Quite a lot," "Some," and "Very little," and then combines the top two responses for the direct measure the "pressured" number is only 68%—that is 68% of the public say either "A great deal" or "Quite a lot." Using that as the "direct measure" would drop the estimate of social desirability bias by about 10 percentage points to an effect of 17%.[3]

Following Imai (2011), Blair and Imai (2012), and Tsai (2019), one can use multivariate regression to explore how this apparent social desirability bias varies by type of respondent. The multivariate analyses include a set of binary variables for respondents' veteran status, military family members, party identification, gender, race, education level, and region as well as continuous variables for age and political ideology.[4] The technical appendix reports the results of robustness checks that confirm the experiment met the conditions Blair and Imai (2012) set for using these techniques.

This technique analyzes both the treatment and control groups together, relying on the fact that the same control items were asked of both groups to increase statistical efficiency. Table 7.2 displays the results of this combined model in the "Sensitive Item" and "Control Items" columns. The results of the "Sensitive Item" column can be thought of as capturing the relationships between each independent variable and the "true" measure of confidence, devoid of any social desirability bias. The coefficients in the "Sensitive Item" column predict whether someone will answer yes to the sensitive item in the list experiment—confidence in the military. The larger the coefficient, the more likely respondents of that type will express high confidence in the military even in situations when they should *not* be feeling social pressure to do so. Thus, older and more conservative respondents were much more likely to express true confidence in the military, while women, African Americans, and respondents with a graduate degree were much less likely to express unbiased support. The coefficients in the

---

[3] The smaller effect measured using the Gallup version of the question is closer to the 14% generated by the list experiment conducted in Wave 1. Normally, I would report only the most conservative result rather than the largest one, but in this case the larger effect comes from the experiment that more closely meets best practices, as identified by Blair and Imai (2012). See the Technical Appendix for Tables and Figures based on the Gallup version of the question.

[4] The model was developed using the R package, *list*, which implements the item count techniques described in Imai (2011) and Blair and Imai (2012).

Table 7.2 **Multivariate Analysis of the List Experiment and the Direct Question (2020)**

Variable	Sensitive Item Est	(SE)	Control Items Est	(SE)	Direct Question Est	(SE)
Veteran	0.76	0.57	0.06	0.07	**0.93***	**0.22**
Military in family	0.32	0.29	−0.05	0.04	0.03	0.09
Republican	−0.52	0.47	**0.22***	**0.06**	**1.04***	**0.15**
Democrat	−0.08	0.46	0.07	0.06	0.11	0.13
Ideology	**0.67***	**0.25**	**−0.08**	**0.03**	**0.41***	**0.07**
Age	**0.37***	**0.15**	−0.01	0.02	**0.16***	**0.04**
Woman	**−0.97***	**0.28**	−0.05	0.04	**−0.22**	**0.09**
Black	**−0.69***	**0.38**	0.04	0.05	**−0.22***	**0.12**
Hispanic	−0.58	0.39	**−0.15***	**0.05**	**−0.36***	**0.12**
Asian	0.13	−0.04	−0.10	0.12	**0.43***	**0.22**
College	0.22	0.31	**0.15***	**0.04**	0.08	0.10
Grad	**−0.83***	**0.45**	**0.29***	**0.06**	0.09	0.14
West	−0.87	0.45	**0.15**	**0.06**	0.05	0.13
South	−0.34	0.38	0.06	0.05	**0.39***	**0.12**
Northeast	−0.56	0.46	0.05	0.06	0.02	0.13
Constant	−0.01	0.61	**−0.25***	**0.08**	0.28	0.18

"Control Items" column predict the number of nonsensitive items with which respondents would agree. The coefficients in the control and sensitive columns are on different scales, and the correlates of the control items are not central to the understanding of confidence in the military.

The next step is to generate a second multivariate logit model of biased support using responses to the direct question, the results of which are displayed in the "Direct Question" column of Table 7.2. Since this intermediate step is essentially replicating the previous analyses in Chapters 2 and 3, the results of the logit model are not further discussed here.

Using the results of these regression models, one can then generate predicted probabilities of unbiased and biased support. The first set of predicted probabilities estimated unbiased support for the sensitive item (confidence) by respondent characteristics using the sensitive item model. The second estimated predicted probabilities using the direct question model, which can be thought of as being contaminated by social desirability bias—if it exists—since they do not rely on the results of the list experiment. The differences between the first unbiased estimate and the second estimate, based on the direct question, represent the size of the social desirability bias, controlling for other demographic characteristics.

Figure 7.2 presents the key results of the subgroup analysis by plotting the predicted probabilities and the resulting differences in the top half and the relative sizes of the subgroup differences in the bottom half, with the largest differences on the left of the figure and the smallest on the right of the figure. The dashed line represents the aggregate model estimate of social desirability bias; subgroups with estimates about the dashed line exhibit "higher than average" social desirability bias, and those with estimates below the dashed line exhibit "lower than average" social desirability bias. The dotted line at zero on the y-axis indicates no social desirability bias detected; whenever a 95% confidence interval crosses the dotted line at zero on the y-axis, the difference for that subgroup between the responses when asked indirectly and when asked directly is not statistically significant, meaning that there is no statistically significant amount of social desirability bias. Following Blair and Imai (2012), the model used 10,000 Monte Carlo simulations to estimate confidence intervals for estimates of both models as well as for the differences in effects.

Figure 7.2 depicts that the large social desirability bias detected in the aggregate is composed of a widely disparate amount of bias spread across the various demographic subgroups that make up the American adult population. Figure 7.2 provides an estimate of how social desirability bias might be operating among different demographic groups by estimating what would happen if it were possible to change one variable in a hypothetical respondent's profile while holding all other variables at their means. For instance, if one could pick a hypothetical "average" person on race, gender, region, ideology, and so on, then the "Republican" coefficient would show how much social desirability bias that individual might experience if one were to change that person into a Republican.

There are groups that exhibit essentially no statistically significant amount of bias, meaning that an average individual on other dimensions would likely feel very little social desirability pressure to pretend they have high confidence in the military if they were to change their demographic status on that one dimension. Some in this category—men, veterans, conservatives, those over 60 years old—are also the populations that show statistically significant higher levels of confidence on average. In other words, there is a military confidence base that is solid and apparently unmoved by considerations of political correctness.

At the other extreme are groups that seem to feel a fair degree of social pressure to claim that they have confidence in the military when they apparently in fact do not. Some in this category—black, women, no military in the family,

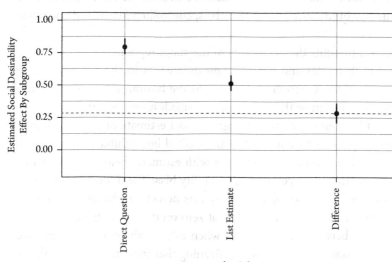
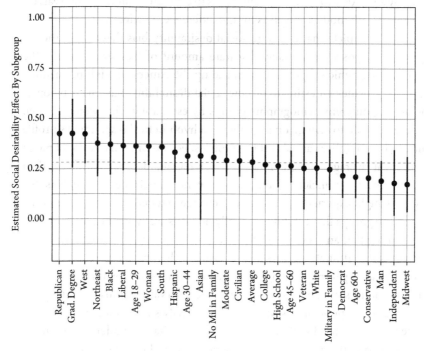

Figure 7.2 Multivariate Estimates of Aggregate and Subgroup Social Desirability Bias from List Experiment (2020)

liberals, younger than 45 years old—are also the groups that show statistically significant lower levels of confidence on average. In other words, the famous fact that the public overall has high confidence in the military is, at least in part, propped up by groups that admit to lower levels of confidence on average and even then might be overstating their true confidence.

Finally, there are also some groups that report misleadingly high levels of confidence on average because that is propped up by a considerable amount of social desirability bias. The group exhibiting the most pronounced version of this are Republicans. In Wave 2, some 84% of Republicans claimed to have "a great deal" or "quite a lot" of confidence in the military. However, the multivariate analysis conducted above suggests that average individual, who happens to be a Republican, would face a great deal of social pressure to express confidence in the military. This suggests that the now well-known fact that Republicans express extremely high levels of confidence in the military may be obscuring a degree of hollowness in that support—that is, that high expressed confidence in the military among Republicans is also somewhat an artifact of social desirability bias.

Conclusion

In short, there is clear evidence that public support for the military is partly due to social desirability bias. When respondents are primed to reflect on the high levels of confidence other Americans had expressed, confidence in the military increased by more than 8 percentage points. Despite the expectation that the analysis would find some social pressure to support the troops, it is still surprising to see an 8-point shift given the already high levels of confidence expressed by the control group. When respondents were informed that confidence in the military among other Americans had dropped by 10 points in recent years, however, confidence fell by 5 points, notable given the relatively weak treatment.

More dramatically, the list experiment also found evidence that Americans in the aggregate inflate their support for the military because they feel social pressure to do so. This bias shows up in most subgroups in the population, but it is most pronounced among the highly educated, minorities, women, younger people, and those with no family in the military. And, perhaps counterintuitively, this is especially pronounced among Republicans. The analysis suggests that ideology plays a big role, especially within the GOP. In other words, there is almost no bias among conservative members of the GOP, but there is quite a bit of bias among moderate members of the GOP.

These findings—coupled with the drop in expressed public confidence among Republicans in polls conducted after the 2020 survey on which this analysis is based—raise interesting questions about why Republican confidence may have dropped in recent years. Is this just a social desirability bias bubble that is popping with pressured Republicans finally feeling free to express their views? Or were groups that were formerly not experiencing much social pressure—say older, white, conservative Republicans—genuinely expressing that their confidence had declined once their champion, Donald Trump, had left office or perhaps because of the disastrous exit from Afghanistan? This would be an intriguing question to pursue in future research.

For now, it suffices to point out that these findings provide clear evidence of what might be called "hollow confidence": astronomical numbers of public support that reflect a certain amount of social pressure, with at least some individuals pretending to register confidence because they think that is the socially correct opinion to express. Even after accounting for social pressure, however, these are still high levels of confidence in the aggregate compared to other institutions. Most other institutions would love to have a "problem" like this one.

Yet these findings suggest that the remarkable staying power of high public confidence may mask a foundation more brittle—and a confidence that is more hollow—than is generally understood. Social pressure and social desirability bias is not all of the story, as the other survey experiments demonstrate, but it is an underappreciated part of the story. To be clear, no one is suggesting that the American public's persistently high level of confidence in the military is entirely attributable to social desirability bias. On the contrary, as argued in Chapters 5 and 6, there are multiple reinforcing props undergirding this high level of confidence.

Nor is anyone suggesting that social desirability is *the* most important prop. Yet the evidence presented here strongly suggests that it is *an* important part of the story, and perhaps one that deserves greater scrutiny than it has hitherto received from scholars and practitioners of civil-military relations in the United States. These findings raise interesting questions about what gives rise to such a social condition and how it might manifest in other related attitudes. The existing data do not provide conclusive answers to all of those questions, but Chapter 10 takes up one important thread: the taboos about the military and its role in society that the public embraces and the taboos that the public rejects. Before turning to that matter, the stage can be set by first exploring other ways public confidence in the military might be linked to things that are of intrinsic importance—material support for the military (Chapter 8) and the role of the military as an instrument of foreign policy (Chapter 9).

PART III

WHY CONFIDENCE IN THE MILITARY MATTERS

8

Whether and How Confidence Shapes Concrete Support for Raising and Maintaining the Military

> I love the troops because if they weren't the troops, I would be the troops. And I would be the worst troops.
> —Comedian Mike Birbiglia (2014)

Senior leaders in the military pay close attention to levels of expressed public confidence in the military. The oldest and wisest veterans remember that it was not always so in American history. Indeed, within the lifetime of many veterans—and within the professional lifetime of the senior-most leaders on active duty—there was a period when the military was not enjoying high social esteem. In the aftermath of the Vietnam War, the prevailing cultural images of the military were negative: the My Lai massacre; the National Guard shooting unarmed college students at Kent State University; helicopters rescuing Americans while leaving behind South Vietnamese allies; helicopters left to burn in the Iranian desert in a botched hostage rescue attempt. The movies—whether lowbrow (*Stripes*) or highbrow (*Apocalypse Now*) often depicted the military as bumbling idiots or worse, war criminals and borderline insane. Some of these depictions continued well into the 1980s, with antiwar movies like *Platoon* (1986), *Full Metal Jacket* (1987), and *Born on the Fourth of July* (1989) continuing to offer conspicuous and highly acclaimed critiques of the Vietnam War and many of the US military personnel who fought there.

But the public mood began to shift late in the 1980s, and this Reagan-era optimism was captured well in movies like *Top Gun* (1986), *Heartbreak Ridge* (1986), and others that depicted the military heroically exorcising the ghosts of Vietnam to enter a new period of pride and confidence. While *Top Gun* was far from the first movie on which the Pentagon collaborated—providing access to fighter planes, aircraft carriers, technical assistance, and military safety training in exchange for creative input into key aspects of the storyline and script—the movie was a watershed moment in Hollywood's cooperation with the military (American Homefront Project 2020; Campbell 2001).[1] Hollywood paid heed to the commercial success of these movies and the military basked in the glow of this newfound recruiting tool and source of respect. By the early 1990s, Phil Strub—the head Pentagon liaison to Hollywood—told the *Hollywood Reporter* that requests for support from the movie industry had increased by 70% (Sirota 2011). And largely positive portrayals of the military have continued in pop culture during the post-9/11 era (Bechtel 2020; Urben and Golby 2020).

Of course, the military likes to be liked and respected. At the most superficial level, there may not be much more to it than that. Yet, one level down, surely the military cares about public attitudes for the understandable intuition that confidence in the military is correlated with other attitudes the military rightly cares about for more material reasons: willingness to resource the military in financial and human capital terms and willingness to use the military in pursuit of foreign policy objectives. Moreover, public confidence may be correlated with other attitudes that the military might also consider advantageous, albeit in more subtle material and nonmaterial terms: the privileges, prerogatives, and other advantages that accrue when the public elevates the military onto a higher and separate plane.

This chapter explores the connections between public confidence in the military and the most obvious material benefits the military needs to be successful—manpower and budget—as well as public views on the military as the "means" toward certain foreign policy "ends."[2] Put another way, this chapter explores whether public confidence in the military is related to the mission-critical elements that enable the military to fulfill its purpose of providing for national security. The analyses in the previous chapters have already established that part of the reason the public has high confidence in the military has to do with the public's assessment that the military fulfills that mission in a competent manner. This chapter explores whether the causal arrow might move in the other direction as well, with higher confidence leading the public to support higher resources for the military. Because of limitations with the survey data, I cannot make strong claims about causation. But I am able to identify a number of correlations that align well with the intuition that people with high confidence in the military are more likely to want to provide the material support the military needs. The next chapter explores whether confidence shapes the way

---

[1] Filmmakers do reimburse the Pentagon for all material costs involved in production.
[2] Portions of this chapter were presented as Golby and Feaver (2021c).

the public wants the military to be used. Then Chapter 10 digs into the murkier, and perhaps more problematic, ways that confidence might be linked to public deference to the military in other domains and in other ways.

Support for Raise and Maintain

The US Constitution directs the federal government to "raise and support" an army and to "provide and maintain" a navy to protect the country. In the post–World War II era, these responsibilities have blurred and been merged in practice. "Raise" entails identifying potential soldiers and sailors/marines (and now air and space personnel) from among the civilian population, somehow bringing them into the uniformed ranks, training them to fulfill military missions, and ensuring that their most basic human needs (food, clothing, medical care) are adequately provided. "Maintaining" entails giving the members of the armed forces a living wage and equipping them with the weapons and logistical support they need to conduct successful military operations wherever and whenever called upon. As the mixed history of American military experience attests, the United States has had both stunning success and shocking failures in the raising and maintaining of adequate military capability over 240-plus years.

For most of the history of the Republic, the country relied on a very small and relatively underequipped, permanent, semiprofessional military made up of individuals who chose this as their career—or perhaps as the lesser of two evils when confronted with possible incarceration. When more military muscle was needed, this small force would be augmented by callups of ordinary civilian citizens who would rapidly form into military units; some of these would already be part-time soldiers in the state-level militias—later the National Guard and service reserves—but most would be brought in directly from civilian life, voluntarily or through a draft. From the beginning of the Republic through to the earliest days of the Korean War, this practice had produced mostly strategic success but at high human and financial cost. Much of what was saved during peacetime by keeping the military institution small would be paid in the butcher's bill of the opening days of the war, when the small, ready-on-day-one American forces would discover how unprepared and underequipped they were relative to the enemy they confronted. To be sure, if the war was a major one that lasted some length of time, by the end the Americans could harness an "arsenal of democracy" to produce the best military in the field. But it took time, and the toll on the first responders was horrific.

Even before the Korean War proved that the old American way of defense preparedness might not be workable in the atomic age, the Truman administration was in the process of pivoting to a whole new approach, which successive administrations, Republican and Democrat, have continued to this present day: maintain powerful armed forces indefinitely, even in "peacetime," as defined by the absence of a major shooting war that necessitated total mobilization. The Founders of the country deemed such a strong "standing army" to be a menace to liberty in the new republic (Kohn 1975). The architects of American grand strategy during the Cold War deemed it a necessity without which liberty could not be preserved (Friedberg 2000). When the Cold War ended, the debate was rejoined, but the side advocating for an indefinite extension of American "peacetime" military strength largely won out.

Of course, even within a bipartisan agreement to sustain indefinitely a military posture that the Founders would have thought risky, there was still plenty of room for political and partisan disagreement as to how to raise the requisite military strength and "how much was enough" to maintain it. These debates were sometimes won by hawks, who wanted a larger and more capable force, and sometimes won by doves, who wanted a smaller and less expensive one. The purpose here is not to trace the history of those debates, let alone align with one side or other on the merits. Rather, the focus is on where those debates intersect the subject of this book: how does public confidence in the military correlate with the public's support for the hawkish or dovish approach to raising and maintaining?

Does Public Confidence in the Military Affect the Ability to "Raise" the Armed Forces?

In terms of raising, the debate largely concerned whether to rely on a draft and, if a draft, whether a uniform draft calling up every male within a targeted age range, or a selective service draft using a lottery to only call up the unlucky. The draft also raised questions of what sort of exemptions would be allowed and whether those exemptions would contain implicit class and racial discrimination. Debate over national service resulted in the Selective Service Act of 1948, which, despite its name, called up a very broad cross section of males with only limited exceptions; the Korean War intensified the need for manpower, resulting in the Universal Military Service and Training Act of 1951, which reduced exceptions further. And then President Eisenhower reduced exceptions still further in 1953. The draft continued for another two decades, but with ever increasing selectivity creeping back in. In the last years of the draft, which coincided with intense public protest of the Vietnam War, the system was widely seen as unfair and discriminatory.

In 1973, the draft ended and was replaced by the all-volunteer force (Flynn 1993; Rostker 2006). Men still must register with the Selective Service Administration upon reaching their 18th birthday, in case the country ever decides to move back to a draft. But on a day-to-day basis, for the past nearly five decades, the military has had to recruit every individual into its ranks. Studies confirm that the dominant driver of propensity to join the military is the degree of economic opportunity outside of the military (Warner 2012; Tomsic 2012). The better the economy is in the civilian sector, the harder it is to recruit individuals into the military sector; but when jobs are hard to come by, military service looks like a more attractive option. Yet the military must field a capable force in good and bad economic times and so must meet its quota of recruits even when the abundance of civilian jobs makes potential recruits resistant to the attractions of military life. It is called the "all-volunteer force," but in practice it is the "all-recruited force," with billions of dollars spent trying to persuade men and women in the right age range and capable of meeting the stringent demands of military service that joining the military is a desirable thing to do. For decades, every American who watches television or attends large-public gatherings like sporting events and national holiday celebrations has consumed a large diet of marketing promoting the US military.

As King and Karabell (2003) and others (Schake and Mattis 2016a) pointed out, there are obvious and intuitive links between the effort to recruit personnel into the all-volunteer force and public attitudes about the military in general. On the one hand, recruiters have long understood that propensity to join is affected by what other "key influencers" are telling individuals about the military (Orvis et al. 1996). On the other hand, the marketing is designed to make more people want to join the military, and the more they want to join the military the higher the level of confidence they express in it. However, I am not aware of data that would dispositively confirm this simple story. Certainly it is easy to document the amount of money spent on directly marketing the military through recruiting advertisements and sponsorships. For instance, the National Defense Authorization Act for fiscal year 2020 provided for $706 million for direct recruiting and advertisements (National Defense 2019). It is harder to track the value of indirect marketing, of the sort that comes from movies and TV shows that enjoy military cooperation and portray the military favorably—in part because of the Department of Defense's active cooperation.[3] The most famous anecdata—the spike in navy recruiting success after the phenomenally popular and favorable *Top Gun* movie—underscores the potential (King and Karabell 2003, 70–79). More recently, the air force launched a major recruiting effort around *Captain Marvel*, hoping to capitalize on the Marvel Comics story of a female fighter-pilot who becomes a superhero (Pawlyk 2020). But some

---

[3] Each military service branch has its own "Hollywood office," which coordinates military assets and marries them up with film companies (Lange 2018).

critics have expressed doubts about the utility of these efforts and have even proposed scaling back the high-profile partnerships between the US military and Hollywood (Sirota 2011) and between the US military and professional sports (US Government Accountability Office 2016; Bryant 2018; Coffee 2018).

It seems likely that the massive marketing campaign does help in recruiting efforts in the way intended: motivating individuals who would not have come up with the idea otherwise to explore joining the military. Although data to assess whether these military public affairs campaigns directly translate into higher enlistments among potential recruits is lacking, the new proprietary surveys do provide at least some evidence that Hollywood and pop culture might be creating positive attitudes among a portion of their target audience: younger Americans who might consider serving in the military.

Wave 2 asked respondents: "How have you, personally, learned most of what you know about the military?" As noted in Chapter 3, only 8% of the public reported that they learned most of what they know about the military from "movies and television" shows. As Figure 8.1 shows, however, there is a noticeable difference across age groups, with younger Americans far more likely to learn about the military through pop culture than are older citizens. Nearly one-fifth of Americans between the ages of 18 and 24 report that movies and television are their primary source of information about the military, but almost all older Americans turn to other sources for their information about the armed forces.

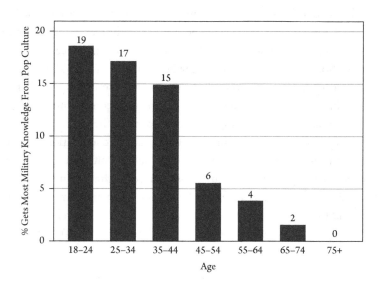

Figure 8.1 Percentage of Americans Who Report They Have Learned Most of What They Know about the Military from Movies and Television Shows

As discussed in Chapter 2, confidence in the military has declined significantly among millennials and subsequent American generations since shortly after the beginning of the Iraq war. Figure 8.2 suggests that Pentagon recruiting programs and the related efforts to foster positive coverage in popular culture may help push against this trend—at least among the subset of younger Americans who learn about the armed forces primarily through popular culture. Of course, this slice of the recruiting age population simply may be more inclined to watch movies or television shows portraying the military in a positive light because they already have confidence in the military. But the fact that younger Americans who receive most of their information about the military from movies and television shows have significantly more confidence than others in their cohort who receive military information primarily from news sources, friends and family who served, or personal experiences remains notable, especially given the patterns discussed in Chapter 3.

These new surveys do not allow one to explore the direct link between pop culture and recruiting. However, it is possible to examine whether or not changes in public confidence are related to changes in younger Americans' stated propensity to serve by drawing on an underexploited data source, the University of Michigan's "Monitoring the Future" survey. This study has interviewed high school seniors since 1975, and it has consistently asked students a number of questions about their future career prospects, including whether they intend to

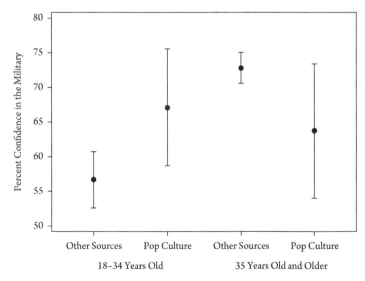

The difference in means between the 18–34 year old groups for a two-sided t-test is statistically significant at the 95% confidence level.

Figure 8.2 Percentage of Americans By Age Who Report They Have Learned Most of What They Know about the Military from Movies and Television Shows (2020)

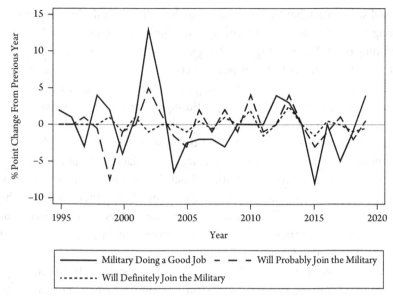

Figure 8.3 Change in Propensity to Serve in the Military and Change in Perception of Whether the Military Is Doing a Good Job for the Nation (Monitoring the Future, 1995–2019)

join the military. These surveys do not include a direct confidence question, but they do include a different question that can serve as a close proxy: "How good or bad a job is being done for the country as a whole by the US military?"[4]

Figure 8.3 shows the relationship between the change from the previous year in the percentage of high school seniors saying the military is doing either a "very good" or a "good" job and the change in those saying they "definitely will join" or "probably will join" the military after they graduate. As the figure shows, the percentage of respondents saying they definitely will join the military stays relatively steady, with no more than a 2.5-point move in any given year and only a weak correlation (.12) with the annual change in the percentage of respondents saying the military is doing a good job. There does appear to be a relationship between the year-to-year movement in the percentage of high school seniors saying the military is doing a good job for the nation and the percentage saying they probably will join the military, however, with a moderate correlation (.39) between these two measures over this 25-year period.

Figure 8.4 depicts these changes at a more granular level, showing the percentages of high school seniors stating they will definitely (left) or will

---

[4] The percentage of high school seniors responding to this question with either "Good" or "Very Good" from 1998 to 2018 is highly correlated (.71) with the percentage of millennials expressing a "great deal of confidence" in the military in the General Social Survey referenced in Chapter 2.

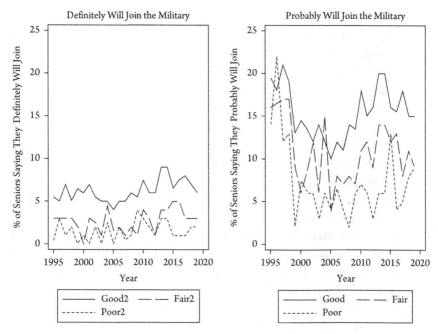

Figure 8.4 High School Seniors Saying They Will Join the Military by Satisfaction with the Job the Military Is Doing on Behalf of the Country (Monitoring the Future, 1995–2019)

probably (right) join the military broken down by whether they assessed the job the military is doing as good, fair, or poor.[5] Throughout the period, the percentage of those reporting they definitely will join the military is consistently higher among those seniors assessing the military as doing a good job for the country, though there appears to be a brief moment of convergence following the initiation of the Iraq war in 2003. There is much greater variation among those stating they "probably will join" the military, beginning with a clear drop among all three groups in 1999 around the time the US government began discussing potential intervention in the Kosovo War. In the late 1990s, there appeared to be little relationship between respondents' propensity to serve and their assessment of the military. Following September 11, some separation between these groups began to appear, though high school seniors assessing the military as doing a fair job became individually more willing to state they might join the military in 2002 and 2004 after the US launched interventions in Afghanistan and Iraq,

---

[5] Unless otherwise noted, all analysis in this chapter reduces the five-point military satisfaction scale to a three-point scale (combining the categories "good" and "very good" into one response and combining "poor" with "very poor." Disaggregating the scale does not change the substantive analysis but complicates visual presentation of the trends discussed above.

respectively. Of course, these students might simply be giving what they think is the "right" answer since these surveys only provide a self-reported propensity to serve. A number of financial, familial, health, and personal factors often intervene in an individual's eligibility and decision to serve (Feeney 2014). But even if the pool of potential recruits increases modestly as a result of increased confidence, it may make the job of military recruiters more manageable—and decreased confidence may complicate their efforts.[6]

It also seems likely that the intended recruitment effect is reinforced by a secondary, indirect effect that operates *through* generalized public confidence in the military. Put another way, it is possible that these military promotional efforts are not only trying to directly move the needle on the hard task of getting a given individual to decide to join the military—the explicit purpose of the effort—but they are also attempting move the needle by creating a more generalized favorable public disposition toward the military. That positive milieu can then assist in recruitment efforts by creating more favorably disposed advisers—family, loved ones, teachers, and other influencers—around any given individual who would reinforce the notion that joining the military is a good idea because they have high confidence in the military as an institution. Prior research has established that an individual's propensity to join the military is heavily conditioned on the advice that individual receives from role models, friends, and family (Orvis, Sastry, and McDonald 1996; Helmus 2018; Oh 1998). And a recent Department of Defense recruiting effort, the "Their Tomorrow" campaign, targets parents and family members specifically.[7] Thus, as the Pentagon is betting, perhaps generalized public confidence in the military helps cause a higher propensity to join the military, and the marketing campaign helps create that generalized public confidence.

Moskos (2003, 42) has suggested that the shift to an all-volunteer force, which allowed many segments of society to avoid military burden altogether, combined with a marketing campaign that reaches everyone but persuades few, only succeeds in creating "patriotism lite"—the combination of high expressed support and low propensity to serve. Liebert and Golby (2017) have likewise noted that there is a pronounced partisan skew in self-reported propensities to join the military. The 2013 Hoover Institution survey (Schake and Mattis

---

[6] Controlling for other factors in 2019, the relationship between individuals' assessment of the military and their reported propensity to serve (separately for "definitely" and "probably") is statistically significant at the 95% confidence level in a logistic regression, even when controlling for other factors.

[7] This recruiting campaign is not the first time the Department of Defense has focused on persuading parents and family members that the military provides worthwhile opportunities for younger Americans, but it is the largest such effort of which I am aware (NGAUS 2018).

2013) as well as data collected for another project (Golby, Feaver, and Dropp 2017) can shed additional light on this issue. The Hoover survey asked respondents whether they have ever considered joining themselves and whether they would advise a close friend or child of a close friend to join the military. (For reasons that are not clear, the survey did not ask whether respondents would advise their own child to join.) As many as 44% of respondents said that they had "considered joining," a remarkably high number that hints at the possibility of social desirability bias—especially the finding that fully 58% of men report that they considered joining (Schake and Mattis 2013).[8] However, respondents were markedly less likely to recommend that others join the military. Overall, only 37% claimed they would advise a close friend or child of a close friend to join, and Democrats were even less likely—only 23% responded in the affirmative.

As reported in Figures 8.1 and 8.2, there is suggestive evidence that demonstrates the earlier stage in the causal chain—from advertisements or direct marketing campaigns to public confidence. There is even better data to assess the later link—from confidence to propensity to recommend the military as a career path. In addition to asking the basic confidence question, the survey also asked a battery of questions assessing whether the public had other positive or negative views of the military. As discussed in Chapter 6, high confidence in the military was indeed associated with other positive attitudes about the military, for instance, believing that the military is good at what it does and maintains high ethical standards and is generally truthful.

However, it is possible to go further than estimates of general positive affect to get closer to the attitude of interest here—support for serving in the military—because the survey also asked whether they would encourage others to join the military. Both survey waves asked, "Would you advise a close friend or relative or the child of a close friend or relative to join the military?" And Wave 1 asked whether respondents would agree with the statement, "I would be proud if a member of my family or a close friend joined the US military" as well as "I would be disappointed if a member of my family or a close friend joined the US military."[9] The topline results are reported in Tables 8.1 and 8.2.

As expected, people with high confidence in the military are far more likely to advise a close friend or relative to join the military and vice versa. In both waves, roughly half of respondents with confidence in the military report that they would advise a close friend or family member to join the military. Only

---

[8] The partisan breakdown is striking, with only 36% of Democrats reporting that they considered joining.

[9] The survey also included a question about whether individuals who serve in the military are "patriotic" in Wave 1. The results for this question follow the same pattern observed in Tables 8.1 and 8.2 so are omitted for the sake of parsimony.

Table 8.1 **Overall Responses to a Question about Whether a Respondent Would Advise a Close Friend or Relative to Join the Military by Confidence (% a great deal + quite a lot)**

	2019			2020		
	Overall	Confident	Not Confident	Overall	Confident	Not Confident
Yes	45%	**51%**	29%	36%	**48%**	11%
	(280)	**(235)**	(45)	(201)	**(183)**	(18)
No	26%	19%	48%	39%	26%	66%
	(163)	(89)	(74)	(214)	(100)	(113)
Not sure	28%	30%	23%	25%	26%	23%
	(173)	(138)	(36)	(139)	(100)	(40)
Total	100%	100%	100%	100%	100%	100% (171)
	(616)	(462)	(154)	(554)	(383)	

Note: The relationship between confidence in the military and a binary "advise" variable is statistically significant at the 99% confidence level in a logistic regression, controlling for standard demographic variables and military contact variables from Chapter 3.

Table 8.2 **Overall Responses to Feelings about Family Member Joining the Military Questions by Confidence (2020, % agree)**

	Proud			Disappointed		
	Overall	Confident	Not Confident	Overall	Confident	Not Confident
Agree	72%	84%	41%	14%	10%	31%
	(221)	(184)	(37)	(44)	(23)	(21)
Neither	21%	11%	45%	21%	16%	38%
	(64)	(24)	(40)	(64)	(38)	(26)
Disagree	7%	5%	14%	65%	74%	31%
	(22)	(10)	(12)	(200)	(179)	(21)
Total	100%	100%	100%	100%	100%	100%
	(307)	(218)	(89)	(308)	(240)	(68)

Note: The relationship between confidence in the military and "proud" and "disappointed" variables is statistically significant at the 99% confidence level in separate ordered logistic regression models, controlling for standard demographic variables and military contact variables from Chapter 3.

29% of respondents without confidence in the military stated they would advise someone to join the military; some might consider this to be a high degree of propensity to recommend service, given a lack of confidence in the institution one is recommending to someone else, but it is worth noting that this number dropped to 11% in 2020. These reductions appear largest among Democrats, independents, women, and minorities, and it is notable here that the second wave occurred in the midst of a divisive election contested along partisan and racial lines. This suggests that this attitude might be rather volatile, indeed more volatile than the topline confidence number. Perhaps in ordinary times there is some social desirability bias at work with respondents not wanting to admit that they would recommend against fulfilling what some consider to be a badge of patriotism, but this weakens in times of social stress. Respondents with high confidence in the military likewise are significantly more likely to say they would be proud if a member of their family or a close friend joined and much less likely to be disappointed, though only a small number of respondents—14% in the aggregate and 31% among those without confidence in the military—stated they would be disappointed if a family member joined the military.

Conventional wisdom holds that a strong predictor of whether one is willing to join the military oneself is whether one has close family or friends who have served (Gibson et al. 2007; Oh 1998). The survey did not ask the question about propensity to join oneself, but it is possible to assess whether propensity to recommend that others join and whether pride in having one's family join are similarly linked to these social ties. As shown in Table 8.3, individuals with connections to the military are much more likely to advise others to volunteer for military service. A majority of each group said they would advise friends and family to join the military, with willingness to advise growing stronger the closer one's direct connection to the military. This pattern appears to operate in reverse as well. The weaker respondents' connection to the military becomes, the more likely they are to not recommend military service. Among each of these "outgroups"—civilians, no military family, and no work connections to the military—a no response is the plurality answer to the question of whether they would advise a friend or family member to volunteer for military service. That said, it is also worth noting that sizable minorities (roughly one-third of those with a personal/family link, one-quarter of those who just have a work link) of people with a connection to the military nevertheless claim they would not recommend that their close friend or relative join the military. Compared to people without connections, they are markedly less likely to respond that they are unsure about the matter, suggesting that they are more likely to have thought about it before the survey posed the question to them. The logical inference is that military connections have something of a bivalent effect, making most people

Table 8.3 **Responses to Question about Whether a Respondent Would Advise a Close Friend or Relative to Join the Military by Military Service Connections (2020)**

	Veteran		Family Member Served		Worked with Military in Last 30 Days		Worked with Military in Last Year	
	Yes	No	Yes	No	Yes	No	Yes	No
Yes	58% (24)	35% (177)	55% (76)	31% (119)	55% (124)	23% (65)	51% (114)	28% (87)
No	32% (13)	39% (200)	31% (43)	43% (166)	28% (63)	49% (137)	24% (55)	50% (156)
Not sure	10% (4)	26% (135)	14% (19)	26% (102)	17% (37)	27% (75)	25% (55)	22% (69)
Total	100% (41)	100% (511)	100% (138)	100% (387)	100% (223)	100% (276)	100% (224)	100% (311)

Note: The relationship between each of the "military connection" variables and a binary "advise" variable is statistically significant at the 99% confidence level in a logistic regression model of the whole sample, controlling for standard demographic variables and treatment conditions. In a model using only the control group, all the "military connection" variables are significant at the 95% confidence level, but veteran status is not.

more inclined to recommend service but also making a sizable minority more assuredly opposed to making that recommendation.

As discussed in Chapter 3, these same social contact variables may also be connected to public confidence in the military, but mostly on the margins and not always in intuitively obvious ways. Yet it is also possible that public confidence in the military has an independent effect on an individual's willingness to recommend military service to others or to express hypothetical pride at the thought of a family member service. That is, perhaps those who have high confidence in the military, whether or not they have a personal connection to the military, are more willing to recommend military service to others than are individuals with low confidence. Figure 8.5 shows that this argument is plausible. Figure 8.5 further reinforces the idea that connections, confidence, and propensity to recommend service are all linked but analytically separable concepts. Note, for instance, that having a personal connection to the military seems to make the propensity to recommend service attitude more robust to declines in confidence. While the propensity to recommend service drops with declining confidence in all groups, it drops lower and faster with declining confidence among people without a personal connection (the cluster of bars on the

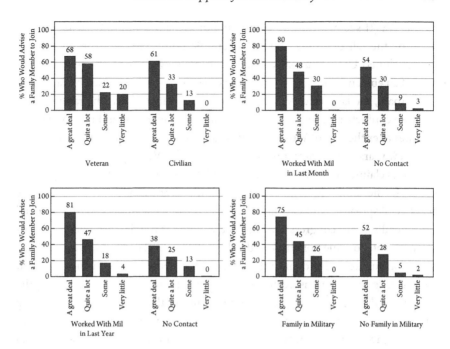

Figure 8.5 Percentage of Respondent Who Would Advise a Close Friend or Relative to Join the Military by Confidence and Military Service Connections (2020)

right in each figure) than it does among people with a personal connection (the cluster of bars on the left of each figure).

In short, the data suggest that—even apart from personal connections to the military—public confidence is also strongly correlated with both an individual's propensity to consider military service and with a family member or mentor's willingness to recommend military service. These findings by themselves do not make confidence in the military an important value worth keeping at all costs. But they do reinforce the military's intuition that public confidence is valuable and that it helps them in their assignment of raising armed forces adequate to the nation's needs, especially in an era of an all-recruited force.

Does Public Confidence in the Military Affect the Ability to "Maintain" the Armed Forces?

It is one thing to raise enough men and women to serve. It is another thing—and a very expensive thing, indeed—to pay them and properly equip them for success on the battlefield. For most of the history of the Republic, defense outlays were quite small, only to increase to astonishing levels at the height of total mobilization and war before returning to prewar levels. The demobilization after

World War II seemed to fit that pattern, but the shock of the Cold War, made vivid by the fall of China, the Soviet atomic bomb test, and the invasion of Korea, shifted US defense spending to a whole new plane. To be sure, the pattern of an ebb and flow tied to war efforts remained—as witnessed by ramp-ups in Vietnam, the late Cold War, and Iraq/Afghanistan, followed by ramp-downs as those conflicts receded. Yet the "low points" in defense spending in the seven decades after the end of World War II would have looked like high points for all but a few years in American history up until World War II.

Doves claimed the ramp-ups were too high and the ramp-downs too halting. Doves further objected that defense spending was artificially propped up by the practice of spreading out expenditures from the defense budget so they reached into literally every congressional district. A vote for the defense budget, in this view, is a vote to bring pork back to the district. Hawks claimed that the ramp-ups were inadequate and the ramp-downs were too deep. Hawks further objected that defense spending was treated as part of the "discretionary budget"—as if the defense of the Republic was an optional luxury in the way that public funding of the classical arts might be—and that defense priorities suffered accordingly. It matters not for my purposes here who was right, only that military leaders had good reason to be focused on defense spending—and not merely for the trivial reason that bureaucracies always like to see their budgets grow. Getting defense spending right is a matter of life and death for those sent to fight the next war, and it may well help deter that war from happening.

If overall defense spending levels are an important metric to track, it follows that public tolerance or even support for maintaining those spending levels is also a vital metric. And it raises the obvious intuition that public confidence in the military itself could be a contributing factor to overall public support for defense spending. The precise dynamics of the relationship might logically change depending on the context. For instance, at the nadir of the post-Vietnam period of malaise, a hawk might report that she has low confidence in the military (because it has been grossly underfunded) and thus wants a significant ramp-up in defense spending; that same hawk a decade later could report high confidence in the military (because of the late-Carter/Reagan military buildup) and still want to see more defense spending—or at least oppose any cuts. Contrastingly, a dove might report low confidence in the post-Vietnam era but also not want to increase spending—and then report higher confidence in the late Reagan era but still oppose increases and maybe even support decreases. However, in general, one would expect that those individuals—whether hawk or dove—with higher confidence in the military would prefer more defense spending relative to those with lower confidence in the military, all else equal. In other words, Americans who trust the military may not always want to increase military spending, but

Figure 8.6 Public Confidence in the Military and Support for Increased Military Spending over Time (Gallup)

they should typically want more defense spending than those who do not trust the military to use its resources wisely.

Figure 8.6 shows two separate trend lines, drawn from Gallup opinion data. The solid line tracks public attitudes related to defense spending: the percentage who say defense spending is too low.[10] The higher the line goes, the more public sentiment is tilted in the direction of increasing the defense budget. The second line tracks the percentage of Americans who express a "great deal" of confidence in the military.[11] The higher the line goes, the higher overall public esteem for the military is. The two trends appear to be nearly orthogonal, with essentially no correlation between them (.00) across the full time period. A closer look, however, suggests that the trends depicted in Figure 8.6 indicate a negative relationship between confidence in the military and public demand for increased military spending before September 11 and a positive relationship after.

---

[10] Note: sensitivity analyses were done with a different dependent variable—the percentage of those who say defense spending is too high minus those who say defense spending is too low. In all cases, the patterns are substantively the same; these two measures of the dependent variable, "too low minus too high" and "too low," are very highly correlated (.94). Here only the percentage who say spending is too low is reported for ease of presentation.

[11] Again, sensitivity analyses looked at total confidence—those expressing either "a great deal" or "quite a lot" of confidence. These variables are also highly correlated (.89), and the one case where the results of the regression analysis differed is reported in Table 8.4.

Table 8.4 **Predictors of Support for Increased Military Spending over Time**

	(1) Total	(2) Pre-9/11	(3) 1979–1981 Omitted	(4) Post-9/11
Log (Confidence)	−0.74*	−1.79**	−1.03	1.92**
	(0.42)	(0.67)	(0.61)	(0.72)
Post-9/11	0.87***			
	(0.17)			
Years since War Onset	−0.01	−0.26*	−0.23*	−0.04***
	(0.01)	(0.13)	(0.11)	(0.01)
Republican President	−0.21***	−0.18	−0.22*	−0.01
	(0.08)	(0.13)	(0.12)	(0.10)
Log (DoD Budget)	−1.73***	−1.41**	−1.20**	−0.72
	(0.32)	(0.55)	(0.47)	(0.50)
Log (Federal Deficit)	−0.05**	−0.05**	−0.06***	−0.19*
	(0.02)	(0.02)	(0.02)	(0.11)
Constant	9.60***	7.05***	6.07**	6.19**
	(2.03)	(3.62)	(3.05)	(2.51)
Adjusted R²	0.66	0.71	0.73	0.60
N	45	26	23	19

Note: Each model is estimated using OLS regression with the log (% defense spending too low) as the dependent variable. Other robustness checks are depicted in the technical appendix.

*** = p < .01; ** = p < .05; * = p < .1 for one-tailed tests.

This pattern may represent a potential case of "Simpson's Paradox," in which trends appear in several separate partitions of data but disappear or reverse when the groups are combined. In most cases, instances of this paradox are caused by a lurking confounding variable: the classic case being that of disproportionate applications by women to "competitive departments" at the University of California, Berkeley, reversing the appearance of gender bias that manifests in the aggregate (Bickel, Hammel, and O'Connell 1975).

Table 8.4 suggests one possible confounding variable: the exogenous shock of September 11.[12] Column (1) in Table 8.4 shows a strong negative correlation between confidence and public desire to increase defense spending, after inclusion of a binary variable dividing the pre- and post-9/11 periods and accounting

[12] The variable is coded as 1 for the Vietnam War years, the Gulf War (1991), and the period since September 11, with all other years coded as 0.

for a number of other variables known to influence public attitudes about the defense budget: the number of years since the last war started, the party of the president in a given year, and separately the log of the defense budget and the log of the federal deficit to capture changes in the broader fiscal environment. However, as Columns (2) and (4) show, the correlation between confidence in the military and public support for defense spending reverses when the sample is divided into pre-9/11 years and post-9/11 years. The huge spike in demand for increased defense spending at the end of the 1970s—just before army chief of staff General Shy Myers testified that his force was a "hollow army" and the Desert One debacle revealed major deficiencies in the US military—certainly contributed to this relationship; in fact, Column (3) shows that the correlation is no longer statistically significant when those years (1979–1981) are omitted from the model for the pre-9/11 period. The massive increase in defense spending as a percentage of GDP—from 4.95% percent in 1979 to 6.81% in 1982—also certainly dampened appetites for further increases. Of course, this evidence is far from definitive, given the extremely small number of years in the sample. Nevertheless, there is at least some suggestive evidence that the relationship between public confidence in the military and defense spending changed after the planes struck the World Trade Center and the Pentagon on September 11, 2001.

To explore this dynamic further, it is worth turning to yet another underexploited source of data, this time the American National Election Survey (ANES). During every presidential election year from 1980 to 2008, the ANES asked respondents to assess whether defense spending should be increased or decreased on a 7-point scale and to rate their feelings toward the military on a 100-point thermometer (a plausible proxy for confidence). Figure 8.7 displays the relationship between these two variables for the periods before and after September 11, 2001, broken down by respondent party identification. Among Democrats, the relationship between one's affinity for the military and one's expressed support for increased defense spending remains essentially unchanged before and after 9/11. Although Republicans already were more supportive of filling the Pentagon's coffers in general, confidence in the military and support for defense spending became more closely correlated among Republicans after September 11 than they had been before.

As explained in Chapter 2, confidence in the military became more polarized across the two parties following the terrorist attacks in 2001, largely because confidence among Republicans grew faster than it did among Democrats. At the same time that confidence in the military was spiking among the GOP faithful, however, confident Republicans were also becoming even more committed to relatively higher levels of defense spending. Less confident Republicans, on the other hand—although far fewer in number—were developing a more skeptical

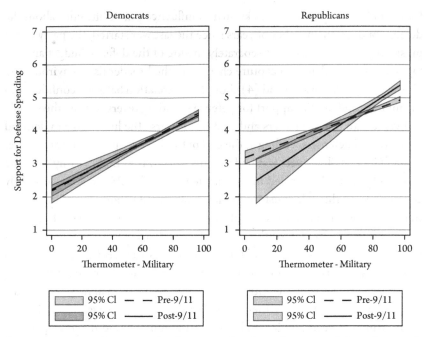

Figure 8.7 Support for Increased Military Spending by Feelings toward the Military and Party before and after September 11, 2001 (ANES)

view of Pentagon spending. Partisan sorting may have been part of the GOP story, but the lack of a corresponding shift among Democrats suggests that this increased commitment to defense spending among Americans on the right likely also moved in lockstep with surging confidence in the military. While the ANES data does not provide any evidence to support the idea that the relationship between confidence in the military and support for defense spending flipped after September 11, it does suggest that 2001 may have been a watershed moment that shaped how Republicans viewed the military itself as well as the issue of defense spending more broadly.

Because the ANES stopped asking the defense spending and thermometer questions in the same surveys in 2008, there is not good data to track these trends through the Obama and Trump administrations. However, the new proprietary surveys do allow for exploration of the intuitions about the relationship between confidence and defense spending at a particular point in time—the present. In addition to the standard question about confidence in the military, Wave 2 also asked respondents to indicate their level of agreement with a few statements regarding defense spending, namely:

1. The military receives too much money in terms of pay and benefits.
2. The US government should cut spending for the State Department in order to increase spending for the Department of Defense budget.

Table 8.5 **Support for Military Pay by Level of Confidence (2020)**

	Military Receives Too Much in Pay			Military Receives Too Little in Pay		
	Overall	Confident	Not Confident	Overall	Confident	Not Confident
Agree	10%	11%	7% (5)	**63%**	**70%**	48%
	(26)	(20)		**(178)**	**(133)**	(44)
Neither	28%	20%	47%	24%	23%	27%
	(77)	(37)	(40)	(68)	(43)	(25)
Disagree	**62%**	**69%**	46%	13%	8%	25%
	(168)	**(131)**	(38)	(37)	(14)	(23)
Total	100%	100%	100%	100%	100%	100%
	(271)	(188)	(83)	(283)	(191)	(92)

Note: For both the "Military Receives Too Much" and "Receive Too Little" results, the relationship between confidence in the military and the outcome variable is statistically significant at the 99% confidence level in an ordered logistic regression controlling for standard demographic variables.

To guard against agreement/acquiescence bias, the survey asked half of the respondents the questions worded as above and half with the sentiment reversed, e.g., "the military receives too little money..." and "the US government should cut spending for the Department of Defense in order to increase spending for the Department of State budget" (Paulhus 1991; Weijters, Baumgartner, and Schillewaert 2013). Reversing the direction of the responses to account for this generates a rough-and-ready scale of hawkish versus dovish attitudes on defense spending. In this lexicon, a hawk would agree that the military receives too little money, disagree that the military receives too much money, agree that the US government should cut spending on State to increase it on Defense, and disagree that the government should cut spending on Defense to increase it on State.[13] A dove would have the opposite views.

As shown in the previous discussion, the question thus reduces to this: are respondents with higher confidence in the military today more likely to be hawks or doves on defense spending? Table 8.5 presents a first cut answer.[14] Regardless of the question phrasing, the pattern is clear: Americans with confidence in

---

[13] A fair critic could charge that a true hawk might wish to increase spending on both Defense *and* State. As designed, the survey is unable to account for this issue, and it is worth exploring in future work. The relatively crude measure presented here probably captures well enough the sentiment under study to be confident in the findings presented above. But future work utilizing a longer battery of questions could parse the dynamic more precisely.

[14] Unless otherwise noted, the results of all regression models referenced in this chapter hold for a model using only the control group and for a model of the full sample, including controls for all experimental treatment conditions.

the military are much more likely to disagree with the notion that members of the military receive too much in pay and far more willing to suggest service members receive too little compensation. Among those who express high confidence in the military, 69% disagree with the "too much pay" statement and 70% agree that the military receives "too little pay." But there is fairly strong support for military pay even among respondents who do not express confidence in the military, with a strong 48% plurality of these respondents agreeing that the men and women who serve in the military receive too little in pay and benefits.

But it is relatively easy to express support for higher military pay when there are no trade-offs involved. Table 8.6 instead puts the question to the respondents in more concrete terms, asking them whether they would be willing to cut the State Department budget to increase funding for the Department of Defense, and vice versa. In this case, respondents were somewhat reluctant to make a call. As Table 8.6 shows, the plurality response among both high- and low-confidence groups is "neither agree nor disagree" for both versions of the question. Respondents with confidence in the military were somewhat more likely to express support for cutting diplomats' funding than those without confidence in the military, however. The difference between agree-disagree responses for cutting the State Department is –3% among Americans with high confidence in the military and –20% for those who do not hold the military in such high esteem. Approximately a quarter of both high-confidence and low-confidence respondents agreed with cutting the military's budget to increase diplomatic

Table 8.6 **Support for Trading Funding for the Department of State to Increase Funding for the Department of Defense by Level of Confidence (2020)**

	Cut State to Increase DoD Funding			*Cut DoD to Increase State Funding*		
	Overall	*Confident*	*Not Confident*	*Overall*	*Confident*	*Not Confident*
Agree	22% (60)	26% (49)	14% (11)	24% (69)	24% (45)	26% (24)
Neither	48% (128)	45% (84)	52% (44)	45% (128)	41% (79)	54% (49)
Disagree	30% (82)	29% (54)	34% (28)	30% (86)	35% (68)	20% (18)
Total	100% (270)	100% (186)	100% (84)	100% (283)	100% (192)	100% (91)

Note: For both the "Cut State" and "Cut DoD" results, the relationship between confidence in the military and the outcome variable is statistically significant at the 95% confidence level in an ordered logistic regression controlling for standard demographic variables.

funding, but Americans with high confidence in the military were more likely to disagree with that proposal, at 35%, than were respondents without confidence, at just 20%. Thus, while the pattern is not dramatic, it is discernible: on the whole, respondents with lower confidence in the military are more likely to be doves on defense spending while respondents with higher confidence in the military are more likely to be hawks.[15]

Since other research has established that attitudes toward defense spending are linked to partisanship and other demographic variables (Leal 2005; Kafura 2020; Bartels 1994), one must control for them to isolate the marginal effect of public confidence. The full details of the multivariate analysis are available in the technical appendix (available here: https://dataverse.harvard.edu/dataverse/pfeaver). For simplicity, Figure 8.8 displays the State and Department of Defense funding questions conditioned on party identification. As noted above, confidence in the military is highly correlated with support for more hawkish budget policies, even after controlling for party, standard demographic variables, and the military contact variables explored in Chapter 3.

One staple of previous studies of public attitudes toward spending on foreign policy is that the general public is not well informed about overall levels. For instance, large majorities often say they support reductions in spending on foreign humanitarian and economic aid, but then peg as the desired amount a level many multiples of what is actually spent (Kull 2011). In similar fashion, some studies have found that the public makes similar misestimates regarding spending on defense (DoD) and diplomacy (State) (Negin 2020; Pocan 2020; Cary 2017). Because Wave 2 separately asked respondents to answer a few factual questions regarding the size of the budgets for the Departments of Defense and State respectively, it can shed some additional light on this topic. Table 8.9 shows the results of public attitudes to defense spending, sorted by whether they knew the actual level of spending in these areas.[16] The slices of the pie broken out below highlight the "correct" answers at the time of the survey, approximately $700 billion for the Pentagon and approximately $55 billion for the

---

[15] There is a chicken-and-egg issue here: does being a hawk give you higher confidence in the military, or does having higher confidence in the military make you a hawk, or does the causal arrow run in both directions depending on the individual (as I suspect). The survey design does not allow a ready resolution of this issue. However, resolving it may not be necessary to answer the basic policy question at the heart of this chapter, namely whether the military should even care about public confidence in the military. Of course, military leaders might prefer to have the detailed knowledge of the electorate that parses all of this in such granular detail as to answer the causal arrow question, but that is not practical. For them, I have shown that the frequently asked "confidence" question is a good proxy indicator for all these other things that they also value and want to know. And keeping it high is desirable, whether the causal arrow moves in only one direction or both.

[16] The sample sizes for the DoD and DoS budget questions are 2,276 and 2,181 respondents.

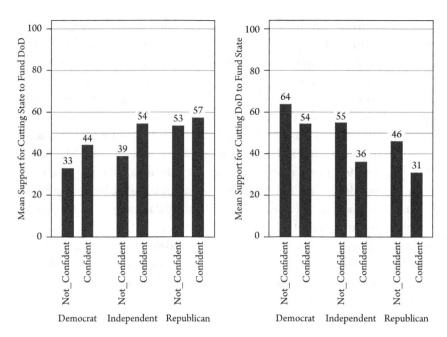

Figure 8.8 Effect of Confidence on Defense Spending Attitudes Conditioned on Party (2020)

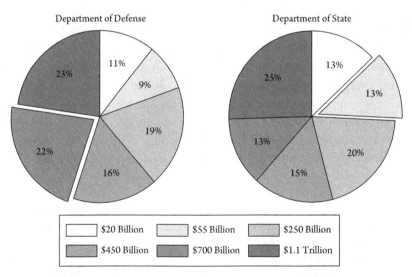

Figure 8.9 Responses to Questions about the Size of the Budgets for the Departments of Defense and State (2020)

State Department.[17] Consistent with previous research, this survey confirms that Americans are largely unaware of what the US government spends on national security and foreign policy, even when given multiple choice options from which to choose. Only 22% of Americans correctly chose the right answer for the DoD budget and a paltry 13% of respondents identified the right amount of funding for the Department of State. Additionally, the percentage of Americans identifying the State Department budget as $1.1 trillion was larger than, though not statistically different from, the percentage of respondents who said the same of the Department of Defense—even though the fiscal year 2020 budget for the Pentagon, which exceeded $700 billion, was far closer to that figure than the State Department budget for the same year, which was just 5% of $1.1 trillion.

Figure 8.10 shows that respondents' confidence in the military has little to do with their understanding of the size of the defense budget, however. Those

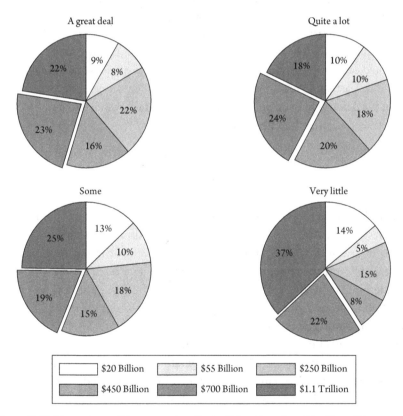

Figure 8.10 Percentage of Responses to a Factual Question about the Size of the Department of Defense Budget by Confidence Level (2020)

---

[17] The total FY2020 budgets for the Departments of Defense and State were $718.3 billion and $56.4 billion, respectively.

with "a great deal" or "quite a lot" of confidence in the military are not significantly better able—with 23% and 24% of them selecting the right answer, respectively—to identify the correct size of the Department of Defense budget than are those with only "some" or "very little" confidence in the military. The only notable difference in Figure 8.10 is that respondents with "very little" confidence in the military are somewhat more likely to overestimate the size of the defense budget, with 37% of that group answering that the Department of Defense budget comes in at $1.1 trillion compared to 25% or less in every other group.

Although not displayed, one other statistically significant relationship emerged, though it is not directly related to confidence. Respondents who answered the DoD budget question correctly were statistically less likely to support cutting the State Department budget to increase funding to the Department of Defense, even when controlling for confidence level, party, and the other standard demographic and military contact variables used to model the relationship in Table 8.6. This relationship was even stronger when the model included not only respondents who noted the correct answer, but also those who overestimated the defense budget at $1.1 trillion. Since the factual question was asked early in the survey before the budget trade-off question, this suggests there is at least some relationship between respondents' perceptions about the size of the defense budget and their willingness to take resources from the State Department in order to better fund the Pentagon.

Conclusion

Military leaders are wise to monitor overall public confidence in the military. The question is asked often enough and reported dutifully in the press to make it a ready indicator for situational awareness about the public mood. And as shown above, public attitudes about confidence in the military track closely with other attitudes military leaders rightly must prize: the public's support for raising and maintaining strong armed forces and public attitudes about the sort of missions the military should be assigned to conduct.

While the data do not permit drawing neat causal arrows between military public affairs campaigns and military cooperation with Hollywood that attempt to boost confidence in the military and individual recruiting decisions, there is enough evidence that exposure to portrayals of the military in popular culture is linked with higher confidence among younger Americans of recruiting age. Moreover, other Americans—the parents, friends, or aunts and uncles of potential recruits—with high levels of confidence in the military are more likely to advise friends and family members to consider military service than are those with low confidence.

This confidence effect also appears to shape attitudes about the military budget, though often in relative rather than absolute ways. More confident Americans—and this is especially true of Republicans in the post-9/11 era—are more likely to support higher military budgets, but other fiscal and domestic factors likely shape the context of budget debates in even more critical ways.

In sum, this chapter marshaled both longitudinal and survey evidence to suggest that military leaders have good reasons to pay attention to what Americans think of them. The personnel, fiscal, and political support the military requires will likely be boosted—or lowered—depending on fluctuations in the level of confidence Americans place in their military.

Of course, support for raising, maintaining, and using strong armed forces is just one set of attitudes that are important for policy. Just as important are views on whether and how the military should be used as an instrument of foreign policy. The next chapter explores the links between public confidence and those policy concerns.

9

Whether and How Confidence Shapes Views on the Military as an Instrument of Foreign Policy

> During a campaign swing through Ohio this week, former vice president Joe Biden promised that if he is elected president, he will let "the troops decide" where the United States should invade next. "For too long, political leaders from both sides of the aisle have used the military in questionable adventures overseas, often in the pursuit of ambiguous strategic goals," said Biden to supporters. "That's not likely to change, to be honest. But what we can change is how we choose where we're going. Who here wouldn't rather invade, say, Rio de Janeiro for some sweet oil instead of Fallujah. . . ." The Trump administration dismissed the idea as costly and misguided. "Biden is completely out of touch with what the troops want," said White House spokesperson Kaleigh McEnany. "Here's the deal: Make America Great again in November, and we'll let them invade the Blue State of their choice. California may be full of radical Democrats, but it has some incredible beaches."
> —Fake news report on satirical military website Duffelblog (2020b)

The previous chapter explored public attitudes toward giving the military what it needs, that is, the "means," to do its job and how confidence in the military might be linked to those attitudes. This chapter explores the connections between public confidence in the military and views on what the military's job ought to be, that is, the "ends" to which the military might be put.[1] A core principle of national security is that the military is not an end to itself. The military sees itself—and the public sees the military—as a means to other ends, most fundamentally preserving the conditions for American citizens to enjoy peace and prosperity. In other words, the military is a tool, a very capable and adaptable tool, but a tool to be wielded for discrete purposes. How does confidence in

---

[1] Portions of this chapter were presented as Golby and Feaver (2021c).

the military relate to the ways the public thinks about the military as a tool, and what does this tell us about the policy impact of rising or declining confidence in the military?

Support for Using the Military

For Americans to enjoy peace and prosperity, the constitutional order must be secure. Officers who join the military swear to defend the Constitution against all enemies, foreign and domestic, and the day-to-day business of being a member of the armed forces is preparing for the day when that kind of action is necessary. While almost everyone would agree that this is the intended purpose of the military, there is wide disagreement about what is the best way to approach applying military means to these larger societal ends.

The common hawk-versus-dove label is a heuristic that intuitively captures some of these dynamics; compared to doves, hawks generally view proposed missions as more important, view the military as more useful on any given mission, view the military as more useful across a wider range of missions, and are more committed to seeing a given mission through to a successful conclusion. A respondent's underlying hawkish or dovishness is likely to shape how that respondent might approach any given use of force, with hawks being more inclined to support the use of the military (because they think the mission is important and think the military is useful in addressing this problem) than are doves. Once military force is committed, moreover, a hawk generally would be more inclined to continue the mission to a successful conclusion, while a dove would be more willing to abandon the fight and cut one's losses.[2]

However, American public attitudes do not fit neatly along a single hawk-dove dimension. It is possible that some individuals may be hawkish on particular types of missions (e.g., overseas humanitarian missions), but not on others (e.g., overseas counterterrorism operations) and vice versa. Prior research has shown that views on the best uses of the military can be distinguished along a "realpolitik" to "humanitarian" spectrum (Holsti 1996). The realpolitik view

---

[2] Hawkishness can be measured on an individual mission basis or as an overall orientation. Thus, some are "hawkish on climate change," assessing it to be a major threat and believing that the military has a crucial role to play in addressing it. It is logically possible to be a "climate change hawk" but otherwise quite dovish, believing other threats to be overhyped and not amenable to military solutions. But the wider the range of threats one deems urgent priorities, and the more one sees a role for the military in confronting the threats, the more hawkish one is. Thus, someone who wants the military at the forefront of confronting climate change, rising China, and transnational networks of militant islamist groups is more "hawkish" than someone who only thinks China or climate change or terrorism is a threat worthy of a military role.

holds that the military is best reserved for "conventional" military threats such as those posed by great power rivals, or rogue states pursuing weapons of mass destruction, or foreign terrorists who are willing to strike against US interests at home or abroad. The humanitarian view holds that those conventional missions are not the only important assignments for which the military must prepare; in addition are other tasks, such as providing humanitarian and disaster relief at home or abroad, intervening in civil wars abroad, and so on. An extreme humanitarian view might go so far as to say that the traditional uses are receding in importance and have been replaced by these other tasks as the primary role for the military.[3]

One can describe a significant portion of the national security conversation since the fall of the Soviet Union as one long debate over the relative importance of realpolitik versus humanitarian missions for the US military.[4] At least in the post–Cold War era, the military as an institution has tended to believe that "realpolitik" missions are the more important and urgent ones, and thus the appropriate focus of their efforts; of course, the military has also conducted many "humanitarian" missions over the past three decades, but more begrudgingly. Civilian elites, however, have been more open to humanitarian ones (Feaver and Gelpi 2004; Recchia 2015). This pattern, however, may be heavily shaped by an underlying partisan divide along this same dimension, with Republicans favoring a realpolitik approach and Democrats favoring the humanitarian approach (Golby 2011), at least during the post-Cold War era.

In recent years, however, dissatisfaction with the cost and ambivalent outcomes of the foreign military interventions launched in response to the 9/11 attacks raised a new (or perhaps better described as renewed) attention to the question of whether the United States should be focused at home or abroad (Kupchan 2020). President Obama campaigned and won on a claim that "it is time to start nation building at home" (Obama 2012a). He won reelection while mocking Mitt Romney's warning about renewed geopolitical tensions and boasting about ending combat operations abroad (Holland 2012; Rayfield

---

[3] The realpolitik vs. humanitarian typology is something of a continuum. Even within the realpolitik category, one can array different tasks along the spectrum of threats, with great power conflict at one end, transnational terrorists threats at the other end, and rogue state nuclear programs somewhere in between. Likewise, within the humanitarian category not all tasks are equally demanding or controversial. For instance, the military services have generally not resisted low-demand humanitarian relief operations—for instance, delivering aid after earthquakes and tsunamis—as much as they have resisted interventions in bloody civil wars.

[4] Of course, the conventional or traditional labels are themselves misleading. Since the founding of the Republic, the US military has been used in missions that fall along every part of the spectrum. One of the very earliest uses of the American military once independence was secured was to put down civil conflict arising from a tax on whiskey (Kohn 1975).

2012). Obama was succeeded by Donald Trump, the candidate who promised an "America First" approach that would be the biggest break with the foreign policy platforms of the Republican and Democratic presidential nominees of the post–Cold War era (McTague and Nicholas 2020). To be sure, Trump also promised to take the gloves off in any foreign fights with terrorists and likewise promised to confront China more directly than any previous American leader had done. There were enough contradictions within the Trump platform to make coding it on any scale an imprecise task. Yet the cumulative effect of the last dozen years of foreign policy debate within the United States clearly points to the need to expand the rubric beyond the procrustean bed of realpolitik versus humanitarian.

Accordingly, the argument here is that the range of debate can better be captured by measuring differences of opinion along two dimensions. One dimension is the orientation, whether outwardly focused on dealing with problems "over there" before they become problems "over here." In terms of military missions, this translates into foreign involvement, whether focused on the realpolitik missions of great powers or the humanitarian missions of intervening in civil wars. The other dimension is the focus, whether on threats, such as great power rivals and domestic disorder, or on values, such as the plight of refugees abroad or social discrimination at home. These two dimensions can intersect to produce a familiar two-by-two matrix, with each cell amounting to a possible mission priority for the military. Viewed this way, the realpolitik-versus-humanitarian debates that dominated the first 15 years or so of the post–Cold War era were largely about options from within a menu of outwardly oriented tasks; domestic missions were in the mix, to be sure, but far less salient. In the last 15 years, a set of inwardly oriented missions has grown in prominence, and this trend intensified in the later years of the Trump administration.

The different mission priorities are summarized in Table 9.1. In theory, an individual might believe that the military should prioritize just one of the cells. In practice, however, political leaders might see an advantage in combining the cells when making their appeals to constituents. Trump, for instance, mostly emphasized the threats vector, warning about foreign terrorists and great power

Table 9.1 **Range of Potential Mission Priorities for the Military**

		Orientation	
		Outwardly Oriented	*Inwardly Oriented*
Focus	**Threat-based**	Realpolitik	Homeland Security
	Values-based	Humanitarian (Foreign Social Work)	Domestic Social Work

rivalry with China, as well as emphasizing the alleged dangers of illegal immigration at home. In doing so, he attacked so-called globalists or internationalists, who might share some of his concerns about a rising China, but who also may be concerned about the plight of refugees abroad while being comparatively less concerned about immigration. Trump also attacked both those who prioritized values-based missions involving humanitarian intervention abroad and those who thought the military should play a key role in addressing long-standing racial justice concerns at home.

Although this framework provides a useful tool to categorize and assess public attitudes about various military missions, there is not a strong theoretical reason to expect that public confidence in the military would operate in different ways across each category. It does seem likely, a priori, that confidence shapes support for all these missions. To explore this relationship, one must disaggregate support into two related, yet analytically distinct attitudes: (i) the importance of the mission, and (ii) the usefulness, or effectiveness, of the military in accomplishing this mission. It is logically possible that some individuals will view a particular mission or set of missions as important but still believe that military tools are mostly ineffective—or at least not very useful—in fulfilling that mission; or vice -versa, that the military is actually a quite capable tool in achieving a certain mission, but it is not important enough to be a priority for the military.

What is not known is how public confidence in the military relates to these attitudes. Logically, one can imagine several plausible patterns. For instance, someone with high confidence in the military might think the military is good at anything and everything and so would embrace the both-and form of the older humanitarian approach. But it is also possible that people with high confidence in the military might be more likely to think about these matters in the manner that many in the military themselves view them, namely by favoring a realpolitik approach. And it could be that partisanship interacts with confidence, so Republicans with high confidence are the most wedded to the realpolitik approach and Democrats with high confidence are the most wedded to the humanitarian approach. In any case, the expectation here is that confidence in the military would have its greatest effect in shaping views about how *useful* the military was in conducting various missions, and only less of an effect, if any, in shaping views about what sorts of missions are *important*. At the same time, people with especially low confidence in the military would likely think the military is not very useful in any of these missions.

The results from Wave 2 of the survey shed considerable light on these matters. The survey asked respondents two batteries of questions, each covering a range of possible uses of the military: "The following are some possible uses of the military. Please indicate <u>how important</u> you consider each potential role for the military. A. Very important. B. Somewhat important. C. Not very important.

D. No opinion." Next, the survey asked respondents, "Here are those same possible uses. Please indicate how useful the military is in addressing these issues, regardless of how important a role you consider it to be. For instance, something can be very important, but the military may be very limited in addressing it; or the military may have great utility, but the issue is of low importance. A. Very useful. B. Somewhat useful. C. Not very useful. D. No opinion." This battery of possible uses was adapted from Feaver and Gelpi (2004), which itself built on Holsti (1996), but then added several new questions to capture whether respondents distinguish between different configurations of the orientation of the mission (domestic or international) and the focus of the mission (threat-based or values-based):

1. To fight and win our country's wars.
2. To redress historical discrimination, for instance against African Americans and women.
3. To provide disaster relief within the United States.
4. To address humanitarian needs abroad.
5. To deal with domestic disorder within the United States.
6. To intervene in civil wars abroad.
7. To combat drug trafficking.
8. To compete with great powers like China and Russia.

This battery is mapped on to the Orientation versus Focus dimensions as indicated in Table 9.2. The correlation matrices reported in the technical appendix

Table 9.2 **Mapping Questions onto the Potential Mission Priorities of the Military**

		Orientation	
		Outwardly Oriented	*Inwardly Oriented*
Focus	**Threat-based**	Realpolitik	Homeland Security
		1. Fight and win 8. Compete with great powers	5. Domestic disorder 7. Drug trafficking
	Values-based	Humanitarian (Foreign Social Work)	Domestic Social Work
		4. Address humanitarian needs 6. Intervene in civil wars	2. Address historical discrimination 3. Disaster relief

(available here: https://dataverse.harvard.edu/dataverse/pfeaver) reveal that the paired questions in three of the boxes in the table hang together reasonably well, with correlations for each pair of at least .42 on the importance questions and at least .52 on the usefulness questions; the questions in the Humanitarian square (.38, .39) hang together slightly less well. Factor analysis including all questions from both the Importance and Usefulness scales allows a further exploration of the validity of this framework. The technical appendix contains all factor loadings as well as the scree plot. This analysis revealed four latent factors. The first was a factor centered on the Usefulness scale, with especially high loadings on usefulness questions related to disaster relief, humanitarian intervention, drug trafficking, and domestic disorder. The next two factors largely mirrored the threat-based categories in the framework focused on importance. However, the Realpolitik scale also included a high, but negative factor loading for the racial discrimination question, and the Homeland Security scale also included a moderate, but negative factor loading for the humanitarian intervention abroad question. The final factor focused on the importance and usefulness of intervening in civil wars, though the importance of disaster relief was also a highly loaded, but negative factor on this scale.

On the whole, the factor analysis reveals several interesting things. First, although the Importance and Usefulness scales are correlated, respondents do make a distinction between these two dimensions of military missions. Second, respondents also appear to draw clear distinctions between threat-based missions abroad and at home, though values-based missions sometimes overlap in unexpected ways. For the most part, however, respondents do seem to think about domestic and overseas missions somewhat differently. And finally, respondents appear to treat intervention in civil wars as a somewhat special case in terms of both its importance and usefulness.

Accordingly, this typology seems sufficiently useful to serve the purposes here—namely to see how confidence in the military is related to how Americans think about using the military on operational assignments—even though further research is necessary to establish this construct as the optimal way to sort public attitudes toward the use of force more generally.[5] Accordingly, the following

---

[5] At the beginning of the analysis, the baseline assumption was that the familiar Realpolitik vs. Humanitarian scale would suffice and so this new typology was not discussed in the registration of the survey with Evidence in Governance and Politics (EGAP) (Ref #: 20200909AA, accessible here: https://osf.io/58gz6). When preliminary analysis discovered that the familiar scale was not working as well as it had in previous studies, that led to a reconsideration of the larger question in light of what is known about foreign policy debates over the past decade. That led to the theorization of this new typology before determining whether the data supported it. This is a fruitful area for future research and I encourage other scholars to see if this typology might add value to other types of foreign policy analysis.

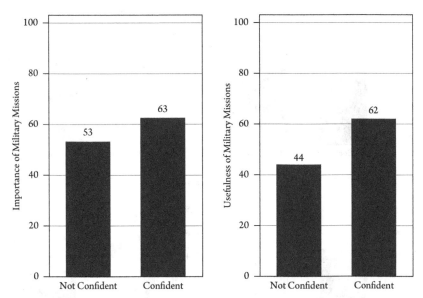

The relationship between confidence and the scale variables is statistically significant at the 99% confidence level in an OLS regression model of the whole sample, controlling for standard demographic variables and treatment conditions.

Figure 9.1 Overall Importance and Usefulness of Military Missions by Confidence Level (2020)

analyses use this construct, noting only a few cases where scaling would otherwise obscure important insights.

Figure 9.1 displays the mean support of aggregate Importance and Usefulness scales, where 0 reflects the lowest possible rating for importance or usefulness and 1 captures the highest possible assessment.[6] The pattern for both scales is clear: confidence in the military is a positive and statistically significant predictor of individual support for both the importance and usefulness of the military missions asked about in the aggregate. While both scales display a similar pattern, the slope of the Usefulness scale is slightly more positive than the Importance scale, reflecting the fact that confidence in the military plays a more significant role in shaping how people think about the military's utility than it does in determining how critical they believe potential missions to be. This

---

[6] All the figures presented in this chapter code 0 as those respondents who expressed "no opinion" on the question. Sensitivity analyses with those respondents omitted did not change the substantive results. Because those stating that they had "no opinion" are correlated with those expressing "very little" confidence in the military, including them distorts the appearance of most figures by causing a "spike" among respondents with "very little" confidence. Since there are not many of those respondents, that spike has very large confidence intervals and does not fundamentally change the results of the statistical models.

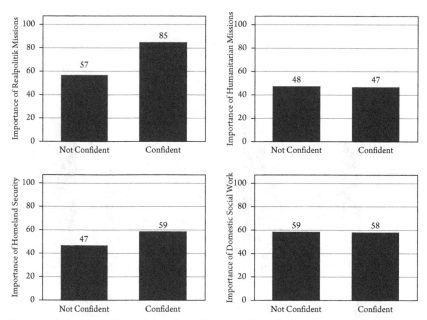

The relationship between confidence and the scale variables is statistically significant at the 99% confidence level in an OLS regression model for only the threat-based scales.

Figure 9.2 Importance of Different Military Missions by Confidence Level (2020)

result is consistent with the findings in Chapters 4 and 5, which demonstrated that military competence—both real and perceived—is one of the most important factors undergirding elevated confidence levels.

Figure 9.2 displays the relationship between confidence in the military and the importance of all four mission priorities displayed in Table 9.2. As expected, the threat-based Realpolitik and Homeland Security mission scales have the most support—.89 and .74 on a one-point scale among those respondents with a great deal of confidence in the military—as well as strong and statistically significant relationships with public confidence. Although confidence in the military is still positively related to both the Humanitarian and Domestic Social Work missions, the relationship between confidence and support for the values-based missions is far more modest. Confidence is a statistically significant predictor of support for humanitarian missions, but not for military missions on the Domestic scale.

To a large degree, however, the weakness of this relationship is the result of answers to the question about the importance of the military in redressing historical discrimination. Figure 9.3 displays both questions in the Domestic scale, and the difference between the two patterns is stark. There is strong agreement that domestic disaster relief is an important military mission in general as well as a clear and statistically significant relationship between respondents' confidence

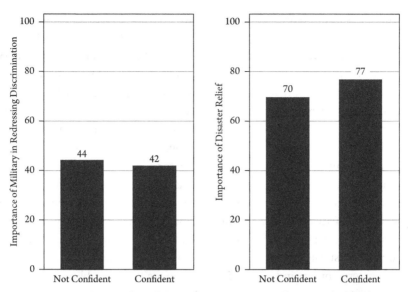

The relationship between confidence and the scale variables is statistically significant at the 99% confidence level in an OLS regression model only for the disaster relief variable.

Figure 9.3 Importance of Domestic Military Missions by Confidence Level (2020)

in the military and the degree of importance they assign to disaster relief as a military mission, even when controlling for other factors in multivariate analysis. In contrast, the desire to have the military redress historical discrimination as part of its mission is middling, with the mean of respondents' support for this type of mission hovering near the middle of the one-point scale across all levels of confidence.[7] The .56 scores among those with a "great deal" and "quite a lot" of confidence are not statistically different from the .51 mean among those respondents expressing "very little" confidence in the military.

---

[7] This result was not anticipated, but it is possible this survey result reflects the highly charged racial environment of the post–George Floyd era and, in particular, the debate over the use of troops to deal with the protests that erupted over the summer of 2020. For decades, the military enjoyed a positive reputation in the area of race relations. The success and prominence of General Colin Powell, the nation's first African American chairman of the Joint Chiefs of Staff, underscored a larger narrative that the military, through diligent effort, had made great strides in dealing with the scourge of racism within its ranks (Moskos and Butler 1996). Asking the public about using the military "to redress historical discrimination, for instance against African-Americans and women" in the Powell era or shortly thereafter might have evoked this understanding. But when the survey was conducted in September–October 2020, after a summer of sharply polarizing debates over race and the use of the military in response to public protests over race, the frame may have shifted in the public mind. And later, after the January 6 attacks on the US Capitol raised questions about how pervasive were sympathies for white supremacist ideology among serving military and veterans, the frame may have shifted yet again. This is another issue worth investigating further in follow-on work.

There is some interesting variation across parties in terms of both overall support for certain military missions and in terms of the relationship between confidence in the military and enthusiasm for the importance of particular missions. As you can see in Figure 9.4, Republicans and Democrats are about equally likely to support realpolitik missions as being important for the military. However, Democrats are more likely to believe that missions involving values-based goals are important for the military, while Republicans are more likely to approve of homeland security missions. For each of these three mission categories, confidence is also a weaker predictor of mission importance among the party expressing greater support than it is among respondents from the less enthusiastic party: confidence has more of an impact among Democrats for homeland security missions and among Republicans for values-based missions. This pattern does not hold for the Realpolitik category, where confidence is a large and statistically significant predictor of mission importance. A variation of this pattern appears in Figure 9.5, too, where neither Republican support for interventions in civil wars nor Democratic support for overseas humanitarian missions is dependent on confidence in the military.

Figure 9.1 shows that the relationship between confidence in the military and respondents' rating of how useful the military would be for a given mission was strong and statistically significant, even stronger than it was for their ratings of how important particular categories of missions are. This positive, statistically significant relationship holds across all mission priorities, even when controlling for party and other demographic variables. The only exceptions to this pattern are shown in Figure 9.6. Although confidence is a strong predictor of whether independents and Republicans think the military will be useful for overseas humanitarian and domestic disaster relief missions, Democrats believe the military is useful for these missions regardless of their level of confidence. In part, this result may indirectly depend on value trade-offs. While Democrats may be more likely to be "hawkish" on these types of values-based missions, Republicans may be hesitant to use the military in these situations out of fear that it would make military personnel or resources less available for the threat-based missions they see as more important.

While there are some differences across parties with respect to particular mission priorities, the results so far suggest that more confident respondents are generally more hawkish than less confident respondents. Confidence did have a significant impact on how respondents rated the importance of mission priorities in almost all cases, but this effect was even stronger and more consistent across mission priorities with respect to how useful, or effective, the military would be if called to play a role in a particular type of mission.

As shown in the analysis of defense spending, however, asking respondents to grapple with trade-offs, particularly the trade-offs between military and

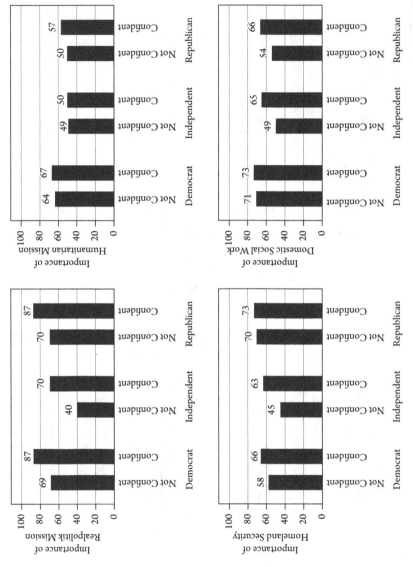

Figure 9.4 Importance of Military Missions Categories by Confidence Level and Party (2020)

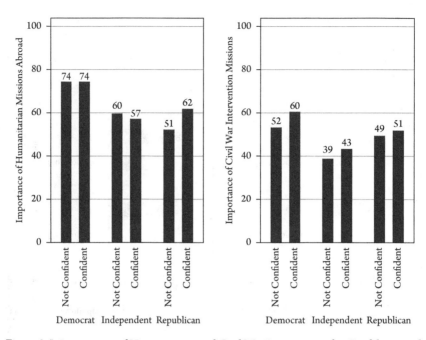

Figure 9.5 Importance of Humanitarian and Civil War Interventions by Confidence and Party (2020)

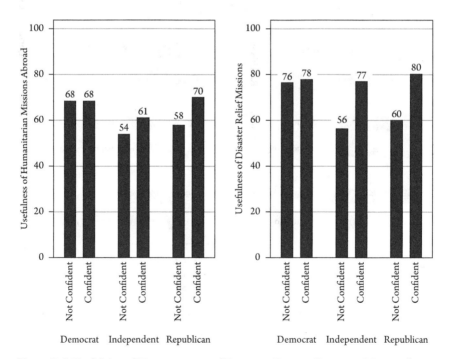

Figure 9.6 Usefulness of Humanitarian and Domestic Disaster Response Missions by Confidence Level and Party (2020)

Table 9.3 **Views on Whether Diplomacy or Military Force Causes More Problems**

	More Problems with Diplomacy			More Problems with Military Fornbce		
	Overall	Confident	Not Confident	Overall	Confident	Not Confident
Agree	24%	28%	11%	39%	41%	33%
	(74)	(66)	(8)	(121)	(91)	(30)
Neither	37%	35%	44%	44%	40%	56%
	(115)	(85)	(30)	(137)	(87)	(50)
Disagree	39%	37%	45%	17%	19%	11%
	(119)	(89)	(30)	(52)	(42)	(10)
Total	100%	100%	100%	100%	100%	100%
	(308)	(240)	(68)	(310)	(220)	(90)

diplomatic capabilities, can help clarify their preferences. Wave 1 of the survey put the question to the respondents more or less directly, asking them to indicate their level of agreement with the following statements: "A. There tend to be more problems when you use non-military tools like sanctions and diplomacy than when you use military force to address foreign policy issues. B. There tend to be more problems when you use military force than when you use diplomatic tools like sanctions and diplomacy to address foreign policy issues." The results are in Table 9.3.

Across the board, respondents were skeptical of military force relative to diplomacy. Regardless of how the question is phrased, nearly 40% of respondents agreed that military force causes more problems than diplomacy. Another 40% chose to neither agree nor disagree when forced to choose between diplomacy or force, while 19%–28% of respondents chose the more "hawkish" response depending on which version of the question they received. Respondents who expressed confidence in the military were more hawkish than their less confident counterparts, though only moderately so. Among confident respondents, 28% agreed that diplomacy causes more problems than military force while 37% disagreed—a nine-point difference—compared to a 34% net difference among those who do not express confidence in the military. When asked in terms of whether military force causes more problems than diplomacy, however, the difference between confident and less confident respondents was similarly modest but in a counterintuitive direction—with 41% of confident respondents agreeing that military force causes more problems, compared to only 33% of those who did not express confidence in the military. Confident respondents were also slightly more likely to disagree with the statement, however, making

Table 9.4 **Support for Drone or Special Operations Forces Attacks against Overseas Threats**

	Support Drone Attacks			Support SOF Attacks		
	Overall	Confident	Not Confident	Overall	Confident	Not Confident
Yes	62%	72%	28%	74%	80%	58%
	(191)	(172)	(19)	(226)	(175)	(51)
No	10%	6%	25%	9%	5%	19%
	(32)	(15)	(17)	(28)	(11)	(17)
Not sure	28%	22%	47%	17%	15%	23%
	(84)	(52)	(32)	(54)	(33)	(21)
Total	100%	100%	100%	100%	100%	100%
	(307)	(239)	(68)	(308)	(219)	(89)

Note: The relationship between confidence and the outcome variable is statistically significant at the 99% confidence level in a logistic regression, controlling for standard demographic variables.

the net support among both confident and not confident respondents roughly the same at 22%. On the other hand, the fact that the choice between diplomacy and military force as the nation's tool of first resort is so close might be evidence, in and of itself, of the extent of hawkish tendencies within the American populace—or perhaps just evidence that the public harbors a substantial dose of skepticism about the record of diplomacy alone in addressing thorny global problems.

Further evidence comes from questions related to potential uses of military force taken from contemporary headlines. Wave 1 put a number of questions to respondents related to the use of targeted killings—via drones or special operations forces—in other countries against people deemed a threat to the United States.[8] As discussed above, a hawk is someone who is relatively more supportive of the use of force or someone who opposes the withdrawal of troops who are currently engaged overseas. Table 9.4 displays the results.

Respondents in the survey were overwhelmingly supportive of targeted killings overseas against people deemed a threat to the United States, regardless of the means: 62% of respondents said they supported drone attacks, and 74% of respondents said they supported attacks by special operation forces while

---

[8] The two questions posed were: (1) Do you think the US government should be allowed to use drones to carry out attacks in other countries on people deemed a threat to the United States? and (2) Do you think the US government should be allowed to use special operations forces to carry out attacks in other countries on people deemed a threat to the United States?

only 10% reported that they opposed these practices. Once again, confidence in the military is a major and statistically significant predictor of support for these questions. A total of 72% of respondents with confidence in the military are supportive of drone attacks, compared to only 28% of those who do not express confidence, a 44-point difference. Although a majority 58% of respondents who do not express confidence in the military still support special operations attacks against overseas threats, the gap between confident respondents and those without confidence is 22 points. Regardless of the means of attack the military uses, there is a large and statistically significant relationship between confidence and support for targeted killings against threats to the United States overseas.

Across the two waves, the survey also asked specific questions about several potential—or ongoing—military missions. As Figure 9.7 shows, confidence in the military is a statistically significant predictor of support for potential strikes against Iran's nuclear program, a hypothetical invocation of the Insurrection Act that would allow federal troops to conduct law enforcement tasks against protestors on domestic soil, and the 2018 troop deployment to secure the southern border—even when controlling for party identification. For all missions, however, support among Republicans remains high overall compared to Democrats and independents. In fact, Republicans without confidence in the military are not statistically different from Democrats or independents who do express confidence for the Iran strikes and Insurrection Act mission, and members of the GOP are significantly more supportive of the mission on the southern border than either Democrats or independents. Although one's party identification does appear to play the dominant role in shaping one's attitudes about the use of force in these scenarios, confidence also plays an important supportive role.

Given the importance of both the Afghanistan and Iraq wars in ongoing debates about national security since September 11, Wave 1 also asked respondents for their retrospective assessments of these wars. Half sample were asked: "Do you think the United States made a mistake sending troops to Afghanistan in 2001?" The other half instead answered: "Do you think the United States made a mistake sending troops to Iraq in 2003?" These results are in Table 9.5.

Overall, respondents remain generally supportive of the initial decision to initiate the war in Afghanistan in 2001 and somewhat mixed on the question of whether the choice to launch the 2003 Iraq war was a good idea. In the aggregate, 44% of respondents disagreed that the Afghanistan war was a mistake, while only 29% of respondents agreed it was. There was also a slight, but not significant, advantage for supporters of the Iraq war: 41% responded that war was not a mistake, whereas 37% said that it was a bad call. Even controlling for party and other demographic factors, however, confidence in the military again was a strong and significant predictor of retrospective judgments about

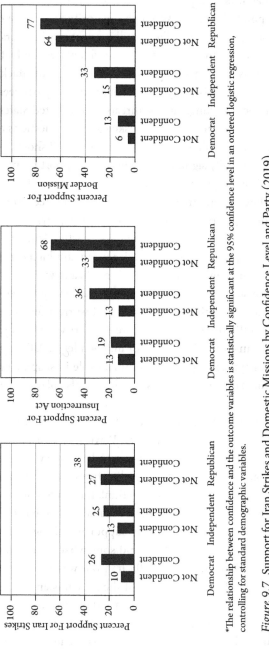

Figure 9.7 Support for Iran Strikes and Domestic Missions by Confidence Level and Party (2019)

*The relationship between confidence and the outcome variables is statistically significant at the 95% confidence level in an ordered logistic regression, controlling for standard demographic variables.

Table 9.5 **Retrospective Attitudes about the Afghanistan and Iraq Wars in 2019 by Confidence Level**

	Afghanistan Was a Mistake			Iraq Was a Mistake*		
	Overall	Confident	Not Confident	Overall	Confident	Not Confident
Yes	29%	26%	41%	37%	34%	44%
	(90)	(62)	(28)	(113)	(74)	(39)
No	44%	50%	24%	41%	46%	30%
	(136)	(120)	(16)	(128)	(101)	(27)
Not sure	27%	24%	35%	22%	20%	26%
	(82)	(59)	(24)	(67)	(44)	(23)
Total	100%	100%	100%	100%	100%	100%
	(308)	(240)	(68)	(308)	(219)	(89)

* Denotes that the relationship between confidence and the outcome variable is statistically significant at the 99% confidence level in a logistic regression, controlling for standard demographic variables.

the wisdom of initiating these two wars. A 50% majority and a 46% plurality of confident respondents said the wars in Afghanistan and Iraq were not a mistake, respectively.

Throughout this chapter, a consistent pattern has emerged: Americans who express more confidence in the military also espouse more hawkish attitudes about various aspects of military policy. Table 9.6 shows the results for a set of two questions about the wars in Afghanistan and Iraq that do not appear to follow this general pattern. Wave 1 not only asked respondents about whether they believed the decision to start the war was a mistake, but also about whether they would support the removal of all US troops from these two nations. One group of respondents was asked: "If the President authorized the removal of all US troops from Afghanistan, would you support that decision?" and a second group was asked, "If the President authorized the removal of all US troops from Iraq, would you support that decision?"

As Table 9.6 shows, in the summer of 2019, there was broad support for withdrawal from Afghanistan and Iraq—with narrow majorities supporting withdrawal from both nations. The survey treated the wars separately, and the results do show at least some differentiation between how the public views each; but it is possible that respondents also mentally group them together under some sort of "endless wars" pejorative label. For the purposes here, however, of greater interest is the relationship between confidence in the military and support for troop withdrawals. Although confident respondents were more supportive of removing troops from Afghanistan, even this difference was not statistically

Table 9.6 Support for Withdrawing Troops from Afghanistan and Iraq in 2019 by Confidence Level

	Support Afghanistan Withdrawal			Support Iraq Withdrawal		
	Overall	Confident	Not Confident	Overall	Confident	Not Confident
Yes	55%	59%	45%	50%	49%	53%
	(170)	(130)	(40)	(153)	(118)	(36)
No	24%	23%	24%	13%	15%	10%
	(72)	(51)	(21)	(42)	(35)	(7)
Not sure	21%	17%	31%	37%	36%	38%
	(66)	(38)	(28)	(113)	(87)	(25)
Total	100%	100%	100%	100%	100%	100%
	(308)	(219)	(89)	(308)	(240)	(68)

Note: The relationship between confidence in the military and support for withdrawal from Afghanistan (or Iraq) is not statistically significant in a logistic regression, controlling for standard demographic variables.

significant after controlling for party and other demographic variables in a logistic regression model. Nor was there a statistically significant relationship between confidence and support for withdrawal from Iraq.

Given the consistency of the relationship otherwise demonstrated between confidence in the military and hawkishness, these results are somewhat surprising. It is even more perplexing that Republicans—who have expressed more hawkish attitudes and sometimes have shown a stronger relationship between confidence in the military and these hawkish opinions—appear to be the ones most responsible for this reversal. One clue to explain this puzzle may be the fact that this reversal is largest for the case of Afghanistan, where President Trump invested a large amount of political capital in an effort both to reduce troop levels and to reduce support for the war. In the aggregate, approximately 55% of both Democrats and Republicans said they supported complete troop withdrawals from Afghanistan in 2019. While there were no differences between confident and not confident Democrats, Republicans who reported confidence in the military were 13 points higher at 58% than were those Republicans who did not express confidence in the military at 45%. Although it is possible that the relationship between confidence in the military and withdrawal decisions operates differently than it does for the other measures we have explored throughout the chapter, it seems more likely that Donald Trump's messaging played a key role in altering the views of many members of the GOP, at least on these specific issues. It remains unclear whether, or how long, Trump's cross-cutting narratives will continue to influence foreign policy views within the Republican Party.

Conclusion

Respondents with high esteem for the military are more likely to think the military is an important and useful tool across a range of potential military missions. Confidence is a marginally better predictor of the military's usefulness, regardless of mission type, which is consistent with previous findings in Chapters 4 and 5 that a respondent's perception of military performance is a strong predictor of confidence. Once again, however, partisan considerations often intervene depending on the focus and orientation of the mission. Indeed, as with many other issues in American politics, partisanship likely is doing quite a lot of the work in driving attitudes regarding how and when to use the military. In general, Republicans tend to be more hawkish than Democrats on threat-based missions, while Democrats tend to be more hawkish than Republicans on values-based missions. Although confidence is uniformly a good predictor of military importance and usefulness across parties for realpolitik missions, a respondent's partisan identification mitigates the effects of confidence for other types of missions. Confidence is not a good predictor of Democrats' views about the importance or usefulness of the military for values-based missions, but it is for Republicans. The same holds in reverse for homeland security missions, with confidence driving attitudes about using the military for Democrats but not for Republicans. Somewhat perplexingly, however, neither confidence nor party provides clear and consistent results on withdrawal decisions from Iraq and Afghanistan. It seems highly likely that President Trump's rhetoric about withdrawal played an important role in shaping these attitudes, but whether those changes were fleeting or persistent—and whether new dynamics emerged after the chaotic end to US involvement in Afghanistan in August 2021—is a question for future research.

Of course, the surveys focused on the long-lasting conflicts of the global war on terror. By 2019, the initial public enthusiasm for both conflicts had long since abated, and very few elites were making strong and prominent arguments to buck up public support. On the contrary, elite debate had shifted to the possibility of higher-intensity conflict against a near-peer rival, especially China. And by 2022, the public was gripped with the reality of a Russia/NATO scenario after Putin's unprovoked invasion of Ukraine. Future research should explore whether the dynamics identified here hold across high-intensity war or whether they are just an artifact of the unusually long-lasting, but relatively low-cost wars of the global war on terror.

The analyses in this and the previous chapter established that confidence in the military is linked to a range of views that are quite properly priority concerns for civilian and military leaders alike: support for raising, maintaining, and using strong armed forces. However, public confidence in the military may also be linked to other attitudes that have a profound impact on the military as an institution: the set of prerogatives and privileges that the military as an institution enjoys—in some cases, uniquely enjoys—in American society. The next chapter engages those issues head-on.

10
Whether and How Confidence Shapes Intangible Benefits Enjoyed by the Military

> If you wanna go after General Kelly, that's up to you, but I think that—if you want to get into a debate with a four-star Marine general, I think that that's something highly inappropriate.
> —White House press secretary Sarah Sanders, October 2017 (Merica 2017)

In October 2017, President Trump made a telephone call to a widow of a soldier killed while on patrol in Niger. The president intended to provide some comfort to the widow, and used language suggested to him by his chief of staff, retired four-star marine general John Kelly—someone who knew from firsthand experience the pain of losing a close loved one in combat. The telephone conversation did not go well, and the widow accused the president of insensitivity. In response, Kelly gave a rare, televised press conference criticizing the member of Congress who overheard the widow's conversation with Trump and accusing both the member and the widow of politicizing the tragedy. The press conference itself went poorly, and critics counteraccused Kelly of insensitively attacking a member of Congress and misstating some of the facts of an earlier interaction he had had with the member (Drezner 2017). Soon the White House was doubly on the defensive, defending Trump's original phone call and Kelly's own unsuccessful efforts at damage control. In the heat of that rhetorical battle, White House press secretary Sarah Sanders offered an extraordinary challenge to reporters, quoted in the epigraph to this chapter.

Even to modern ears, Sanders's suggestion that members of the US military were beyond critique was a bit off-key. But viewed in historical context, in light of the deep background of the Republic's founding and the long history of American civil-military relations, Sanders's effort to deploy the prestige of the military as an impenetrable shield was jarring. Leading figures in the Revolutionary era were reflexively skeptical of armed forces—at best viewing a standing professional military as a necessary risk and at worst viewing it as an enduring threat to liberty.[1] Ever since, one can trace a strong strand of antimilitarism throughout American culture, especially political culture (Ekirch 1956). To be sure, the public also lavished affection and favors on the military, particularly the citizen-soldier military mobilized during major wars—the Civil War, World War I, and World War II. And there was certainly the occasional military hero from among the professional ranks—in the Civil War, General Lee for Southerners and General Grant for Northerners, or in World War I, General Pershing, or in World War II, Generals Marshall, Eisenhower, Bradley, and above all MacArthur. MacArthur, in particular, seems the best historical precedent for an individual military professional who thought himself above criticism and who enjoyed enough popularity to sustain that view, at least for a while (Brands 2016). Yet, on the whole, the professional standing army was viewed more equivocally than the citizens mobilized in times of crisis . . . until the last three decades, when those professionals started to enjoy a special status that would have struck earlier generations as highly unusual and perhaps even un-American.

Policymakers view public confidence in the military as important because, as explained in the previous chapter, they have reason to believe that confidence is linked to public endorsement for the material support—recruits and budget—that the military needs to complete its mission. It also is linked to how the public views using the military to safeguard the country's security interests at home and abroad, which is the very purpose of the military and is therefore a central preoccupation of civilian and military leaders. This chapter explores whether public confidence is important in yet another way: how it might contribute to what one might call the "ideational benefits" enjoyed by the military.[2]

The term "ideational benefits" refers to a range of perks—some tangible, such as preferential seating in public venues, but most intangible, such as an insulation from criticism—that the public confers on the military. The perks can be explicit, as with the aforementioned preferential seating or preferential access to jobs. A case could be made that benefits this considerable could be thought of as part of the "concrete support" analyzed in the previous chapter. But they

---

[1] As Samuel Adams put it, "A Standing Army, however necessary it may be at some times, is always dangerous to the Liberties of the People. Soldiers are apt to consider themselves as a Body distinct from the rest of the Citizens. They have their Arms always in their hands. Their Rules and their Discipline is severe. They soon become attached to their officers and disposed to yield implicit obedience to their commands. Such a Power should be watched with a jealous Eye" (quoted in Kohn 1975, 2).

[2] Portions of this chapter were presented as Golby and Feaver (2021d).

seem better considered as "ideational" because they are more often implicit or voluntary, arising from the way the public thinks about the military. And more to the point, the public apparently thinks of these as part and parcel of the proper response to the willingness of the military to serve. The previous chapter, then, looked at the public's willingness to provide the military with the basic building blocks to provide for national security—people, budget, and mission. This chapter looks at how the public responds to that provision of national security, specifically the forms of gratitude, respect, and deference that the public believes the military has earned through its service.

This chapter examines the explicit and implicit forms this public response takes and explores the extent to which those forms might be linked to "confidence in the military." As explained earlier in Chapter 7, the fact that most Americans in recent decades profess high confidence in the military has achieved something like the status of a social fact that everyone knows—one that, to a certain extent, reinforces itself through peer pressure. This chapter explores whether public confidence in the military covaries with these other attitudes about the military's place in society, perhaps contributing to a perpetuation of these perks and social benefits.

Ideational benefits can be grouped into five baskets: (i) *privileges*, the special benefits and deference shown to the military in social settings; (ii) *pedestalizing*, the degree to which the military is venerated and held up as an ideal superior to civilian society (and worthy of emulation by civilian society); (iii) *prerogatives*, the degree to which the public is willing to grant to the military advantages or deference in the policymaking process it does not grant to others; (iv) *policy preferences*, the degree to which military endorsements affect public support for other policies; and (v) *pinning blame*, the degree to which the public blames or credits the military for policy outcomes.

The common theme across all these categories is civilian deference to the military: deferring to the military in airports, deferring to the military in the area of values, or deferring to the military in the policymaking and political process. The lines between these categories are blurry but are meaningful. For instance, privileges and pedestalizing are very closely linked phenomena related to the idea that the military services deserve special status because of the special sacrifices entailed in the military; privileges mostly refer to material perks that come with that status, whereas pedestalizing mostly refers to the mental posture that comes from viewing the military this way—especially the mental comparisons and contrasts one must make between civilian and military. The last three categories all involve the military's role in the policymaking or political process and capture the extent to which the public is willing to grant to the military, explicitly or implicitly, an advantaged position vis-à-vis civilian counterparts.

Ideational benefits may, in fact, *not* be beneficial for the military as an institution—or the nation—regardless of whether individual service members enjoy having them. Civil-military specialists have long worried that treating the military in an exalted fashion may be corrosive of the norms on which healthy democratic practices depend (Ricks 1997; Feaver and Kohn 2001; Golby, Cohn, and Feaver 2016; Robinson 2018; Golby and Karlin 2020; Friend 2017; Dunlap 2019) and may even be a sign of militarism (Ekirch 1956; Bacevich 2005; Brooks 2016; Carter and Schulman 2016; Friend and Hicks 2017). Whether civilian deference to the military crosses a line to the point of undermining civilian control is a normative judgment on which reasonable people can differ (Brooks, Golby, and Urben 2021a, 2021b; Schake 2021; Feaver 2021). The analyses in this chapter shore up the empirical foundation on which such normative debates must rest.

In brief, the results are a cause for concern but not for alarm. With some exceptions, noted below, the ideational benefits mostly covary with confidence in the military in intuitive ways: the higher the confidence one has in the military, the more one is willing to confer this or that perk on the military and the more willing one is to defer to the military in the policymaking process. The military shows some discomfort with the deference but also shows some comfort looking down on society from the pedestal on which civilians have placed it. It is true that the public claims it is willing to defer to the military in the policymaking process in a way that violates the norms of some democratic civil-military theory, but that deference has not reached the point where civilian governance is in doubt. When it comes to actual policy debates that have been thoroughly aired in the public—for instance, debates about using force against Iran or allowing transgender individuals to serve in the military—the public seems inclined to defer to military views only minimally and on the margins; partisanship seems a much stronger predictor of attitudes than any generalized inclination to defer to the military.

The one area where the ideational benefit seems most consequential has to do with the way the military may be insulated from public criticism—and thus, perhaps, from some healthy public accountability—regarding the conduct of the post-9/11 military operations. In short, there is not strong evidence that high confidence in the military leads to what could be called "militarism," but there is evidence that high confidence buys the military perks—and possibly protection from criticism—that have defined its exalted place in society, for good and for ill, over the past several decades. The military advantages in this partisan blame game are not conducive to healthy civil-military relations in a democracy. They create an incentive for the military to avoid meaningful and constructive accountability and for political partisans to engage in only the worst, performative theater versions so familiar to televised hearings.

Privileges

The title of this book, *Thanks for Your Service*, evokes the familiar ritual, reproduced hundreds of thousands of times in recent years, when an American civilian encounters someone who has in the past or is now serving in uniform. Almost reflexively, the civilian is likely to offer words of gratitude and may, if circumstances allow, go further than that—offering to buy a cup of coffee or other libation as a way of expressing thanks for what the military member has done or is doing for others. Such privileges are formalized in the now-standard practice of allowing military personnel traveling in uniform access to board onto airplanes ahead of most other customers. And the veterans' privileges are even more substantial than that, with lavish benefits such as lifetime access to subsidized medicine, stipends for education, and head-of-the-line status in applying for government jobs. Politicians keep voting for these benefits for the military likely because they are believed to be popular. And some citizens keep honoring the rituals for the same reason. As demonstrated in Chapter 7, this social pressure to support the troops may be a key prop that undergirds public expressions of confidence in the military.

Many observers have noted that these customs make for awkward civil-military interactions (Ricks 2010; Fisher 2010; Samet 2011; Kinzer 2014; Coale 2015; Livingston 2015; Richtel 2015; Olsen 2016; Melcher 2017; Millsap 2020; Worsencroft 2020; Lemar 2020). Of course, the difficulty of the interactions between those who went off to war and those who stayed behind has been a theme of literature ever since Homer's *Odyssey*, and the ancients' engagement on the issue has become a staple of our contemporary era as well (Batuman 2020). Hollywood has weighed in, including with the 2017 *Thanks for Your Service* movie that explores post-traumatic stress disorder and how that complicates society's desire to elevate returning veterans to hero status. The analyses here home in on one aspect of this familiar and wide-ranging topic: the privileged status that society grants the military or veteran and the issue of whether nonveterans can ever merit such privileges.

The survey allows an assessment of how public confidence in the military props up this privileged status. It asked respondents to indicate their level of agreement to a battery of statements that directly address the issue of these privileges:[3]

---

[3] The statement regarding extending privileges to nurses and doctors was rotated between a positive and negative formulation to avoid acquiescence bias. In the reported results, responses are reversed responses, as needed, so they can be grouped together. They are further coded in the same direction so that higher levels of agreement are associated with higher levels of support for the military enjoying privileged status. Thus, someone who disagrees strongly with the idea that doctors and nurses should enjoy the same preferential treatment in restaurants is coded as strongly supporting military privileges.

- Members of the military should not get preferential treatment in airports and restaurants. (Wave 1)
- Military veterans should not get special treatment when they look for jobs in the civilian world. (Wave 1)
- All Americans should say thank you for your service to members of the military when they meet them. (Wave 2)
- Saying thank you for your service to troops can make it harder for Americans to have a real conversation with military service members. (Wave 2)
- Doctors and nurses who treated patients during the COVID-19 pandemic should get the same preferential treatment in airports and restaurants that members of the military receive. (Wave 2)

Table 10.1 summarizes the results, both in the aggregate and broken down by the level of confidence respondents had previously indicated they had in the military. The first column reports the percentage of respondents who answered "agree" or "strongly agree" with the specific question about privileges; the next columns report the percentage of respondents who both agree with the privilege and report that column's specified level of confidence in the military.

The pattern is notable. The higher the level of confidence one expresses in the military, the more one supports the military enjoying these privileges. With regard to the relatively minor privilege of preferential seating at airports and restaurants, support overall in the aggregate is high enough that there is relatively little distinction among groups with different levels of confidence. The same pattern holds—and is, in fact, even stronger—for giving veterans the more substantial privilege of preferential access to jobs. Interestingly, the custom of saying thanks to the military is almost uniformly embraced by those with high levels of confidence in the military, whereas only a quarter of those with low levels of confidence support it. Yet there does not appear to be much of a difference across the groups regarding whether the custom produces awkwardness in conversations—somewhere between only a quarter and a third of respondents agree this might be the case, regardless of the level of confidence they express.

This pattern of endorsement of privilege extends all the way to what might be considered the limiting case: a reluctance to extend these same privileges to other "heroes," namely the medical professionals who were fighting the pandemic at the time of the survey. Logically, it would seem plausible that individuals would want to honor all heroes, military and medical, with similar favors; honoring the medical professionals need not detract from honoring the military. The survey suggests that there are indeed some Americans who view it that way, but there are others who wish to elevate the military alone to the first rank—and those Americans are notable for their high professed confidence in the military.

Table 10.1 **Responses to Privilege Questions by Level of Confidence in the Military (% agree or strongly agree)**

	Overall Agree	Very Little Confidence	Some Confidence	Quite a Lot Confidence	Great Deal Confidence
Should not get preferential treatment in airports and restaurants*	12% (545)	18% (66)	14% (132)	10% (152)	11% (195)
Should not get special treatment when they look for jobs in the civilian world	8% (349)	14% (49)	7% (67)	6% (92)	8% (141)
All Americans should say TFYS to members of the military when they meet*	66% (1501)	27% (43)	44% (232)	69% (563)	85% (664)
TFYS can make it harder for Americans to have a real conversation*	26% (584)	30% (46)	27% (144)	27% (219)	23% (176)
Doctors and nurses should get the same preferential treatment	55% (1227)	57% (102)	54% (281)	58% (462)	52% (382)
Doctors and nurses should not get the same preferential treatment*	28% (625)	15% (27)	20% (108)	29% (231)	34% (259)

* Denotes that the relationship between confidence in the military and the outcome variable is statistically significant at the 95% confidence level in an OLS regression controlling for standard demographic variables.

At least some of these patterns persist, even when controlling for partisan identification and the other demographic variables that play such a large role in shaping public attitudes. As reported in the technical appendix (available here: https://dataverse.harvard.edu/dataverse/pfeaver), level of confidence was not a statistically significant differentiator for the first and fifth questions, once one controlled for other demographic factors; the confidence level was strongly significant in the other four questions. Additionally, the first question was statistically significant when confidence is included in the models as a binary variable (confident, not confident), but not as a categorical variable. Since these six questions just represented alternative wordings of three underlying ideas and since confidence remained statistically significant for one of the wording formats for each idea, the results can be interpreted collectively as supporting the idea that confidence matters and in the intuitively obvious way.

Younger veterans who served after 9/11 think about these ritualized privileges differently than do civilians who have not served in the military—and differently than do the older veterans who served before the era of the global war on terror. As indicated in Table 10.2, older veterans and civilians are basically comfortable with the custom of saying, "Thanks for your service." They generally see it as a laudable practice, and one's support for this courtesy varies in an intuitive way along with confidence in the military—the higher the confidence, the more likely you will agree with it. Younger veterans, however, express somewhat

Table 10.2 Thanks for Your Service by Veteran Status (% agree or strongly agree)

		Overall Agree	Very Little Confidence	Some Confidence	Quite a Lot Confidence	Great Deal Confidence
All Americans should say TFYS to members of the military when they meet	Civilian*	66% (1892)	26% (133)	44% (451)	70% (679)	86% (629)
	Pre-9/11* Veteran	68% (249)	47% (13)	67% (27)	61% (86)	74% (123)
	Post-9/11 Veteran*	55% (112)	51% (3)	25% (13)	45% (43)	72% (53)
TFYS can make it harder for Americans to have a real conversation	Civilian*	25% (1889)	30% (130)	27% (452)	26% (679)	21% (628)
	Pre-9/11* Veteran	29% (249)	34% (13)	42% (27)	25% (86)	29% (123)
	Post-9/11* Veteran	64% (112)	80% (3)	56% (14)	56% (43)	71% (52)

* Denotes that the relationship between confidence in the military and the outcome variable is statistically significant at the 95% confidence level in an OLS regression controlling for standard demographic variables.

less support for the custom and are far more likely to see it as inhibiting rather than facilitating conversation across the civilian-military divide. The number of respondents in some of the cells is small, so one should not lean too hard on this finding, but it is suggestive of a pattern that shows up frequently in the data: younger veterans are different from older veterans in the way they view the military's place in society. Of course, younger veterans only have personal experience with the era of good public feelings toward the military and that may lead them to view it with some skepticism or even take it for granted. Older veterans may better remember the reception given the Vietnam War cohort, and this may make them embrace latter-day privileges more enthusiastically.

Pedestalizing

A closely related phenomenon is the degree to which the public puts the military on a pedestal—as an object worthy of veneration that is not shown to other high-status professions, or, indeed, to other professions that serve the society in difficult and dangerous ways. Of course, the impulse to place the military on a pedestal is inherent in the privileges discussed just above—it is far more common, for instance, to offer to buy a soldier a cup of coffee in the airport than it is to similarly treat an inner-city middle-school teacher or an asbestos-remover or an itinerant farm laborer, even though those jobs likewise contribute to society, involve at least some hardship, and perhaps even entail personal risk. Americans literally put statues of soldiers on pedestals in town squares all over the country, and few other professions are destined for similar treatment.

The new proprietary survey asked a battery of questions designed to tap into this pedestalizing of the military, to measure the extent to which the public wants to elevate the military above the rest and hold it in special esteem as somehow better than the civilian society itself. The survey asked respondents to indicate their level of agreement with the following statements:

- Military leaders care more about the people under their command than leaders in the non-military world care about people under them. (Wave 1)
- In general, I respect people who have served in the military more than I respect those who haven't served. (Wave 1)
- Through leading by example, the military could help American society become more moral. (Wave 1)
- The military needs to become more like American society. (Wave 1)
- All Americans should stand for the national anthem because it shows respect for our military. (Wave 1)

- The military gets more respect than it deserves from civilian society. (Waves 1 and 2)
- The military gets less respect than it deserves from civilian society. (Wave 2)
- Eligible Americans who do not volunteer to serve in the US military when the nation is at war should feel guilty for not serving. (Wave 2)

Table 10.3 presents the total percentage of respondents who indicated that they "agree" or "strongly agree" with the statements, according to the level of confidence the respondents had already indicated that they have in the military.

Two distinct inferences emerge from the pattern presented above. First, as expected, lower levels of confidence are correlated with a lower propensity to put the military on a pedestal. This relationship is quite strong and statistically significant across a broad range of questions, with the move from "very little" to "a great deal" corresponding with shifts of nearly 50 points for some questions. These results are even more dramatic than the ones found and presented above regarding "privileges." If public confidence in the military were to decline markedly, one would expect to see a correspondingly lower pedestalizing of the military.

Second, that said, the pedestalizing impulse does not disappear altogether even among those who express "very little" confidence in the military. Confidence and pedestalizing thus appear to be separate but related attitudes that move in tandem but not in lockstep, and even some Americans who otherwise have very little confidence in the military do not want them knocked off the pedestal altogether. At the same time, it is notable that the questions directly comparing the military to society are those with some of the smallest shifts as confidence varies. Americans with confidence in the military are comfortable saying positive things about the military, but they seem less inclined to extend that comparison directly to themselves, especially when it might imply an unflattering contrast.

On one crucial question, there is a marked veteran-versus-civilian divide that is different from others found in the data. As shown in Table 10.4, when the survey asked respondents whether Americans who chose *not* to serve when the nation is at war should feel guilty, only 22% of civilians—almost a quarter of those who presumably made a choice not to serve—agreed. A plurality (43%) of pre-9/11 veterans thought that the civilians should feel guilty, and nearly a supermajority (59%) of post-9/11 veterans concurred. At least in this one respect, veterans were inclined to look down from their pedestal on the civilians who put them up there. The small sample size cautions against pushing this finding too hard, but it could be a harbinger of the alienation across the societal-military divide that is captured well in the aphorism, "1% went to war and 99% went to the mall." In their survey of West Point cadets, Bryant, Haney, and Urben

Table 10.3 Public Pedestalizing of the Military by Confidence Level (% agree or strongly agree)

	Overall Agree	Very Little Confidence	Some Confidence	Quite a Lot Confidence	Great Deal Confidence
Military leaders care more about the people under their command than nonmilitary people would* (Wave 1)	47% (1,046)	15% (26)	40% (189)	43% (319)	61% (513)
I respect people who have served in the military more than I respect those who haven't served* (Wave 1)	47% (1,071)	30% (55)	24% (114)	47% (347)	60% (565)
Through leading by example, the military could help American society become more moral* (Wave 1)	45% (1,030)	38% (69)	36% (156)	41% (303)	53% (502)
The military needs to become more like American society* (Wave 1)	23% (521)	39% (71)	31% (135)	18% (136)	19% (179)
All Americans should stand for the national anthem because it shows respect for our military* (Wave 1)	56% (1,266)	21% (37)	33% (160)	56% (416)	78% (653)
The military gets more respect than it deserves from civilian society* (Wave 1)	15% (336)	31% (53)	21% (102)	11% (83)	12% (98)
The military gets more respect than it deserves from civilian society (Wave 2)	19% (433)	24% (43)	18% (93)	20% (158)	19% (139)

(continued)

Table 10.3 **Continued**

	Overall Agree	Very Little Confidence	Some Confidence	Quite a Lot Confidence	Great Deal Confidence
The military gets less respect than it deserves from civilian society.* (Wave 2)	58% (1,311)	22% (40)	40% (215)	59% (469)	78% (587)
Eligible Americans who do not volunteer to serve in the US military when the nation is at war should feel guilty* (Wave 2)	24% (525)	13% (26)	17% (94)	25% (188)	31% (217)

* Denotes that the relationship between confidence in the military and the outcome variable is statistically significant at the 95% confidence level in an OLS regression controlling for standard demographic variables.

Table 10.4 **Attitudes about Guilt for Not Serving by Veteran Status and Confidence (Wave 2, % agree or strongly agree)**

	Group	Agree	Neither	Disagree
Eligible Americans who do not volunteer to serve in the US military when the nation is at war should feel guilty	Civilian	22% (448)	28% (577)	50% (1,013)
	Pre-9/11 Veteran*	43% (48)	25% (28)	33% (37)
	Post-9/11 Veteran*	59% (22)	17% (6)	23% (8)
	Overall	24% (518)	28% (611)	48% (1,058)

* The difference in means for both the pre-9/11 veteran and post-9/11 veteran groups for a two-sided t-test is statistically significant at the 99% confidence level when compared to the civilian group. The post-9/11 veteran group is significant at the 95% confidence level when compared to the pre-9/11 veteran group.

(2021) likewise find evidence of incipient alienation of this sort, which they cluster under attitudes of "increased isolation," "unequal burden-sharing," and "exceptionalism"; they find it in both cadets and midgrade officers, both of whom would fit our "post-9/11 veteran" category, and in some cases find it more pronounced in the most junior officer ranks.

Prerogatives

The foregoing sections addressed public views of the military's special status in commercial, social, and general public settings. The military's special status also extends to the domain of politics and policy. The reference here is to the public's willingness to grant the military advantages that are not, in fact, spelled out in the Constitution or that otherwise flout the norms of democratic civil-military relations. Previous research has established that, to a remarkable degree, the public is not well aligned with normative civil-military relations theory. The public embraces as acceptable certain behavior that theorists view as contravening norms—and the public is reluctant to embrace other principles that the theorists deem bedrock for democratic civil-military relations. For instance, Feaver and Kohn (2001) found that civilians supported the military playing an advocacy role in which the military could "insist" on its preferred outcomes during policy deliberations rather than merely the advisory role that normative theorists like Eliot Cohen (2002) identify as proper. Golby, Cohn, and Feaver (2016), showed that increasingly the public wanted the president to defer to the military in wartime rather than exert civilian control over military operations. Krebs and Ralston (2020), and Krebs, Ralston, and Rapaport (2021), found that large portions of the public did not support the idea that civilian preferences should prevail over military preferences in the setting of policy, the basic hallmark of civilian control according to numerous civil-military theorists (Desch 1999; Cohen 2002; Feaver 2003). A number of scholars have even suggested that such public support for deference to the military on policy matters could have detrimental democratic effects (Krebs, Ralston, and Rapport 2021; Karlin and Friend 2018).

Of course, these attitudes could be generously described as simply granting the military a great deal of autonomy in its area of expertise—something Huntington (1957) himself thought was advisable and consistent with overall civilian control of the military, especially when confined to issues related to national security and foreign policy. However, other research has found that a small but notable minority of American citizens support something closer to "army rule," and the number expressing support for this position tripled from 6% in 1995 to 18% in 2017, with the highest levels among those who are "disaffected, disengaged from politics, deeply distrustful of experts, and culturally conservative" (Diamond and Drutman 2019).

Public ignorance of—or, more charitably, public reluctance to embrace—basic civil-military norms may merely reflect a general decline of civics education in society at large. When, if ever, would the typical citizen engage a civil-military question in any depth inside or outside the classroom? Views might, in this regard, resemble what Converse (1974) called "nonattitudes," topics on which the public genuinely does not hold a stable opinion and only generates in response to a survey question, which then gets wrongly interpreted as an actual viewpoint when it is merely a quasi-random response. The growing number of respondents who answer "don't know" or "no opinion" to questions about civil-military norms—a phenomenon observed in a 2014 survey (Golby, Cohn, and Feaver 2016) that occurs again in the current surveys—suggests that this may indeed be going on in some of these questions and in other surveys about the military where respondents are not provided a "don't know" option. For Converse, the problem of nonattitudes shows up not in respondents who say "don't know," but rather in respondents who give another answer, perhaps to avoid some embarrassment at not having a genuine opinion. The fact that a large portion of the public is willing to admit to not knowing or not having an opinion on questions about military policy suggests these nonresponses may themselves be an indication of a growing "familiarity gap."

However, for those who are willing to express an opinion, something else might be going on—something that makes the overall "confidence in the military" opinion particularly important. Later theories of mass opinion, particularly Zaller's (1992) "receive-accept-sample" model, addressed Converse's problem of nonattitudes by suggesting that the public may employ a variety of heuristics to generate valid, if only lightly considered, opinions on topics that are far from their day-to-day areas of expertise and familiarity. Thus, individual respondents may not have thought very much about the specific question being asked, but they might have a rule of thumb that they find trustworthy and that, once applied to the novel question, leads them to an answer that genuinely reflects an underlying view. Overall public confidence in the military could serve as one of these heuristics, providing respondents with a ready rule of thumb on which to rely when encountering questions and topics they have not closely studied. The thought process might go something like this: "How should a war be conducted? I don't really know, but I do have high confidence in the military, so I am inclined to let them decide."

The new survey provides some evidence of this dynamic at work.[4] It asked respondents to indicate their level of agreement with a wide range of statements of military prerogatives—claims that civilians should defer to the military in the policymaking process rather than keeping the military subordinate to the civilian, as democratic civil-military relations theory requires. Chapter 6 already explored in some depth one aspect of this topic: military criticism of the

---

[4] Constraints on survey length made it impossible to analyze this dynamic using the structural equation approach advocated by Zaller (1992). As a consequence, these results are suggestive and worth investigating in greater depth in follow-on studies designed explicitly to home in on this one issue.

civilian commander in chief, the president of the United States. Recall that the pattern observed was that civilians were more willing to accept military criticism of the president provided the president was of the opposite party of their own preference; Democrats tolerated military criticism of Trump and Republicans tolerated military criticism of Obama—and neither particularly welcomed military criticism of their own party's standard bearer. The analyses here explore other dimensions of those norms of civil-military relations. The survey asked a battery of questions regarding the proper role of the military in the policy advising and executing process and the degree to which the military should feel free to publicly criticize civilian leaders along the way:

- Members of the military should not publicly criticize senior members of civilian branches of the government. (Wave 1)
- It is proper for the military to advocate publicly the military policies it believes are in the best interests of the United States. (Wave 1)
- In general, high-ranking civilian officials rather than high-ranking military officers should have the final say on whether or not to use military force. (Wave 1)
- In wartime, civilian government leaders should let the military take over the running of the war. (Wave 1)
- Military leaders do not have enough influence in deciding our policy with other countries. (Wave 1)
- A system in which the military rules the country would be a good way of ruling this country. (Wave 1)

Table 10.5 presents the survey responses for those in the main experiment's control group—that is, who did not receive a prompt designed to nudge up or down their confidence in the military—broken down by the degree of confidence respondents indicated that they had in the military. For each of the first three questions, the table also includes responses from an earlier survey YouGov conducted in 2012.[5] The pattern is consistent with the idea that a respondent's overall level of confidence may be doing a fair bit of work as a heuristic when an individual is asked a thorny question regarding best practices in civil-military relations, with a statistically significant relationship for all three of the questions

---

[5] YouGov conducted a nationally representative survey of 2,750 respondents from July 12, 2012, to July 28, 2012. YouGov interviewed 3,079 respondents who were then matched down to a sample of 2,750 to produce the final data set. The respondents were matched on gender, age, race, education, party identification, ideology, and political interest. YouGov then weighted the matched set of survey respondents to known marginals for the general population of the United States from the 2007 American Community Survey. See Golby, Dropp and Feaver (2012, 2013, and 2017).

Table 10.5 **Attitudes about the Military Role in Policymaking by Level of Confidence (% agree or strongly agree)**

		Overall Agree	Very Little Confidence	Some Confidence	Quite a Lot Confidence	Great Deal Confidence
Public Advice	Members of the military should not publicly criticize senior civilians.* (2012)	42% (2,251)	28% (93)	36% (391)	42% (701)	45% (1,066)
	Members of the military should not publicly criticize senior civilians. (2019)	44% (310)	26% (21)	42% (69)	42% (101)	50% (119)
	It is proper for the military to advocate publicly for military policies* (2012)	52% (2,852)	27% (90)	39% (418)	53% (893)	61% (1,451)
	It is proper for the military to advocate publicly for military policies* (2019)	49% (308)	21% (21)	34% (68)	57% (100)	56% (119)
Use of Force	High-ranking civilians should decide whether to use military force* (2012)	34% (1,865)	40% (131)	35% (377)	34% (575)	33% (782)
	High-ranking civilians should decide whether to use military force (2019)	30% (307)	23% (26)	13% (41)	26% (106)	41% (134)

Table 10.5 **Continued**

		Overall Agree	Very Little Confidence	Some Confidence	Quite a Lot Confidence	Great Deal Confidence
	In wartime, the military should take over the running of the war* (2019)	39% (308)	7% (21)	21% (68)	47% (100)	47% (119)
Policy Role	Military leaders do not have enough influence in foreign policy (2019)	39% (310)	25% (21)	47% (69)	49% (101)	29% (119)
	A system of military rule would be a good way of ruling this country* (2019)	19% (307)	9% (26)	10% (42)	8% (106)	32% (133)

* Denotes that the relationship between confidence in the military and the outcome variable is statistically significant at the 95% confidence level in an OLS regression controlling for standard demographic variables.

in 2012 and half the questions in 2019 even when controlling for standard demographic variables. Moreover, if one sets aside the matter of criticizing civilians for a moment, the pattern of responses aligns with the basic intuition: the greater the confidence in the military, the more one is inclined to grant the military prerogatives that civil-military relations theorists find problematic.

The questions about whether it is proper for the military to criticize senior civilians seemed to elicit a different pattern—albeit one that is not statistically significant when controlling for other demographic variables. Yet upon closer inspection this indicates the influence of partisanship and not some underlying public embrace of proper civil-military relations norms. For starters, support for the long-standing norm of military deference in public in the form of not publicly criticizing civilians is fairly weak overall; less than half of the respondents agreed with that norm. It is easy to think of historical examples when this long-standing norm of military deference in public was violated in a prominent way, especially if we include recently retired members of the military—every president since Truman has borne the scars of a scathing critique from a recently retired military figure, and some even experienced the same from active-duty military leaders. Apparently, these incidents do not generate as much concern among the public as they do among civil-military relations theorists.

However, even this shaky public embrace of the norm is strongly tinged with partisanship. Recall the discussion in Chapter 6 about how partisans supported more restrictive norms when it benefited their party leader and opposed them when it did not. The same thing seems to be happening here with respect to criticism of civilians. Agreement increased from 44% among Republicans with "very little" confidence to 71% among Republicans with "a great deal" of confidence in 2019, with no clear agreement between confidence level and agreement among Democrats. In 2012, with a Democrat in the White House, this pattern reversed: agreement among Democrats increased from 34% to 59%, while agreement among Republicans hovered around 35% regardless of confidence level.

Partisanship is also doing a fair bit of work in some of the attitudes shown in Table 10.5. For every 2019 question in Table 10.5 except the questions about "military rule," Democrats were more likely to grant the military greater prerogatives than were Republicans. This partisan split marks a clear reversal from when an earlier survey asked three of these same questions in 2012, during the Obama era. For all three of the questions asked in 2012, however, Republicans were instead more likely to side with the military than were Democrats. In other words, what is going on here is not some principled disagreement on which the parties differ because of some underlying theory of good government. Rather, the survey responses seem to indicate that the public is viewing civil-military relations through the partisan lens of whether the president—thus the preeminent "civilian" in "civilian control"—is a member of their party or not. When the president is of the opposite party of the respondent, then respondents are much more willing to have the military enjoy policy prerogatives that would tie the hands of the president. When it is their party in control of the presidency, the respondents are more inclined to keep the military in a subordinate position. Put another way, respondents seem disinclined to have the military play the role of "adults in the room" when their own party controls the White House but are more open to the idea when the opposing party is in charge.

The overall pattern is that people with a high level of confidence are more inclined to grant the military deference, especially when they perceive it will benefit their party, even if those prerogatives are debated by civil-military theorists. It is particularly alarming that the most extreme prerogative—inverting civilian control altogether and having the military rule civilian society—has support from nearly a third of those in the sample who report a great deal of confidence in the military, with no significant difference across parties. One must not push this finding too far, since it is based only on the admittedly small slice of the sample from the control group. This surprising result could simply be a statistical anomaly—given that no other treatment group contains responses that exceed 23%, with an overall sample average of 17% among those with "a great deal" of confidence. On the other hand, support even in the 17%–19% range for a system of military rule is alarming enough. Note that this question was only asked in the 2019 wave, so the responses cannot be blamed on desperation caused by the global pandemic. Although it is not reported in Table 10.5, it is worth noting that veterans appear slightly less likely to support military rule and, not surprisingly veterans who do not have high confidence in the military are especially opposed to the idea of military rule; however, the small sample sizes are ample reason to treat this characterization of the veteran's viewpoint as suggestive rather than dispositive.

Policy Preferences

If the public is willing to grant the military wide prerogatives in terms of expecting civilian leaders to defer to the military, it is not that much further to go to empower the military viewpoint on policies more generally. This could begin with foreign and national security policy but then extend even to policies that go rather far afield from traditional areas of military expertise. Many observers have noted that Americans are relatively quick to reach for the military tool to confront a wide range of social ills—be it structural racism (Butler and Moskos 1996), drug abuse (Trainor 1989), inequality between men and women (Decew 1995; Moskos 1990), violence in schools (Hui 2018), rescuing a beleaguered public health system during a pandemic (Campa-Najjar 2020; Obradovich, Migliorini, and Wurth 2020; Golby and Friend 2020), and so on (Myers 2020a, 2020b).

As reported in Chapter 6, the survey put the question directly to respondents, asking them to indicate their level of agreement with the statement: "The US government would function better if we allowed the military to take over non-military programs, such as tax collection or public education." The results show little support for this idea, with only 12% of respondents stating they strongly agree or agree with this statement. Support was slightly higher among political independents, at 15%, than for Democrats and Republicans, with 11% support in both parties. But confidence in the military does not appear to be driving even this limited support. Barely 12% of those expressing a great deal or quite a lot of confidence in the military agree with the statement, compared to 14% of those with only some or hardly any confidence in the military, a statistically insignificant difference.

But the ideational benefit of being a high-status institution might accrue in a more subtle way: the extent to which its preferences have influence on a wide range of public attitudes, including attitudes on matters that range far from the institution's legitimate claim of privileged expertise. Earlier research (Golby, Dropp, and Feaver 2017) established that the military serves as an elite cue-giver to the general public when it comes to the advisability of the use of force, at least on the margins. Others have replicated and extended this finding, as was done in Chapter 6 with the experiment on the border deployment (Robinson 2018; Saunders 2018; Jost and Kertzer 2019). The stable pattern is that military influence is mostly a veto player when it comes to the use of force. Hearing that the military endorses a use of force has minimal effect on the public's own views regarding the desirability of military action; but hearing that the military opposes the use of force markedly reduces the public's enthusiasm. This effect is moderated by partisanship; in the study conducted during the Obama administration, Republicans moved more sharply than did Democrats and sometimes even in support of the use of force in response to military cues. Robinson (2018) replicated and extended these results in surveys conducted shortly after the surprising election of Donald Trump. He found that the cueing effect was, indeed, moderated by partisanship but not in the sense that Republicans always trusted the military more than did Democrats.

Left hanging from this previous work are several questions that the new surveys are well positioned to answer. First, did the cueing effect that this earlier work identified persist later in the Trump administration, after the public had more or less adjusted to the new normal of this unusual Republican president? Second, did this cueing extend to other areas of policy, far beyond the military bailiwick of the use of force? Finally, how, if at all, is this cueing effect shaped by the public's overall level of confidence in the military—does the intuition that members of the public who express high levels of confidence in the military are more likely than the rest of the public to respond to cues, or likely to respond in more dramatic fashion, hold up? Recall that Chapter 6 showed how these military cues operate with respect to vote choice in presidential campaigns and in cases of military deployments that have become highly politicized—namely, only at the margins and in a very limited way. This chapter homes in on other uses of force from within the military's traditional bailiwick and beyond into domestic and social issues.

The survey included a number of additional experiments tailored to answer these questions, in the manner described in greater detail in Chapter 5 and the technical appendix. In each case, one can compare the results of how the public responds on topics of interest after being told about military attitudes on that topic as compared to how the public responds without receiving that prompt. Wave 2 asked about a series of topics: the possibility of military action against

Iran;[6] President Trump's restrictions on the ability of transgender persons to serve in the military;[7] and allowing teachers to carry handguns in school to prevent school shootings.[8] Based on earlier research, the expectations were that the cueing on the use of force against Iran and restrictions on transgender personnel would follow the veto and co-partisan patterns. The a priori reasoning was that these were all more or less within the traditional bailiwick of the military, and so the influence of military expertise should operate in more or less similar ways across each issue area. There were less strong priors on how the cues would work on the question of allowing teachers to carry handguns, especially since the treatments focused not on active-duty cues, but rather on cues from veterans' groups. While firearm safety might have some link to the military because individual members receive so much training in how to handle weapons, it also seems likely that the policy topic of firearms in schools was far enough outside the military's direct area of expertise that the cues should be weaker; finding that the cueing still operated would, it would seem, be a sign of a particularly strong "ideational benefit" accruing to military status.

---

[6] **Control** received "We are interested in what you think about the uses of the military. As you may know, US officials have considered initiating military action to destroy Iran's ability to threaten US interests and allies in the region. Do you agree or disagree that the United States should initiate military action against Iran? (Strongly agree, agree, etc.)." Respondents receiving the **military support cue** received this additional piece of information before being asked about their own attitudes: "According to recent reports, the Chairman of the Joint Chiefs of Staff and regional combatant commander support military action against Iran." Respondents receiving the **military oppose cue** received "According to recent reports, the Chairman of the Joint Chiefs of Staff and regional combatant commander oppose military action against Iran."

[7] **Control** received "As you may know, President Trump has implemented certain restrictions on the ability of transgender persons to serve in the US military. Do you agree or disagree that transgender persons should face restrictions on their ability to serve in the military?" **Military support cue:** "According to recent reports, the Chairman of the Joint Chiefs of Staff and other senior military leaders support these restrictions." **Military oppose cue:** "According to recent reports, the Chairman of the Joint Chiefs of Staff and other senior military leaders oppose these restrictions." For this question, some respondents were also primed with information that suggested the military was itself divided on the policy, so a **military divided cue:** "According to recent reports, the Chairman of the Joint Chiefs of Staff and other senior military leaders are divided over whether to support these restrictions."

[8] **Control:** "As you may know, US officials have considered allowing teachers to carry guns in schools to prevent school shootings. Do you agree or disagree the United States should allow teachers to carry guns in schools?" **Military support cue:** "A prominent veteran's organization, Veterans Against Gun Control, has advised elected officials that this step would make school children more safe." **Military oppose cue:** "A prominent veteran's organization, Veterans for Gun Reform, has advised elected officials that this step would make school children less safe." **Military divided cue:** "Veteran's organizations are divided on whether or not this step would make school children more safe."

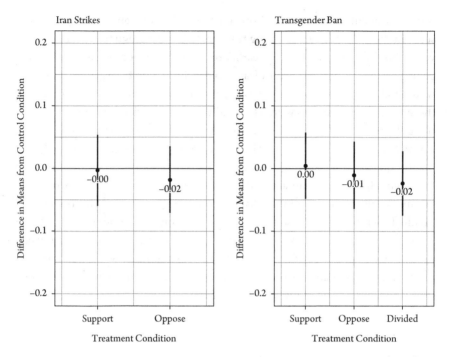

Figure 10.1 Treatment Effects for Iran Strike and Transgender Ban Questions (2020)

Figure 10.1 presents the treatment effects for the experiments that cover policies closest to the military bailiwick. There is no statistically significant effect from the treatment in the aggregate. Support for a strike against Iran is low overall. Only 27% supported a strike, and that did not budge among respondents who were told that the military supported such a move; being told that the military opposed the strike lowered support by two points, but this was not a statistically significant drop.[9] Similarly, on the issue of placing restrictions on whether transgender individuals can serve in the military, only 32% agreed in the baseline. That moved up a point among those told the military supported such restrictions, down a point among those told the military opposed those restrictions, and down two points among those told the military were divided.

Interestingly, the pattern was roughly the same when respondents were asked about a policy that took veterans' groups pretty far out of the domain of traditional national security policy—whether to allow teachers to carry handguns in

---

[9] Although this did not replicate the results of a similar Iran experiment James Golby and I conducted previously, the debate about whether to strike Iran's nuclear facilities was a key issue in US national security in 2012 (see, for example, Kroenig 2012 and Kahl 2012) in a way that it was not in October 2020. Support for hypothetical strikes in 2020 was nearly 15 points lower than it was in 2012, and floor effects left less room for an opposition cue to lower support.

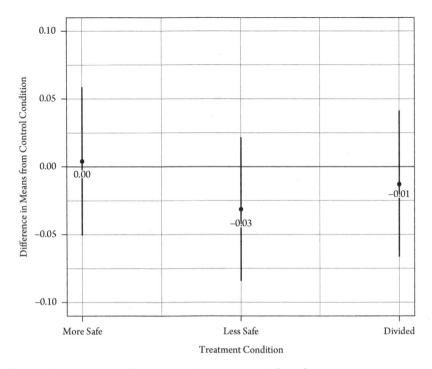

Figure 10.2 Treatment Effects for Handguns in Schools (2020)

school, as shown in Figure 10.2. The cue that the military supported the move nudged up support by a point while the cue that the military opposed the move nudged support down three points and a cue that the military was divided nudged it down a point.

Of particular interest, however, is the extent to which these effects might be conditioned on public confidence in the military itself. Perhaps it is people who have high confidence in the military who are most responsive to military cues on policy, both within the military domain and beyond. Figure 10.3 sheds light on this question. First, regardless of treatment, people with low levels of confidence are markedly less likely to agree with the proposed policy—less likely to support an attack on Iran or restrictions on transgender individuals. The first stance might fit comfortably within a "hawkish" mindset in the traditional hawk-dove formulation, as explored in the previous chapter; the second, on transgender rights, fits at the conservative end of the conservative-progressive continuum. In short, people with high confidence in the military are more inclined toward the hawkish/conservative response than the dovish/progressive response.[10]

---

[10] Across all three questions, the effect of confidence holds even when controlling for party identification and standard demographic variables.

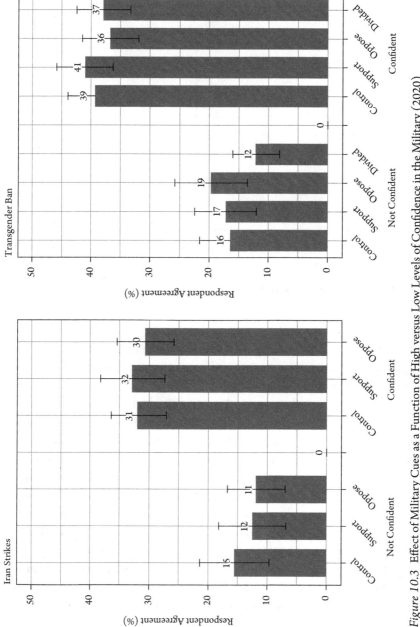

Figure 10.3 Effect of Military Cues as a Function of High versus Low Levels of Confidence in the Military (2020)

Second, people with high levels of confidence in the military respond in a more intuitive way to the military cues. An oppositional military cue nudges support down, and a support cue nudges support up. Of particular interest, the nudge up in support is more dramatic among those who report high confidence in the military than it is in the sample as a whole. People with low confidence in the military do appear to be responding to the military cues, but not consistently in the intuitively expected fashion across the three issues areas. Reporting a military cue drops support for Iran strikes, regardless of whether the cue is in support or opposition to that policy. The cue that the military opposes the policy appears paradoxically to nudge support higher for restrictions on transgender service; however, the cue that the military supports the policy does nudge up support ever so slightly as well. But these effects are not statistically significant in any of the cases, and there is little support overall for the idea that confidence impacts respondents' willingness to listen to military cues across the questions asked here.

As shown in Chapter 6, military cues as a whole tend to be conditioned on partisanship, and that remains the case here as well. Figure 10.4 shows the treatment effect, disaggregated by whether the respondent is a Republican, Democrat, or independent. For clarity of presentation purposes, only the results for the survey experiment regarding restrictions on transgender individuals serving in the military are shown. As expected, Republicans are more supportive of restrictions on transgender service overall than are Democrats, and Republicans with high confidence in the military are more supportive than Republicans with low confidence. Here it is Republicans with high confidence in the military who appear to be responding to the military cues in the intuitively expected way and in a marked fashion, with responses to both cues barely reaching the 90% confidence level; the oppose cue moves Republicans who have high confidence in the military to reduce their support for the transgender restrictions by six points while the support cue moves those high-confidence Republicans to increase their support for the restrictions up five points. Republicans who report low confidence in the military respond to the support cue as expected, albeit more modestly, with a bump up of three points; but Republicans with low confidence in the military respond to the oppose cue in the opposite way as we expected, by increasing their support for the restrictive policies, though this shift is not statistically significant. Democrats, whether with high or low confidence in the military, have lower support for the transgender restrictions than do Republicans; but Democrats with high confidence in the military are more supportive of the restrictions than are Democrats with low confidence in the military. Democrats do not respond to the cues in the intuitively expected way, though none of the Democratic shifts are statistically significant. The "military oppose" cue seems to move Democrat support for transgender restrictions up a tick, whether it is Democrats with high

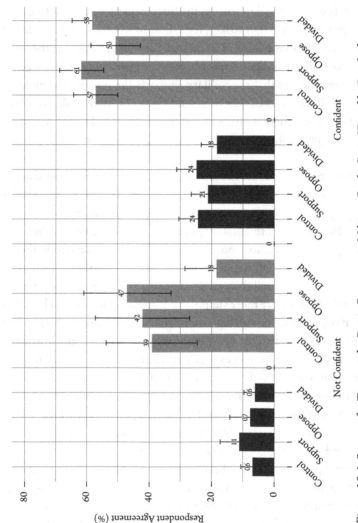

Figure 10.4 Support for Transgender Ban in Response to Military Cue by Party ID and by Level of Confidence in the Military (2020). Darker shaded bars are Democratic respondents and lighter shaded bars are Republican respondents

confidence or Democrats with low confidence. Democrats with high confidence respond in the opposite way to the military support cue, while Democrats with low confidence respond in the expected way to the military support cue, with a statistically insignificant increase in support of four points.

In sum, when it comes to policy preferences, several findings are notable. Overall, there is relatively little movement in response to cues, which is perhaps not surprising since the cue is minor—basically one prompt—and the questions focus on issues that have already been subject to public debate. In the real world, of course, a military cue might be repeated several times and highlighted by pundits on TV and in social media, perhaps amplifying the effect. Even so, one would not expect a dramatic change in attitudes simply on the basis of learning that the military supported a policy, though previous research has shown that military opposition can sometimes modestly decrease public support (Golby, Dropp, and Feaver 2013, 2017). That said, in the aggregate, the differences in the current surveys are not statistically significant, but movement is usually in the intuitive direction: opposition nudges overall support among all respondents down (or at least not up) from control, support nudges overall support up (or at least not down), and divided has a slightly downward effect but less than with an unambiguous cue. People who have high confidence in the military give baseline-higher levels of support for the "hawkish/conservative" answer (strike Iran, maintain transgender ban), and these differences are statistically significant with high levels of confidence across all the questions. People with high confidence respond more in alignment with the military cues—moving up with support and down with opposition—than do people with low confidence, but the "unaligned" movements may be an artifact of low numbers. Partisanship is also in play, since Republicans with high confidence respond even more in alignment than any other sample group; but again, small numbers for Republicans with low confidence make it hard to offer definitive assessments there. In two of the experiments, Republican responses to the military primes are statistically significant at the 90% confidence level, but none are significant at the 95% confidence level.

The literature already has had a lively debate as to whether this influence was inappropriate or excessive (Feaver and Kohn 2001; Feaver 2003; Brooks 2009; Golby 2011; Golby, Feaver, and Dropp 2017; Coletta and Crosbie 2019). The findings here suggest that that debate remains of interest today, though one should take care not to overstate the extent to which the public is cueing off the military. Consistent with previous research, it is likely that military cues will be more salient on newly developing issues for which partisan narratives have not already formed. On issues that have long been part of the public discourse, including most of the scenarios from these survey experiments, any cueing effects may already be baked into public attitudes. The findings do suggest that the military has some influence, especially at the margins and especially among Republicans who have high confidence in the military, however. Moreover, the pattern seems to hold regardless of whether the military is opining on matters well within its traditional area of expertise or whether it is discussing topics away from the core concerns of national security and military expertise, though cues do appear to have a smaller—and rarely statistically significant—effect on these issues.

Pinning Blame

The last possible ideational benefit to consider is arguably the most important: blame or credit for the outcome of military operations. Perhaps high confidence "matters" in the sense that it buys the military some insulation from blame for adverse outcomes and presumption of credit for good outcomes. Burbach (2017) has noted that the public maintained relatively high levels of confidence throughout the post–Cold War era even though military operations produced only uncertain results. The public turned on the wars in Iraq and Afghanistan as prospects for victory receded but did not lower their confidence in the military in a corresponding fashion. Burbach went on to speculate that confidence in the military may have stayed high because the public might differentially blame civilian and military leaders for the results.[11] These new surveys allow for an assessment of these dynamics in various ways and in some detail.[12]

First, one must establish how the public assessed the wars in Afghanistan and Iraq in general—as a success, a failure, or something else. Wave 2 put the question to respondents directly, and then followed up with a specific question about Afghanistan in light of President Trump's deal with the Taliban.[13]

---

[11] Burbach cites the 2014 YouGov survey presented in Golby, Cohn, and Feaver (2016) for findings suggestive of this effect.

[12] All of these new surveys predate the actual American withdrawal from Afghanistan and the complete collapse of the Afghan government soon thereafter. Polls immediately after the collapse initially showed strong support for leaving and a deep ambivalence about the mission itself (Green and Doherty 2021) However, as instability in Afghanistan persisted and the risks of the withdrawal came more in view, public attitudes shifted again somewhat with an uptick in the number of respondents who indicated that perhaps the US military should have stayed after all (Walsh 2021).

[13] "Thinking back on the military operations conducted since the terrorist attack on September 11, 2001—the wars in Afghanistan, Iraq, and operations elsewhere—how well would you say those operations overall have gone? A. They have been very successful. B. They have been mixed, somewhat successful and somewhat unsuccessful. C. They have been very unsuccessful. D. Don't know/ No opinion." Note, to avoid question ordering effects, the survey asked this question about overall success *after* asking the other questions, reported above, regarding the level of candor in battlefield reports and the taboo on criticizing the military.

Table 10.6 Public Views on Success of the Wars in Iraq and Afghanistan
(Wave 2, % agree or strongly agree)

	Overall Agree	Democrats	Independents	Republicans
Very successful	14%	11%	7%	20%
	(619)	(225)	(57)	(336)
Mixed	57%	53%	55%	63%
	(2557)	(1043)	(438)	(1076)
Very unsuccessful	16%	24%	12%	9%
	(715)	(473)	(95)	(147)
Don't know	13%	12%	26%	9%
	(601)	(240)	(204)	(157)
Total	100%	100%	100%	100%
	(4491)	(1980)	(795)	(1716)

Table 10.6 again shows a largely ambivalent public, with 70% of respondents saying either "I don't know" (13%) or reporting that success in the wars was "mixed" (57%). Although not depicted, there were not any statistically significant differences between nonveteran civilians or veterans. There is some evidence that at least a few post-9/11 veterans hold slightly more optimistic views of the wars, however, with 24% claiming the wars have been very successful. The percentages of post-9/11 vets reporting that success in Afghanistan and Iraq was "mixed" or "very unsuccessful" were identical to those of civilians, with the key difference being that less than 3% of those who fought in the current wars said they didn't know.

When respondents were asked the question about success in the war in Afghanistan in a different way, and with fewer choices, the picture that emerged was slightly more negative and the partisan differences were even clearer. Among the entire sample, roughly 39% of respondents said that the United States had not accomplished its goals and another 39% said that they did not know; only 22% agreed that the United States had accomplished its goals. Republicans were more positive than either Democrats or independents, with 33% of Republicans agreeing and 31% disagreeing that the United States has accomplished its goals in the nation's longest war. Democrats were the most negative about the ongoing mission, with roughly half of Democratic respondents saying they thought the United States has not been successful.

It is one thing to view the wars as a mixed bag. It is another thing to assign blame (or credit) for this outcome—what in Washington, DC, policy circles is known as the blame game. One can begin to unravel the rules of the blame game by assessing the public's willingness, in the abstract, to criticize the military. The

Table 10.7 **Public Views on Whether the United States Has Accomplished Its Goals in Afghanistan (Wave 2, percentage of respondents by response category)**

	Overall Agree	Democrats	Independents	Republicans
Yes	22%	15%	16%	33%
	(988)	(297)	(126)	(565)
No	39%	48%	34%	31%
	(1,753)	(941)	(271)	(541)
Don't know	39%	37%	50%	36%
	(1,741)	(732)	(394)	(615)
Total	100%	100%	100%	100%
	(4,482)	(1,970)	(791)	(1,721)

survey asked respondents how they viewed Americans/civilians who criticized the military:[14]

- Americans who criticize the military when troops are deployed to fight a war overseas are unpatriotic. (Wave 2)
- Americans who criticize the military when troops are deployed to fight a war overseas send a bad signal that helps our enemies be more effective. (Wave 2)
- Americans who criticize the military when troops are deployed to fight a war overseas disrespect our service members. (Wave 2)
- Civilians who have not been to war should not question soldiers who have been to war on questions related to foreign policy. (Wave 2)

Table 10.8 reports the results, broken down by level of confidence in the military. The pattern is striking. First, a significant portion of the public—nearly half—takes a dim view of criticism of the military and is willing to equate it with a lack of patriotism or abetting the enemy. Second, such attitudes are more pronounced among those who express a high degree of confidence in the military. Put another way, the higher one's degree of confidence in the military, the more you are willing to shield the military from criticism and to view that criticism as tantamount to undermining the war effort.

---

[14] To avoid acquiescence bias, the survey also asked the same questions in reverse form. Thus: "Americans who support the military when troops are deployed to fight a war overseas are patriotic." "Americans who support the military when troops are deployed to fight a war overseas send a good signal that helps our troops be more effective." And "Americans who support the military when troops are deployed to fight a war overseas respect our service members."

Table 10.8 **Public Views on Criticism of the Military by Level of Confidence (Wave 2, % agree or strongly agree)**

	Overall Agree	Very Little Confidence	Some Confidence	Quite a Lot Confidence	Great Deal Confidence
Americans who criticize troops are unpatriotic*	46% (2,224)	18% (186)	24% (483)	48% (816)	64% (740)
Americans who criticize troops help our enemies*	47% (2,224)	15% (186)	26% (483)	48% (816)	66% (740)
Americans who criticize troops are disrespectful*	52% (2,224)	23% (186)	30% (483)	54% (816)	72% (740)
Civilians should not question soldiers who have been to war*	41% (2,215)	15% (206)	30% (540)	41% (766)	58% (703)

* Denotes that the relationship between confidence in the military and the outcome variable is statistically significant at the 95% confidence level in an OLS regression controlling for standard demographic variables.

Perhaps not surprisingly, veterans feel even more strongly and negatively about the notion of civilians who have not been to war criticizing those who have. Veterans are 23 points more likely (63% to 40%) to think that civilians should *not* be putting the awkward questions to the military. Veterans in this sample are not a pure proxy for contemporary military views; in particular, veterans who served during the draft era or even just before the era of the global war on terror likely experienced military service in profoundly different ways than those serving in uniform today. Yet in the absence of better survey data of the contemporary military, veteran opinion is at least a suggestive indicator—and in this case the results suggest that those who have served, and perhaps those who do serve, in uniform have gotten used to the insulation the military enjoys and would not appreciate if it were to wear out.

These results suggest that the blame game begins on a tilted field, one that clearly advantages the military. Moreover, the more one has confidence in the military, the more one is inclined to tilt the playing field in favor of the military.

Table 10.9 Public Views on Who Deserves Blame/Credit (Wave 1, % agree or strongly agree)

	Blame	Credit
Civilian political leaders	39% (436)	10% (107)
Senior military leaders	9% (96)	38% (417)
Enemies on the battlefield	12% (139)	5% (57)
Don't know	40% (441)	48% (530)
Total	100% (1,112)	100% (1,111)

Next, one can assess the public's willingness, in specific situations, to blame or credit the military for the outcomes of military operations. Wave 1 asked the question directly: "Who deserves the most blame for the outcome of the wars in Iraq and Afghanistan? A. Civilian political leaders; B. Senior military leaders; C. Enemies on the battlefield; D. I don't know."[15] In order to avoid biases related to question-wording effects, a randomly assigned half the sample received the same set of questions but focused on credit instead of blame. The results reported in Table 10.9 depict a public much more willing to blame civilians, and credit the military, for outcomes in the post-9/11 wars. When the question is about blame, 39% of respondents target civilian political leaders, while only 9% blame the military, respectively. Another 12% blame the enemies the military has faced on the battlefield. When the questions instead focus on credit, this pattern reverses, with only 10% crediting civilian political leaders, while nearly four times as many respondents, 38% of the sample, credit the troops. In both frames, however, the plurality answer (40% and 48%, respectively) was "I don't know," again highlighting a public that is either not paying attention to—or afraid to answer questions about—military policy overseas.

The survey dug more deeply into how the public played the blame game by asking respondents to assess the performance of both civilian and military leaders in planning, advising, and executing related to military strategy and

---

[15] Note that since the survey also administered an experiment that primed respondents with information suggesting either that the war in Afghanistan had been a success or a failure, reported here are only the results for respondents who did not receive that earlier Afghanistan outcome treatment.

Table 10.10 **Perceptions of Civilian Leaders' Performance in Afghanistan (Wave 2, % agree or strongly agree)**

	Civilian Political Leaders	Democratic Political Leaders	Republican Political Leaders
Had a good plan	27% (1,540)	27% (1,467)	33% (1,479)
Listened to military advice	26% (1,537)	32% (1,459)	29% (1,478)
Did a good job integrating	28% (1,538)	28% (1,459)	30% (1,476)

operations in Iraq and Afghanistan.[16] Because the wars have spanned multiple Republican and Democratic administrations, it was also important to explore partisan effects. To examine these differences, respondents were randomly assigned into three groups, asking one group questions about "Civilian political leaders," another group about "Democratic political leaders," and a final group about "Republican political leaders."

Table 10.10 summarizes the topline results for the questions that directly asked about blame and outcome. Overall, the public gives civilian political leaders—including both Democratic and Republican political leaders—little credit for the planning and execution of the wars in Iraq and Afghanistan. On every question, one-third of respondents or fewer agreed or strongly agreed that civilian leaders had performed well.

As Table 10.11 shows, the public assesses military leaders as having performed better than civilian political leaders did in planning, implementing, and advising civilian leaders on policies related to the wars in Afghanistan and Iraq. Across all three questions, assessments of the military are about 10 points higher than they were for civilian leaders on their corresponding responsibilities. A 46% plurality of respondents said that military leaders implemented the plan they were given well, 39% said military leaders gave civilian leaders good advice about the wars, and 38% said they did a good job integrating their military operations with

---

[16] "Please indicate to what extent you agree/disagree with these statements about US military operations in Iraq, Afghanistan, and elsewhere since the terrorist attack on September 11, 2001. A. Civilian political leaders had a good plan for these operations. B. The military implemented the plan civilian leaders gave them as well as they could. C. Military leaders gave civilian leaders good advice about military strategy. D. Civilian political leaders listened to military advice as much as they should have. E. Civilian political leaders did a good job integrating military, diplomatic, and economic efforts in Iraq and Afghanistan. F. Military leaders did a good job integrating military operations with diplomatic and economic efforts in Iraq and Afghanistan."

Table 10.11 **Perceptions of Military Leaders' Performance in Afghanistan by Confidence in the Military (Wave 2, % agree or strongly agree)**

	Overall Agree	Very Little Confidence	Some Confidence	Quite a Lot Confidence	Great Deal Confidence
Implemented the plan well*	46% (4,478)	19% (355)	27% (1,063)	50% (1,579)	63% (1,480)
Gave good advice*	39% (4,475)	13% (357)	20% (1,062)	41% (1,578)	57% (1,479)
Did a good job integrating*	38% (4,466)	11% (358)	21% (1,060)	39% (1,571)	55% (1,476)

* Denotes that the relationship between confidence in the military and the outcome variable is statistically significant at the 95% confidence level in an OLS regression controlling for standard demographic variables.

diplomatic and economic activities related to the wars. Moreover, there are substantively large and statistically significant relationships between a respondent's level of confidence in the military and his or her assessments of the military across all three of these dimensions. In every case, confidence was linked in the intuitively obvious way—the higher the confidence in the military, the more one was willing to credit the military with performing well. Perhaps as importantly, few respondents in the survey "disagreed" or "strongly disagreed" that the military has done its jobs well; they were far more likely to place the blame on civilian political leaders, regardless of party. These critical "disagree" answers hovered around 30% for civilian political leaders but dropped to approximately 10% for military leaders.

As discussed in Chapters 4 and 5, the perception that the military "works" in ways that other federal institutions do not is a significant driver of high public confidence in the military. While Chapter 5 showed that priming the public with information about poor military performance can lead to decreased confidence, it is not clear whether the positive perceptions the public currently holds about the military's wartime performance are based on an accurate assessment of battlefield and strategic competence. The findings in Chapters 3 and 7 suggest public pressure, media framing, and pop culture narratives can play a significant role shaping how military performance gets communicated to the public.

Partisanship is also clearly playing a role in shaping the blame game. Figure 10.5 shows that individual attitudes about civilian political leaders are shaped both by the partisan identity of the respondent and by the party of the civilian leaders they are judging. It also indicates that partisanship may be playing a key role in the

Intangible Benefits

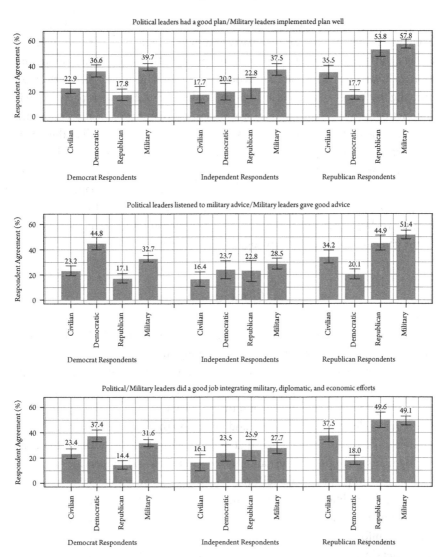

Figure 10.5 Views of War Performance of Civilian and Military Leaders by Partisanship of Respondent (2020)

public's assessments of senior military leaders as well. Overall, respondents did not rate civilian leaders highly in their conduct of the war. But when the generic "civilian" was replaced with the partisan "Democratic" or "Republican" political leaders, then partisan considerations intervened. Democratic respondents rallied to the Democratic leaders and against the Republican leaders; Republicans did the opposite. Respondents in the aggregate thought that civilian leaders had mismanaged the war, but they thought that the civilian leaders of the opposing party had *really* mismanaged the war.

Interestingly, there is also a strong correlation between partisans' judgments of civilian leaders from their own party and their assessments of senior military leaders. Although Republicans are more positive than Democrats about the military's wartime performance in general, they think the military has performed only slightly better than civilian political leaders from their own party in their conduct of the war—and even these differences are not statistically significant. Democrats also think the military has performed just about as well as their own party leaders have, though they rate military leaders' advice a statistically significant 12 points lower than they judge Democratic political leaders' willingness to listen to that advice. However, as the findings presented in Chapters 2 and 3 make clear, while the public is more skeptical of senior leaders than of the military as a whole, they are also hard-pressed to identify military leaders. In this blame game, the public are fairly foggy scorekeepers.

Conclusion

The results presented in this chapter suggest that the military definitely accrues ideational benefits overall, but especially among Americans with high levels of confidence in the military. Put another way, if the public did not have such high confidence in the military, then the public would be less inclined to defer to the military as much as it does—and the military would likely lose some of the privileges, pedestalizing, influence, and insulation that it currently enjoys.

There is also some evidence that—after nearly two decades of frequent deployments in support of the nation's post-9/11 wars—some service members look down from their pedestal onto members of the public who have not served in the military. The large numbers of recent veterans and military service members in the survey who think civilians should not be able to question those in uniform, and who even believe those same civilians should feel guilty for not serving, is alarming. But even among those civilians who have not served in the military, the higher the level of confidence one places in the military, the more one is also willing to support the extension of special privileges and prerogatives to the men and women serving in a military uniform. As the early part of this chapter shows, these tendencies can even make Americans with confidence in the military more reluctant to honor other heroes—including medical professionals and first responders fighting the pandemic or other domestic problems.

Taken as a whole, there is evidence of some deference to the military, but perhaps not at the levels warned about by the most strident critics of American "militarism" (Bacevich 2005; Brooks 2016). As shown in this and the previous chapter, confidence in the military is definitely associated with a greater willingness to support the military materially and a propensity to embrace relatively more hawkish policies in general. But, when facing specific situations or decisions, people often form opinions about policy decisions based on partisan or contextual factors, with direct military cues themselves only playing a supporting role—if they play a role at all. There is not much evidence of military opinion dominating public opinion, with military cues playing a large role in decisively shifting public support for certain policies one way or the other. The modest role found for military cues is fully in keeping with healthy civil-military relations, which would certainly allow for the public to be influenced by input from military experts when considering policy choices within the domain of military expertise.

Adding the separate but related issue of the political-military blame game to the equation, however, opens the door for a different kind of pressure for civilian leaders to defer to the military. As shown in Table 10.8, a significant portion of the public takes a dim view of criticism of the military by civilians. When a policy debate bubbles into public view and civilian leaders go so far as to criticize military leaders for the position they are taking, the survey results suggest this could backfire against those civilians—even though they are nominally in charge under the principle of civilian control of the military.

Indeed, precisely this situation arose in the run-up to the Iraq war, when internal civil-military debates about how large an invasion force was needed reached the public's attention with Army Chief of Staff Shinseki appearing to argue for a larger force in congressional testimony. Secretary of Defense Rumsfeld and Deputy Secretary of Defense Wolfowitz sharply criticized Shinseki for expressing that view, with Wolfowitz calling it "wildly off the mark." A political firestorm ensued, with most of the commentary lambasting the civilians and lionizing Shinseki—a framing that became etched in stone once coalition troops struggled to stabilize Iraq after toppling the Saddam Hussein government, thus appearing to vindicate Shinseki's judgment (Moten 2008; Coletta 2007). Although the army chief had previously failed to express those reservations to President Bush when he was asked directly whether he supported the war plan, the damaging public narrative of a break between senior civilian leaders and Shinseki took hold and civilians in the Pentagon paid a political price when their assumptions proved overly optimistic (Di Rita 2008). As this example illustrates, political leaders have powerful incentives to avoid a public break with the military on use of force decisions, and that gives the military considerable leverage in the policymaking process (Feaver 2011; Recchia 2015). In short, to the extent that public opinion creates pressure for civilian leaders to defer to the military, it may have more to do with perceptions that civilian leaders are ignoring military leaders than with direct shifts in the public's policy preferences that result from military advocacy.

As the militarism critics warned, there also might not be as much accountability of the military for decisions and performance after the fact. While it is outside the scope of this study to assess who deserves the blame—and, in some cases, the credit—for the nation's strategic performance in the wars in Iraq and Afghanistan, the surveys do indicate that the public judges senior military leaders much less harshly than civilian political leaders, especially if those political leaders are members of the opposing political party. In this sense, the logic of political leaders attempting to politicize the military by wielding it as a shield to defend against—or a sword to attack—partisan opponents is clear and well supported by polling data. And the results also resoundingly show that confidence and partisanship often interact to create an open door on which both civilian and military leaders may be tempted to push in the heat of a political dispute. Whether these hypothesized dynamics have been in operation since President Biden's decision to withdraw from Afghanistan cemented the failure of the war effort in Afghanistan remains to be seen.

In sum, the results show evidence of a partisan blame game, but one in which partisans tend to see the military as being "on their side" and thus deserving of some insulation from blame. Thus, partisans credit their own party and blame the other party, but they assess the military to be about the same as (or even a little better than) they assess their own party. Most of these effects are more pronounced among those in the public who express a high degree of confidence in the military. This partisan blame game means that the military avoids some of the criticism for military decisions, but then also some of the accountability. At least for now, the public seems content with this arrangement, since when asked directly, the public takes a dim view of criticism of the military, especially during times of war. As discussed in Chapter 2, however, it is unclear—and probably somewhat less likely—that the public will continue to give the military the benefit of the doubt when the public no longer believes the nation is at war.

11

Conclusion

> Marie Kondo urges nation to thank veterans for their service before discarding them.
>
> —Duffelblog.com (2019)

The American public expresses high confidence in the US military. It was not always so in American history, it may not always be so in the future, but it has been true for several decades now. It is a remarkable fact that such confidence has endured even as the country has been split into hardened political factions and beset with doubts about the health of our constitutional system. In a time of considerable alienation, amid rampant skepticism that the government can deliver what citizens need, confidence in the military is a rarity—a bond that apparently brings Americans of all stripes together.

Or so it seems when viewed at a distance. Viewed more closely, as done in the preceding chapters, a more complex picture emerges, one that seems to be drifting in the direction of "hollow confidence." Yes, the public in the aggregate expresses high confidence, but that masks important divergences across the standard demographic divides in American public opinion. Public attitudes toward the military are not as sharply polarized as other political questions have become, but they are not immune from the influence of partisanship. Indeed, partisanship is consistently a statistically significant covariate for a wide range of public attitudes toward the military—and shapes how public confidence relates to other attitudes of interest as well. Gender, race, and other divides that matter in American politics also show up in public attitudes to the military, if in somewhat muted form.

These results collectively contribute to a better understanding of what the public means when they say they have confidence in the military. More than anything else, it appears that "confidence" means something like this: "the military is able to get the job done, and when that doesn't happen it probably isn't the military's fault." Confidence is not synonymous with "liking" or "positive affect"; of course, those attitudes are linked and probably tend to covary, but it is possible to have confidence in the military as an institution and not particularly like it. Nor is confidence synonymous with "identifying with" or "wanting to be a part of"; again, those attitudes are linked, but it is possible to have high confidence and yet wish not to be a part of the organization, as Mike Birbiglia's joke at the top of Chapter 8 suggests ("I love the troops because if they weren't the troops, I would be the troops" [Birbiglia 2014]). Nor is confidence synonymous with "supporting" or "wanting to fund" or "wanting to use." Again, confidence is linked to these other attitudes, but stands somewhat alone. Public confidence, as a focus of concern, is important because it is one public attitude that has been measured for decades and that has been applied not just to the military but to other institutions as well. And it is widely understood that the public has had notably high levels of confidence in the military even while confidence in other public institutions has waned.

These results also contribute to a better understanding now of what has propped up public confidence over several decades. In short, high confidence in the military is not an iron law in the study of public opinion, and the preceding pages show that there are multiple ways that confidence could dip in the future and may already have crested from the highs it reached during the more intense phase of the war on terror.

The American public has confidence in its military because of six primary drivers: *Patriotism, Performance, Professional Ethics, Party, Personal Contact,* and *Public Pressure*. By *Patriotism* is meant the lingering effects of a rally derived from being a country at war—or at least one that needs the military to actively confront foreign threats. By *Performance* is meant the perception that the military is quite competent in handling those threats while *Professional Ethics* refers to the idea that the military can be counted upon to engage in ethical behavior. To be sure, public confidence has climbed and dipped with good and bad news about military behavior, whether on the battlefront or the home front. But as of 2023, the public had not yet blamed the desultory and worse strategic outcomes in Afghanistan, Iraq, Libya, Syria, and other military campaigns on the military; instead, the default high confidence in the military has provided some insulation from blame, which the public more readily lays at the feet of civilians from the opposite party to their own. Whether that insulation will continue to hold up under the heat of the complete defeat of the US military effort in Afghanistan remains to be seen, yet there was no early evidence that public confidence in the military collapsed alongside the collapse of the war effort. Likewise, myriad scandals have dented but not destroyed that confidence.

Throughout, public attitudes to the military have been strongly conditioned on *Party*, one's partisan identity, as shown in chapter after chapter. As a general rule, Republicans have more positive views of the military than do

Democrats—and often it is independents who are the most skeptical. Some of these attitudes appear to be somewhat durable views that follow the ideological differences between the parties, but others seem to be purely and cynically partisan, by which is meant that when the commander in chief is from your party, you have one set of views about the military, and when the commander in chief is from the opposite party, you have a different set of views.

Confidence in the military is also shaped by *Personal Contact*, one's connection to the military—by which is meant what one knows about the military and whether that knowledge comes from personal experience and friends/family ties or merely through the media. With a few notable exceptions, the stronger and more direct one's connection to the military, the higher the level of confidence. Yet this is all propped up by *Public Pressure*—the influence of social desirability bias where the public seems to know that it is politically correct to express high confidence in the military and so respondents are inclined to do so whether or not, in their heart of hearts, they really do feel that way. The striking evidence of a significant amount of social desirability bias is a key warning indicator that the high professed levels of confidence might reflect a hollow form of confidence. Table 11.1 summarizes these determinants.

These results also contribute to a better understanding of what goes along with that high confidence—and thus what might gradually wane if confidence

Table 11.1 **The Six Determinants of Public Confidence in the Military**

	Meaning	**Where Explored in Book**
Patriotism	A rally round the military in time of war.	Chapter 2
Performance	The perception that the military is good at its mission.	Chapters 2 and 5
Professional ethics	The perception that the military behaves ethically.	Chapter 5
Party	Predictable patterns where Republicans diverge from Democrats.	All, but especially Chapter 6
Personal contact	One's connection to the military.	Chapter 3
Public pressure	Saying you have confidence in the military because you believe others have confidence in the military.	Chapter 7

does dip meaningfully. Public confidence helps drive recruits to the military and helps prop up support for defense budgets. Public confidence seems to help shape what citizens consider to be the proper uses of the military to be. A raft of intangible benefits seem to go along with high confidence as well. It props up support for privileges, helps keep the military on a pedestal seemingly above civilian society, and gives the military considerable insulation from the ravages of the political blame game for strategic missteps on the geopolitical stage. And high confidence may help explain at least part of the reason why the public tends not to embrace the norms that many theorists of democracy believe constitute best practices in civil-military relations: why be punctilious about civil-military taboos if we have a professional and competent military that enjoys the confidence of a broad swath of the country?

This concluding chapter reviews what has been learned and then turns to some questions that are left hanging from the myriad findings presented in earlier chapters. The chapter begins by briefly summarizing the main findings and empirical claims of the research. Then it considers the crucial normative question avoided until now: what level of confidence *should* the public have? Is confidence too high or too low? Next the chapter addresses how policymakers, civilian and military, should make use of these findings, focusing on what they could or should do with regard to shoring up public confidence in the military. The chapter closes by flagging some of the most interesting questions for future research and exploration.

Main Takeaways

Based on this examination of decades of polling, with a particular focus on two large surveys conducted in 2019 and 2020, each designed expressly to explore public confidence in the military, consider the following 15 main takeaways about public attitudes toward the military:

1. **Public confidence in the military is high in the aggregate, but this masks important patterns of variation.** Public confidence is higher among men than women; higher among whites than nonwhites; higher among older than younger generations; higher among Americans from the South than other regions, especially the Northeast; and higher among wealthier and better-educated Americans. One of the most significant demographic patterns on public confidence in the military is the partisan divide between Republicans and non-Republicans (Democrats and independents). Among the former, high confidence has been almost universal; among the latter it is mixed, just a bare majority. Also of considerable importance is the fact that younger

respondents show markedly less confidence than do older generations. The military is losing ground with the cohorts that will matter the most over the long term. And may also be losing ground with Republicans.

2. **Closer connections to, and knowledge of, the military tend to be associated with higher confidence, but the pattern is not absolute.** People who identify with the military—who think the military looks like them or shares their values—tend to have higher confidence in the military than people who feel more distanced. People who trust conservative media have higher confidence than people who distrust conservative media and vice versa with left-leaning media sources. Confidence is higher on average among people who know more about the military, but not for Democrats; for Democrats, higher knowledge/education leads to slightly lower confidence. Confidence is higher among those with personal or social connections with the military than those without such ties, though we cannot be sure whether those connections cause elevated confidence. But when the survey pressed respondents to think about whether those personal ties had a positive or negative effect on their own confidence, a notable number indicated that their personal connection to the military actually *lowered* their confidence.

3. **Public confidence in the military is tied to war.** While one cannot be certain without data from before the Vietnam War, it does seem likely that the relatively low levels of confidence captured by Gallup when it started measuring this attitude at the end of the Vietnam War was, indeed, a reflection of the public's ambivalence about the military's role in that divisive conflict. However, it is notable that public confidence did not reach its nadir until 1980, several years after the war ended. Moreover, while, there was a modest bump up during the Reagan build-up—call it a *Top Gun* effect of more Americans expressing pride and confidence in the military as Reagan sought to exorcise the ghosts of Vietnam—the real jump came with Desert Storm, an actual war in which the American military performed with operational virtuosity. A still further bump up occurred in the wake of the 9/11 attacks as the country shifted to a more or less indefinite war footing to confront both transnational networks of terrorism inspired by militant Islamism (al-Qaeda, al-Qaeda in Iraq, the Islamic State, and so on) and potential state sponsors of terrorists who were seeking weapons of mass destruction (Iraq, Iran, and North Korea). This was not a total-mobilization kind of war, as the country experienced in World War II, nor was it a war that touched society broadly through a universal draft. Instead, this was closer in feel to the Cold War, which involved higher-than-peacetime levels of national security mobilization punctuated by outbreaks of mid- to high-intensity combat operations. And yet, because those combat operations persisted over time—in

9. **Public confidence in the military is shaped by public attitudes about the politicization of the military, but in complex and especially troubling ways. Throughout, as with so many other matters in contemporary American public life, political polarization touches all aspects of public confidence in the military.** Public confidence is not primarily propped up by a belief that the military is apolitical in the sense of staying out of partisan politics. It may be propped up partly by such a belief, but the crucial dimension of this for public confidence may be that "apolitical" is interpreted by individual respondents as "does not align with the opposite party of my own." Individual respondents in this survey showed a disturbing tolerance for a "politicized" military, so long as the military was aligned with those respondents' own political preferences. When respondents were told that the military aligned with *their* party, this raised their confidence in the military modestly rather than raising their concerns about a politicized military; but when the respondents were told that the military aligned with *the opposing* party, then confidence dropped markedly. In other words, partisans become slightly more confident in the military when they believe the military is biased in their favor, and much less confident when they believe it is biased against them. And, perhaps most troubling of all, the public seems willing to draw the military into the gyre of partisan polarization—enforcing norms of civil-military relations only when it benefits one's own party and showing a willingness to flout them to score points against one's political opponents. These findings suggest that theorists were right to worry about the politicization of the military, but the corrosive effects are more subtle and indirect than many theorists had believed. Selective and partisan enforcement of civil-military norms can create cross-cutting pressures that make maintaining a nonpartisan military an onerous task.

10. **High levels of expressed public confidence in the military are somewhat misleading because they are driven by social desirability bias.** A notable percentage of the public seems to claim to have high confidence in the military in part because they believe that that is the socially acceptable attitude to express. When given a chance to subtly signal lower levels of confidence without openly breaking a social taboo, they do so. Precisely how much the overall confidence levels are skewed by this social desirability bias depends on the method used to measure it—the analyses presented here yielded estimates ranging from 8% to 27%—and this may be the type of result that varies markedly with different question wording. But even if the more conservative estimates are closer to the truth, this still suggests that this public support is hollow and could erode sharply, if ever the social bias is weakened and the taboo loses its hold.

11. **The public does not draw especially sharp distinctions between military status or service.** The surveys found negligible differences across the military services (i.e., army, navy, air force, marines). The public shows the highest regard for the military as a whole and in the abstract as compared to specific military statuses—leaders, veterans, retired generals, and so on. But the differences are minor. Besides, the public has very little awareness of who is a retired military officer and who is on active duty, so these might be distinctions without much of a difference in the shaping of day-to-day attitudes.

12. **Public confidence in the military matters, because it is linked to the material support the military needs to function.** People with high confidence in the military are more likely to recommend military service to others, thus helping recruiters fill the ranks of the all-volunteer force. People with high confidence in the military are also more likely to support higher defense spending, especially Republicans in the post-9/11 era.

13. **Public confidence in the military matters, because it is linked to how individuals think about using the military.** People with high confidence in the military are more likely to see the military as a useful tool in addressing foreign policy challenges—and more likely to be hawkish in general about potential uses of the military in particular scenarios.

14. **Public confidence in the military matters, because it is linked to ideational benefits the military enjoys, although whether these are actually beneficial is debatable.** People with high confidence in the military are more likely to want to grant the military privileges and special courtesies in social settings and more likely to put the military on a pedestal above civilian society. People with high confidence in the military are much more likely to wish to insulate the military from criticism from civilians. The public has a tolerance for military criticism of civilians, however, provided that the military is criticizing the political leaders of the opposing party.

15. **Public confidence in the military has not reached the point where the military enjoys decisive sway over public attitudes about national security policies and other political issues more generally.** The public does look to the military as a cue giver on thorny policy questions, but military cues only seem to have a marginal impact. They have a bit more impact when the cue is an unexpected direction or on a topic closer to the core of military expertise. And it is possible that the military could play an important role in emerging issues that become salient among the public quickly, leaving little room for partisan positions to emerge. But—for most of the real-world scenarios explored here—partisan cues are stronger, and partisanship seems to condition the effect of military cues on individual respondents. Although several questions in the survey suggest the public

My reading of normative civil-military relations theory and best practices in democracies sets up the ideal as a situation in which the public has high confidence in a range of institutions, military and civilian, and in which confidence in both is well grounded. Accordingly, I identify four enduring goals with respect to public confidence. First and foremost, work to better ground public confidence in the military so it is fully justified and based on the citizenry holding an accurate and rigorous understanding of military affairs. The military should strive to be trustworthy, not simply trusted. Second, within that constraint, work to ensure confidence reflects that understanding across as much of the population as possible. Third, work against any accountability gaps and lean against pedestalizing the military, so that this high confidence does not unintentionally undermine military effectiveness or civilian control. And fourth, work to close any gaps between the military and other civilian institutions, not by lowering confidence in the military, but by raising confidence in civilian institutions. Here, both military leaders and elected civilian politicians have an important role to play.

The condition today is preferable to many other logically possible configurations, most of which have prevailed in the United States at some point in its long history. Better to have high confidence that is warranted than to have low confidence that is warranted. For that matter, unwarranted high confidence and unwarranted low confidence in the military are not likely to serve the country well, either. Whenever the country could not rely on the military to adequately defend the national interest—whether because antimilitarism had kept it too weak or wishful thinking about the military's capacity to meet the threat the military had resulted in under-resourcing—eventually a horrible butcher's bill came due when geopolitical developments finally woke the country up from its daydreams.

I believe that high confidence in the military is generally beneficial if that confidence is warranted. High confidence in a capable military provides policymakers with the support and flexibility they need to use military tools, as they deem appropriate, to further the national interest. And it helps guarantee a healthier situation on the home front than we saw during the Vietnam War, when the men and women who served did not always receive the respect or support they deserved from the nation that sent them into harm's way. To be sure, high confidence could also lead to overconfidence in the military and this could lead to an overpropensity to resort to military tools. This is precisely what critics of alleged American militarism claim has happened (Bacevich 2005; Brooks 2016). Whether those allegations are true—whether there really is an overpropensity to use force—is beyond the scope of this book. But regardless an optimal policy process should not require undermining public confidence in the military. It may, however, require a rebuilding of public confidence in other